Identity and Community in Biblical World

Biblical Hermeneutics Rediscovered

The Series as the name suggests will focus on Biblical Hermeneutics, i.e., literary works concerned with methods of interpreting the Old and New Testaments of the Bible via different stream of topics like Literature and Poetry, Indigenous Philosophizing, Ethical response towards Ecology, Health and Healing, Science and Technology, Feminist Theology, Sociological approach towards Human Rights, Law and Politics, Arts, History of Ideas, Ancient Civilizations, Cultural Contiguity, Religious Cosmologies and Mysticism, Appraisal of various Theologians, World Peace and Harmony, Global Capitalism, Network Marketing, Cybertheology, Population and Demographics, Epigraphic Studies, Contextualized Education, and many others. We welcome a Mss. on any topic/s mentioned, whether they are original works, scholarly monographs, collections of conference papers, revised dissertations, or translations of historical documents. Through the Series we, the Publishers, are striving to put forward published works that may help Institutions, Academic Bodies, Researchers, Scholars and the World at large in furthering their respective knowledge and understanding on the concerned subject. We welcome your comments on our efforts and further suggestions on how we can enshrine new ray of analysing and explaining the written Texts through our upcoming books.

Biblical Hermeneutics Rediscovered - 26

Identity and Community in Biblical World

Collected Essays on Identity and Community from Biblical Perspectives

Edited by

B. Lalnunzira & Varaprasad Gosala

Society for Biblical Studies in India

&

Christian World Imprints

First Published in 2020 by

Society for Biblical Studies in India, Bangalore
63 Miller Road, Benson Town
Bangalore- 560046
sbsindia1416@gmail.com
Phone: +91 9483743497

&

Christian World Imprints
Christian Publishing & Books from India
C-3, Wazirpur Industrial Area
Delhi-110052
cwidelhi2017@gmail.com
www.ChristianWorldImprints.com
Phone: +91 11 41526079

ISBN: 978-93-5148-437-0 (HB)
ISBN: 978-93-5148-438-7 (PB)

Printed in India.

Contents

Foreword

It gives immense joy to see that scholarly papers presented at the Society for Biblical Studies in India (SBSI) Biennial Conference 2018 held at Aizawl Theological College are published with the help of Christian World Imprints. Since the establishment of SBSI in 1962 it was the first time that a biennial was held in North East region of India, a region were the number of scholars pursuing Biblical studies is increasing. Moreover, it was a good opportunity to counsel the North East Chapter to continue to be in full association with the National forum. The members of SBSI were extremely grateful that the Aizawl Theological College had come forward to host this significant event.

During the Conference the delegates deliberated and discussed the theme: "Quest for Identity in Community Formation: Biblical Perspectives." The quest for identity exhibits a basic human need. Quest for identity structures one's personal identity in relation to others. Quest for identity helps to identify oneself with what lies outside the self. Quest for identity enables one to find roots and establish connections to the past as well as to the future. Glancing through the Holy Bible we perceive that the quest for identity forms a community's personal conviction of what gives meaning to life, belief system, spiritual essence and its own unique life experiences.

As Christians our quest for identity has formed us to a life of unity and order, not to a life fragmented by a mixture of identities. It means we abandon any image of ourselves that is not from God revealed in the person of Jesus Christ. We stop accepting what others say about us or how others label or define us but commit and engage ourselves to Jesus Christ who is the authentic way to find meaning in life.

The present publication affirms the above mentioned idea. This volume, titled *Identity and Community in Biblical World*, contains the Presidential Address delivered at the Conference, Keynote address, nine scholarly papers and three doctoral dissertation synopses. These presentations put in a nutshell the theme of Biennial Conference 2018. The book bears witness to the progress and impact of biblical scholarship that SBSI promotes, fosters and encourages.

I take this opportunity to express our sincere gratitude to Rev. Dr. V. J. John, the president of SBSI for the biennial 2016-18. As the secretary for the biennial 2016-18 it has been a remarkable experience to work with him. I thank the executive committee members of SBSI for the biennial 2016-18, who played a great role in taking forward the activities of SBSI. I very specially place on record the uphill struggle of Rev. Dr. Varaprasad, the treasurer, who meticulously did his job. As mentioned above, it was the first time in the history of SBSI that we had a biennial in North East region. This was possible only because of the great generosity of Aizwal Theological College. Therefore, we remember with gratitude Rev. Prof. C. Lalhlira, Principal, Aizawl Theological College, Dr. B. Lalnunzira, who played a huge role in arranging the biennial and other members of the staff and students of ATC. I also thank the resource persons for their hard work, the time and energy spent to bring out scientific papers. I am very grateful to Dr. B. Lalnunzira and Dr. Varaprasad Gosala for meticulously editing the volume. We acknowledge our heartfelt appreciation of our donors, whose generosity has eased our financial burden in connection with the Biennial Conference 2018. Christian World Imprints deserves special thanks for publishing this volume.

May the grace and peace our Lord Jesus Christ be with us all!

Rev. Dr. Laurence Culas
President SBSI
Archbishop's House (Latin Rite)
Trivandrum 695 003, Kerala, India
lalujculas@gmail.com

Society for Biblical Studies in India (SBSI)
(A Brief Historical Note)

The initial suggestion for forming a Society for Biblical Studies came from Prof. R. A. Martin of the Gurukul Lutheran Theological College, Madras and Rev. T. S. Garrett of the Theological College of Tirumaraiyur in the year 1962. But it was at the "initiative taken by Dr. F. Muliyil, Rev. C. Arangadan and Rev. E. C. John who, at the end of a translation meeting of the Malayalam Bible, sent a circular to various Theological Institutions of India, presenting the need of a Society that 'would foster Biblical studies on scholarly and practical levels.'" The first conference of the Society for Biblical studies (SBS) was held on August 3-4, 1963 at Gurukul Lutheran Theological College, Madras. 47 delegates including theology teachers, postgraduate students, Bible translators and pastors attended. The second conference was held at Serampore College, Serampore where 38 scholars participated. The third was in De Nobili College, Pune, 87 members participated, then, in United Theological College, Bangalore. Conferences were since held in Mumbai, Jabalpur, Hyderabad, Kottayam, Ranchi, Goa, etc. Some of the earlier participants were Dr. F. Mulliyil, Dr. E. C. John, Rev. C. Arangaden, Dr. K. V. Mathew, Dr. M. V. Abraham, Rt. Rev. Victor Premsagar, Dr. K. James Karl, Dr. K. David, Rev. Abraham P. Athyal, Fr. Lucien Legrand, Fr. K. Luke, Fr. Joseph Pathrapankal, Fr. Lucius Nereparambil, Fr. R.J. Raja and Fr. Jacob Theckanath. The only name that I could recollect of the earlier members from the Northeast is Dr. Renthy Kaiser, former Principal of Eastern Theological College, Jorhat.

The decision taken at the Serampore Conference, which interestingly was held after one year of the first meeting, "Two decisions were taken regarding the subsequent meetings. That the Society should meet once in two years and that there be papers on one main theme, besides presentations of the results of the research done by *individual members*." (emphasis added) ("Dr. E. C. John's Message on the Occasion of the golden Jubilee"). He further writes, "It was suggested to theological colleges that they pay the travelling expenses of members of their staff attending the conference. Several colleges paid the whole or part of such expenses."

Fr. R. Van de Walle writes, "Regional and confessional considerations were also reflected in the representation for the management. During the election of office bearers there was always an atmosphere of friendship, tact and diplomacy, first among five members of the nomination committee and during the election proper." He continues, "As for the working of the management committee, this was a real pleasure: there was an obvious family spirit, a dedication to the cause of the entrusted scripture message and to the needs of India."

It was in the year 2012 that we celebrated the Golden Jubilee of SBSI. It was held on the occasion of the 25th Biennial Conference held at Ecumenical Christian Centre, Whitefield, Bangalore, 20-21 December 2012. The last biennial (27th) was held at the Laity Institute for Transformation Education (LITE), Chennai, 21-23 November, 2016. During the biennium, we had a regional conference held at Bishop's College, Kolkata, 16-18 November, 2017 on the theme: "Religiosity and Nationalism: Biblical Perspectives" Nine papers were presented on the theme apart from the keynote address. There were 60 participants including Bishop's College Faculty and post-graduate students of the North Indian Institute of Post-Graduate Theological students (NIIPGTS). Two study circles, namely of the Old Testament and the New Testament at United Theological College, Bangalore and CSI Centre, Chennai. We need to further explore the possibility of increasing the number of study circles and the number of meetings at least once a year. Even regional conference could meet at least at two different venues. Publication of the papers is encouraged and should be explored. The 28th biennial Conference was held at Aizawl Theological College, Mizoram, 23-25 October, 2018 on the theme "Quest for Identity in Community Formation: Biblical Perspectives." Aizawl Theological College is the first Northeast Centre/College that hosted SBSI biennium.

Office Bearers of the SBSI (2018-2020)
President: Rev. Dr. Laurence Culas
Vice President: Rev. Dr. Jesurathnam
Secretary: Rev. Dr. B. Lalnunzira
Treasurer: Rev. Dr. Varaprasad Gosala

Introduction

Society for Biblical Studies in India (SBSI) is a society initiated by scholars of Biblical Studies in India who had great visions to promote Biblical scholarship in India. It is an ecumenical body in which scholars and students of Biblical studies from Protestant, Roman Catholic, and Orthodox Church join together in its endeavour. Though a simple beginning, the society is growing stronger and stronger that regional seminars and national seminars (Biennium) have been regular features of the society.

The SBSI Biennium, 2018 was hosted by Aizawl Theological College during 23-25 October. It was the Biennium hosted in the Northeast Indian soil for the first time. The College hosted the Biennium with great enthusiasm and excellence. Participants who came from all parts of India cherished the hospitality of the Aizawl Theological College. Over 80 participants attended the meeting. The theme for 2018 Biennium was, "Quest for Identity in Community Formation: Biblical Perspectives." Scholars from different parts of India read their papers that focus on the theme from different Biblical and contextual perspectives. In addition to ten scholarly papers, a brief Introduction to Society for Biblical Studies in India (SBSI), Presidential Address, Keynote Address of the Biennium, and three more excerpts and abstracts of Doctoral Dissertations were presented and discussed with great appreciation.

This book is an outcome of Biennium 2018 in which articles presented by scholars and doctoral excerpts are put together for public reading. Authors of the articles have to be found in the last part of the book. As stated above, the theme for the seminar and of this book is Identity and Community Formation. As its introduction, a brief description of the history of Society for Biblical Studies (SBSI) is appended. Presidential address by the then president Dr. V. J. John follows this. Dr. John discusses about identity, community and Biblical narratives in which concept of identity and Biblical images of identity markers are delineated. In a keynote address, Dr. Vanlalnghaka Ralte, principal of Aizawl Theological College highlights issues of identity and the people of God in Biblical tradition.

The ten articles runs as follows: The first four articles are perspectives from the Old Testament. The first article is "Quest for Identity in Community Formation: Ancestral Narratives for Model Communities in the Book of Genesis," by Dr. Jesurathnam. The Second article is contributed by Dr. Jose Varickasseril, which deals with "The Chronicler's Blueprint for Israel's Identity in Community Formation: Reflections from 1 Chronicles 1:1-2 Chronicles 9:31." Another article that reflects on identity is found with Dr. Takayeba, which entitled, "The role of Human being in Identity Formation in Wisdom and Poetry." Dr. B. Lalnunzira's article entitled, "Quest for Israelite Identity in the Exilic Prophets," discuses how exilic literature developed group identity among the exiles and the non-exiles during the exilic period. Five articles that discuss issue of identity and community formation in the New Testament follow this. The first is an article by Dr. Zakali Shohe on "The Matthean Community: Diverse, Complex and Overlapping." From the same Gospel, Dr. Laurence Culas discusses "Early Evidences on the Identity of Matthean Community." "Quest for Identity traits in Community Formation: Luke-Acts," by Virginia Rajakumari Sandiyagu follows the two articles on Matthew. From the Gospel of John, Dr. C. Gregory Thomas Basker contributes the article, "Quest for identity in community formation in the Gospel of John and its Relevance to the Indian Context." There is yet another article on the theme written from Catholic Epistle with the topic, "Identity formation of the Christian Community in 1 Peter: Dialectic of Continuity and Discontinuity," which is written by Dr. Prema Vakayil.

In addition to these articles, three excerpts from doctoral dissertation are appended. The first one is Joseph Lalfakmawia's excerpt entitled "Redefining *Mammon*: Implicit and Ignored Teachings of Jesus on Wealth from Socioeconomic Approach." Another doctoral abstract on the topic is "The significance of Torah in the Book of Proverbs," by Enolyne Lyngdoh. The last article is synopsis of doctoral dissertation by Keciziuying Siang on the title, "The Rich in Matthew: a Socioeconomic Reading."

Biblical Studies seek to explore why and how identity has been a crucial issue in the formation of community right from the time of the people of God in the Biblical world. Therefore, it is our hope that this volume will help readers to explore issues of identity and community formation as it is engraved in the Holy Scriptures and thereby promoting a viable and healthy community in our pluralistic society.

B. Lalnunzira
Varaprasad Gosala

1

SBSI Biennium 2018 Presidential Address Identity, Community and Biblical Narratives

V. J. John

Prelude

Vice President, Rev. Dr. Naveen Rao; Secretary, Fr. Dr. Laurence Culas; Treasurer, Rev. Dr. Varaprasad Gosala; Principal of Aizawl Theological College, Rev. Prof. C. Lalhlira & Vice Principal Rev. Dr. Vanlalnghaka Ralte; Former Presidents & Executive members of SBSI, Resource Persons, Principals, Senior Professors, Distinguished Colleagues, Faculty & Students of ATC, and all Conference Participants, I feel honoured to be standing here before you as the President of the Society for Biblical Studies on the inaugural function of the 28th biennial Conference at this beautiful scenic city of Aizawl, the capital of the land of the Mizos.

It has been our desire to hold a national conference of SBSI in the northeast region for a while. In fact, Fr. R. Van de Walle, SJ wrote in his Reminiscenes of Yesteryears in the SBSI Directory 1998 that "Even Jorhat in Assam was contemplated but the cost of travelling was found prohibitive." It was only on 15-17 November 2013 (nearly 5 years ago) that any gathering of SBSI took place for the first time in the Northeast. It was held at the Pastoral Centre at Shillong, Meghalaya. There were 29 participants and focused broadly on "Tribal Biblical Hermeneutics". This has given birth to the Northeast India Society for Biblical Studies which is now registered and functioning as a forum for biblical scholars from the Northeast to gather and interact. They meet annually for their conference. However, it is again the first time that a national conference of SBSI is being held in the Northeast after 56 years of the formation of SBSI. In that sense it is historic and important event.

The venue of this conference too is symbolically important. Mizoram is among the smallest of the Indian States, earlier known as the Lushai Hills District of Assam. In 1987 it became a full state. Mizoram is known for its folk culture and folk music, bamboo dance by women and men colourfully attired and its beautiful Cane furniture. The land is blessed with a variety of landscapes including, ridges and gorges, hills and valleys, forests and mountains, waterfalls and lakes. With a nearly 100% literacy and with a predominantly Christian population, It not only provides us a beautiful scenic setting, but also a very real life issues of struggles and questions on identity that they have struggled with for several decades until they finally achieved their identity as an independent state within the wider community of the Indian nation. Its various people groups including Hmar, Lushai, Ralte, Pawi, Thadou and Zou serve thus serve as a perfect context for our reflection of "Quest for Identity in Community Formation" from a biblical perspective. The seven sisters too provide us the context. It comprises **seven** states; namely Assam, Tripura, Manipur, Arunachal Pradesh, Meghalaya, Mizoram and Nagaland. ***The reason it is called "seven sisters" is the similarity between the states, in terms of geographical features, and interdependence among them in the political, social and economic spheres albeit there is great ethnic and religious diversity.*** North East India is one of the most ethnically diverse regions of the world

Introduction

The issue of identity has gained immense importance in the struggles for freedom and liberation of the subordinated people around the world. This is not only true of people under dictatorship and autocratic rule, but also in the context of democratic governance where the will of the majority rules, with little or no room for the cause of minorities and other marginalized groups.[1] Interest of the wider and vocal community gets projected over against the genuine aspirations and longings of the less privileged, whether individual or group. Hence emerged the quest for identity and recognition in the struggles for socio-political freedom, economic justice, geographical rootedness and emancipation from cultural domination and spread over to other aspects of life's experiences. We shall try to consider very briefly three questions in this address. 1) What is identity? 2) How is identity portrayed in the biblical

1 See M.N. Karna, ed., *Democracy, Pluralism and Conflict* (Jaipur, Delhi: Rawat Publications, 2006).

narratives? 3) What is the relationship between identity and community as the biblical stories recount?

1. Concept of Identity

What is the nature of identity? According to one definition identity is "who you are, the way you think about yourself, the way you are viewed by the world and the characteristics that define you"[2]. Or as the *Cambridge Dictionary* put it, identity concerns "who a person is, or the qualities of a person or group that make them different from others"[3] In another words, identity has to do with the understanding of self in relation to others and the way one is viewed by others. Hence, Identity is a process of meaning making.[4] For the tribal[5] community their identity is to be understood in relation to the geography, the land of their existence. In the words of Nirmal Minz "The story of land alienation and the tribals being deprived of their homes and hearth throughout history is the key problem in the discussion of tribal identity"[6]

Identity of various kinds determines aspects of people's life today unlike anytime earlier in human history. Moya recognizes this when she remarks in her introduction to *Reclaiming Identity*, the question of "identity" remains one of the most vital and hotly contested issues in the study of literature and culture in recent years as it plays an important role in postcolonial and ethnic studies as well as feminism and queer theory.[7] However, the quest for identity is looked at both from a negative and a positive point of view. For some all identity claims are suspect, and hence "politically and metaphysically problematic" while for others it is significant and real.[8] The important place taken by gender, race,

---

2 http://www.yourdictionary.com/identity

3 *Cambridge Academic Content Dictionary* © Cambridge University Press.

4 Linda M. Acloff, "Who's Afraid of Identity Politics?"in *Reclaiming Identity: Realist Theory and the Predicament of Postmodernism,* Paula M.L. Moya and Michael R. Hames-Gracia, eds., (Orient Longman, 2001), 323.

5 The use of the term "tribal" is seen as a "misnomer" and a "great injustice" to the collective identity of Northeast Indian ethnic groups and proposes the need to rediscover the use of Mongolian instead. See Laiu Fachhai, *Ethnic Squeezing in Northeast India: A Religio-Political Analysis* (Delhi: ISPCK, 2014), 49-66.

6 Nirmal Minz, "Tribal Identity in India", in *Pearls of Wisdom: Selected Essays from Lifetime Contributions by Bishop Dr. Nirmal Minz An Intellectual*, Joseph M. Kujur & Sonajharia Minz, eds. (New Delhi:ISI/ Bangalore: CISRS, 2007), 22.

7 Paula M.L. Moya, "Reclaiming Identity" in *Reclaiming Identity: Realist Theory and the Predicament of Postmodernism,* Paula M.L. Moya and Michael R. Hames-Gracia, ed., Orient Longman (2001), 1.

8 See Linda Martin Alcoff, "Who's Afraid of Identity Politics?" in *Reclaiming Identity*, 312-13.

ethnicity, sexuality, and other forms of identity in academic work including theology and religion indicates its relevance in all areas of study.[9]

In the history of the debate, identity is broadly perceived in three ways; namely, the *essentialist* view, the *postmodernist* view and the *realist* view. For the essentialist, experience is very vital, whether of a "woman's experience", a "Dalit's experience" or a "tribal's experience". The critics see it as problematic as identity categories are "neither stable nor internally homogeneous".[10] They argue, making one group's experience "normative" leads to the marginalisation and exclusion of another. Further they claim that "particular identities will unnecessarily balkanize our society and obscure our shared human attributes."[11] But those who speak in favour of identity consider "identity categories provide modes of articulating and examining significant correlations between lived experience and social action."[12] They point out that Identity *mattered* for the Black Liberation movement and they considered it as at least in some sense *real*.[13] Postcolonialists speak of a "strategic essentialism" to displace "hegemonic knowledge and structures of oppression."[14]

Post modernists, on the other hand, consider it an "error to grant ontological and epistemological significance to identity categories". Being influenced by deconstructionist thesis about the "arbitrariness and indeterminacy" of linguistic reference, they consider "experience" and "identity" are about social relations and as such they are "indeterminate and hence epistemically unreliable". There is no "objective" truth, and knowledge mediated through language cannot be said as objective. [15] They argue, as stated by Moya:

> Social and cultural identities . . . are fictitious because the selves they claim to designate cannot be pinned down, fixed or definitively identified. . . . So to speak of identities as 'real' is to naturalize them and to disguise the structures of power involved in their production and maintenance.[16]

---

9 See Ashish Thomas Koshy, *Identity, Mission and Community* (New Delhi: Christian World Imprints); Cyprian E. Fernandez, *Text, Community and Christian Origins: Searching the Rhetoric of Identity Description in the Markan Gospe*l (Christian World Imprints, 2016); Roji T. George, *Paul's Identity in Galatians: A Postcolonial Approach* (New Delhi: Christian World Imprints, 2016)

10 Moya, "Reclaiming Identity", 3.

11 Moya, "Reclaiming Identity", 4.

12 Moya, "Reclaiming Identity", 4.

13 Linda Martin Acloff, "Who's Afraid of Identity Politics?", 314.

14 See Gayatri Spivak, *In Other Worlds: Essays in Cultural Politics* (New York: Methusen, 1987)

15 Moya, "Reclaiming Identity", 5.

16 Moya, "Reclaiming Identity", 6.

They see "all identities as arbitrary and as unconnected to social and economic structures" and are produced through domination from a conceived common belief of a "linked fate"[17] despite being real and having real effects and constituting key features of our "shared reality" identities.[18] Hence, they insist upon the need to "subvert" identities to destabilize the forces that bring them into being. "[19]

The postpositivist realist view provides an alternative to both. They emphasize the possibility for us to have knowledge about the world without being caught in language to the extent of knowing nothing about the world.[20] They insist on the need to move from the negative emphasis of violence of identification of "wounded attachments" towards the "enabling, enlightening, and enriching structures of attachment and feeling" of cultural identities.[21] To this identity is important. As Moya states, ours and others perception of who we are will determine where we live, whom we marry and the educational and employment opportunities available to us.[22] There is relationship among social location, experience and identity.[23] Therefore, we need to recognize categories of identity that promote structures of inequality so as to make amends to bring about "progressive social change". As our views are influenced by our experiences within the social structure, we need "to distinguish those identities that provide more promising perspectives on the underlying structures of social conflict from those that do not."[24] We cannot just deny identity because of the possibility of a lack of objectivity as particularity and objectivity together constitute identity. Mohanty views observation and knowledge are theory mediated and that a "theory mediated objective knowledge is both possible and desirable".[25] Identity is therefore "epistemic significant and are empowering". The stress should be on critical realism.

2. Biblical Images of Identity Markers

There are a number of images in the biblical stories that serve as identity makers of the individual or community who are its referent. They are broadly of two types: negative images and positive images.

---

17 Linda Martin Acloff, "Who's Afraid of Identity Politics?" 319.

18 Linda Martin Acloff, "Who's Afraid of Identity Politics?" 318.

19 Moya, "Reclaiming Identity", 11.

20 Linda Martin Acloff, "Who's Afraid of Identity Politics?", 315-16.

21 Moya, "Reclaiming Identity"; 8; Satya P. Mohanty, "The Epistemic Status of Cultural Identity: On *Beloved* and the Postcolonial Condition" in *Reclaiming Identity*, 29-66.

22 Moya, "Reclaiming Identity", 8.

23 Moya, "Reclaiming Identity", 17.

24 Moya, "Reclaiming Identity", 9.

25 Moya, "Reclaiming Identity", 12.

1. Negative Images

Among the negative images include: wanderer, stranger, alien, foreigner, slave, oppressed, afflicted and foolish.

a. Wanderer

You shall make this response before the Lord your God: "A *wandering* Aramean was my ancestor; he went down into Egypt and lived there as an *alien*, few in number, and there he became a great nation, mighty and populous. When the Egyptians treated us *harshly* and *afflicted* us, by imposing *hard labor* on us, we cried to the Lord, the God of our ancestors; the Lord heard our voice and saw our *affliction*, our *toil*, and our *oppression*. (Deut. 26:5-7) Translated literally, "my father was a wandering Aramean," it was part of the formula that was recited when the first fruit offerings were brought to the Temple in ancient times. Commentaries on the Haggadah contrast the evil of Laban, who oppressed Jacob, with Pharaoh and see Laban as "a symbol for political, sociological, and psychological evil." While there were disputes as to whether the reference was to Abraham or Jacob what is important to remember is that the Israelites when bringing the first fruits and tithes as an offering before the Lord were to recollect their past experiences of rejection and subjugation.

b. Aliens, Strangers and Foreigners

Then the Lord said to Abram, "Know this for certain, that your offspring shall be *aliens* in a land that is not theirs, and shall be *slaves* there, and they shall be *oppressed* for four hundred years; (Gen. 15:13)

> And I will give to you and to your offspring after you, the land where you are now an *alien*, all the land of Canaan, for a perpetual holding; and I will be their God." (Gen. 17:8)

Aliens, strangers and foreigners are three terms which more or less appear synonyms. One who is a foreigner is an alien and hence a stranger to the place of her/his current residence. The experience of such a person is neglect and rejection and is often vulnerable without support and protection.

Making the covenant with Abram, much like a prophesy God already told him, for three generations (430 years, Ex. 12:40) of oppression his descendants will have to undergo in Egyptian bondage.[26] There they would be aliens and strangers and will be mistreated. The covenant promises a land where they are now aliens, literally, sojourner – a "resident alien", "immigrant" despite his

26 Gordon W. Wenham, "Genesis 1-15", *Word Biblical Commentary* vol. 1 (Thomas Nelson, 1987), 332.

living there a long time.[27] Elsewhere in the chapter the emphasis is on the son, the multitude and fruitfulness of descendants.[28]

> You shall not wrong or oppress a resident alien, for you were aliens in the land of Egypt. (Ex. 2:22 cf. 22:21)

'Alien' here is the compound verb from *sogom* 'linger in one travels' plus *sham* 'there, thither'[29]. As outsiders, aliens were without the protection of their clan. They were permanently without a community of their own and hence vulnerable and often poor. They were defenseless like the poor, the widow and the orphan and were objects of God's special care and provision (cf. Deut. 24:19-22; Ezek. 22:7).

Moses even named one of his sons Gershom in recollection of the fact, "I have been an alien in a foreign land" (Ex. 18:3), "a new comer" the time that he was in sojourn in Egypt. A stricken Job accused of sin by his own friends and kinsmen laments that he was forgotten by his own guests and maidservants who did his daily chores and has become an alien (foreigner) in their sight. He said, "The guests in my house have forgotten me; my serving girls count me as a stranger; I have become an alien in their eyes". (Job 19:15) *zar* means "resident alien" or *nokri* a "foreigner". The high esteem of servants for Job has now turned to contempt.[30] This is the cry of an innocent sufferer who had been given up by his own for his fate.

The experience continued for the people of Israel even when they were exiles in Babylon and under Persians, Greece and Roman empires. While certain amount of freedom may have been enjoyed by the elites the common masses continued to experience subjugation and oppression. They thence longed for freedom and return to their native land.

Jesus too was an alien along with Joseph and Mary when they fled to Egypt fearing harm to the new born Jesus from Herod the Great (Mt. 2:13-18). They continued to stay there until the information of the death of Herod reached them through an angel. Jesus came from a marginal home where his father Joseph was a carpenter. (Mk. 6: 3) It appears that being a too familiar and ordinary person people could not believe his miracles. They questioned about the source of his wisdom and the work of his miracles.

Writing to the Christians at Ephesus, the Gentile reader, in her/his early state was an alien or foreigner (*genos*), stranger or resident alien (*paroikoi*) in

---

27 Gordon W. Wenham, "Genesis 16-50", *Word Biblical Commentary* vol. 2 (Thomas Nelson, 2000), 22.

28 "Genesis" *Jerome Bible Commentary,* (Bangalore: TPI, 1994), 22.

29 John I. Duhram, "Exodus" *Word Biblical Commentary* vol 3 (Thomas Nelson, 1987), 23.

30 John E. Heartly, *The Book of Job* (Grand Rapids, Michigan: William B. Eerdmans, 1988), 268.

relation to Israel (Eph. 4:19). Both terms used interchangeably. The believing community in dispersion, Peter reminds them that they were homeless and aliens in their present experience. They were cautioned to be bewared of the fleshly desires that could turn them against God. He entreated them, "Beloved, I beseech you as aliens and exiles to abstain from the passions of the flesh that wage war against your soul". (1 Pet. 2:11)

c. Slaves

Then the Lord said to Abram, "Know this for certain, that your offspring shall be aliens in a land that is not theirs, and shall be slaves there, and they shall be oppressed for four hundred years. (Gen. 15:13)

The Israelites were not only aliens in a foreign land; they were also slaves of Pharaoh and the Egyptians. As such they laboured in brick kilns and rigorous labour was imposed upon them including collection of firewood for brick making which made their life oppressive. They had to constantly cry to God for mercy and deliverance (cf. Deut. 26:5-7).

d. Oppressed

> The cry of the Israelites has now come to me; I have also seen how the Egyptians *oppress* them. (Ex. 3:9)
>
> You shall not wrong or *oppress* a *resident alien*, for you were aliens in the land of Egypt. (Ex. 22:21)

The more the Israelites were oppressed; the more they increased in number (Ex. 1:12). But they cried to God. God intervenes on behalf of the people because he has seen and heard their cry of suffering. It is the terrible oppression the people had to undergo that led to their cry to God (Judg. 2:18). God was moved because of their suffering. Moses was chosen to deliver the people out of Egypt. God did so because he had heard the cry of the people (Ex. 2:23-25). There was repeated experience of suffering. God raised up judges as deliverers (Judg. 10:8; 12:12; 1 Sam. 12:8). Even the Assyrians and later the Babylonians oppressed them (Is. 52:4). God is always open to the cry of those crushed under the burden of merciless oppression. It is for this very reason that God has prohibited his people from practicing oppression. Their experience of suffering should restrain them from doing the same on others.

e. Foolish

> "For My people *are* foolish, They have not known Me. (Jer. 4:22)
>
> Consider your own call, brothers and sisters: not many of you were wise by human standards, not many were powerful, not many were of noble birth. But God chose what is *foolish* in the world to shame

> the wise; God chose what is weak in the world to shame the strong; (1 Cor. 1:26-27)

Repeated failure of people to be obedient to God, despite divine intervention is termed as foolish (Deut. 32:6; Jer. 10:8). The failure of the disciples on the road to Emmaus to understand Jesus had to die and rise again on the third day was termed by Jesus as foolish (Lk. 24:25) Writing to the Corinthian community who had disputes over allegiance to their respective leaders, Paul reminds them that they need not quarrel among themselves. He advises them to consider their call. It is not because of any of their greatness that they can boast of that they were chosen by God. They were neither of noble birth nor rich. If anything most of them were very ordinary people, foolish by the worldly standards. Yet God chose them to reveal the greater power of God.

It is very interesting that the Gospels portray the ministry of Jesus as taking place amongst the poor, the sick, the blind and the lame, prostitutes and tax collectors. They were the people who have had no identity as most of them belonged to the expendable class. Jesus' ministry was aimed at providing them an identity and recognition as the disciples and followers of Jesus.

2. Positive Images

The positive images that the Biblical stories portray include: citizen and household of God, children of God, follower, disciple, Christian.

a. <u>Citizen</u>

> So then you are no longer strangers and aliens, but you are *citizens* with the saints and also members of the household of God. (Eph. 2:19)

Citizenship in God's city is not determined by political boundaries of city and province. Yet the Christian community in Ephesus was a divided lot on the basis of their roots, whether they came from a Jewish ancestry or a Gentile background. It is the work of Christ that made it possible to bring together the estranged Jews and Gentiles into the same community. Artificial barriers created by human beings whether of race or culture or anything else can hinder the unity and oneness that was brought about by the work of Christ.

As those belonging together we are called the "household" of God. The basic social unit of the Graeco-Roman society was the household consisting of parents, children and slaves. As members of the household, Christians are called God's beloved children. It is in the context of the household that a believer's identity is determined.

b. Covenant Community

> As for me, I am establishing my covenant with you and your descendants after you, (Gen. 9:9)

> Now the angel of the LORD went up from Gilgal to Bochim, and said, "I brought you up from Egypt, and brought you into the land that I had promised to your ancestors. I said, 'I will never break my covenant with you. (Judges 2:1)

The special relationship that God shared with God's people was sealed by the covenant that God established with them. It is part of this covenant promised that the Lord brought them out of the house of slavery and established them in the promise land. They were repeatedly reminded of this special relationship with God whenever they went astray and forsaken God.

c. People of God

> Afterward Moses and Aaron went to Pharaoh and said, "Thus says the Lord, the God of Israel, 'Let my people go, so that they may celebrate a festival to me in the wilderness.'" (Exod. 5:1)

> The woman said, "Why then have you planned such a thing against the people of God? For in giving this decision the king convicts himself, inasmuch as the king does not bring his banished one home again. (2 Sam. 14:13)

> So then, a sabbath rest still remains for the people of God; (Heb. 4:9)

One of the frequently used terms to describe God's relation with the people is as "people of God". It indicates the fact that the people belongs to God. The close relationship that God has had with them was indicated with the use of the title "people of God".

d. Family of God

> and all the members of God's family who are with me, To the churches of Galatia (Gal. 1:2)

> So then, whenever we have an opportunity, let us work for the good of all, and especially for those of the family of faith (Gal. 6:10).

Paul while writing to the church at Galatia addresses them along with the believers with him who are termed as the family of God. Again he desires that as opportunity allows the Galatian church should work for the good of all, particularly the family of God.

e. Children of God

> You are children of the Lord your God. You must not lacerate yourselves or shave your forelocks for the dead (Deut. 14:1)
>
> But to all who received him, who believed in his name, he gave power to become children of God, (Jn. 1:12)

Israel was the chosen people of God, as such Israel were to be different from the rest. They were a holy people and a treasured possession of God. They were not to be participants in the pagan religious practices of the mourners in Canaan. The believers in Christ were called the children of God, a very privileged position indicating the special love and affection that determined their relationship. As the specially privileged ones they were not to be prevented from coming to the presence of Christ. Everyone who becomes like children will only be inheritors of the kingdom of God (Lk. 18:15-17).

f. Disciples

> it is enough for the disciple to be like the teacher, (Mt. 10:25)
>
> and whoever gives even a cup of cold water to one of these little ones in the name of a disciple-- truly I tell you, none of these will lose their reward." (Mt. 10:42)
>
> When it was evening, there came a rich man from Arimathea, named Joseph, who was also a disciple of Jesus.(Mt. 27:57)
>
> A disciple is not above the teacher, but everyone who is fully qualified will be like the teacher. (Lk. 6:40)

The companions of Jesus who heard the call of God and followed Jesus were called the disciples. The title indicates the master and student relationship that existed between Jesus and those who chose to be his followers. The disciples' identity was their master. If the master was well known, the disciples benefitted from the reputation of the master.

g. Followers of Christ

> Then he said to them all, "If any want to become my followers, let them deny themselves and take up their cross daily and follow me. (Lk. 9:23)
>
> Jesus answered, "My kingdom is not from this world. If my kingdom were from this world, my followers would be fighting to keep me from being handed over to the Jews. But as it is, my kingdom is not from here." (John 18:36)

> and it was in Antioch that the disciples were first called "Christians." (Acts 11:26)

The people associated with Christ were called followers of Christ and hence were given the name Christians. Followers were the ones who were closely associated with Jesus and walked with him.

h. Church

> And I tell you, you are Peter, and on this rock I will build my church, and the gates of Hades will not prevail against it. (Mt. 16:18)
>
> And great fear seized the whole church and all who heard of these things (Acts 5:11) That day a severe persecution began against the church in Jerusalem, (Acts 8:1) For, to begin with, when you come together as a church, (1 Cor. 11:18)

The community that Christ established and came together to worship God was called the "church". It was the community of the believers. They were collectively known as the church, whether a group gathered in a particular locality or the collection of beliers as a whole their belonging to the church gave them an identity more so when they were driven out from the Jewish synagogue.

3. Identity and Community in the Biblical Stories

The biblical stories indicate that there was a close connection between the identity of the people and their association and belongingness in the wider community. In another words, the biblical identity was more of a collective identity than an individual one. It is belongingness or lack of it that determined the identity of a person including her/his role and status in the social order. For convenience sake these identities can be clubbed into three groupings. They are: subjugated identity, contested identity and Reclaimed Identity.

a. Subjugated Identity

In the early Israelite history when the people were in Egypt, they were under slavery of Pharaoh. In a foreign land their identity was that of mere slaves. Their survival was depended on the good pleasure of the slave masters and their rulers. As a subordinated people, they had no freedom. They were to do the work of slaves in brick kiln not only making bricks but also procuring the firewood for baking the bricks. This was a subjugated identity. Individual role is determined in association with their clan and tribal identities. A good example is that of Achan's sin that led to the defeat of Israel (Josh. 7:1, 18-24). The person is seen in relation to the community and the entire people suffer for his wrong doing.

Even during the times when the people were in exile, they were in foreign land under Assyria, Babylon, Persia and later Rome. The identity of the people as an independent nation was under threat under all these rulers. People not only had to serve them, they were exploited and oppressed. Despite their commitment to Jerusalem many a people became flexible and adjusted their identity in order to survive. Thus it was identification with local culture to the most was the mode of survival.

b. Contested Identity

Israel's claim as the people of God and the land as a divine promise to them were not readily accepted by all nations surrounding them. God's assurance of a promise land through Moses involved a series of wars with the native people so as to occupy them. Israel claimed themselves as the chosen people of God and the land as given to them by the promise of God. Their identity deeply associated with the land.[31] But this claim to identity associated with the

land came under intense challenge by the natives of the land. It was constantly under test as the many wars and exiles testify.

Even when the people returned after the exile in Babylon, the natives in Palestine, refused to have them occupy the land and rebuild the temple and the wall, by the Samaritans and the Tobias and Sambalat. Israel's claim for lost identity was under context during this period. Under the Roman rule The Maccabean family had to sacrifice their lives for the sake of safeguarding the independence of the people. They succeeded for a period of time.[32]

The early church had to face estranged relation with the synagogue community and was finally thrown out of the synagogue as the Matthean and Johannine community testify. The Jew-Gentile controversy in the early Church had to do with the question of identity. The Jews felt threatened owing to the influx of Gentile Christians and demanded that they first become Jews before they can be Christians.

c. Identity Reclaimed

Conquest of the promise land and the establishment of the nation was an affirmation of their identity although it may have been contested at various points of their history. A mark of affirmation of their identity was the establishment of the monarchic rule despite divine intervention at various points. With this the Israelites become a people like the rest of their neighbours with a king of their own. Repeated battles they had fought, for example, with the Philistines, Midinites, etc and the battles they won were a testimony to

31 See J.H. Christopher Wright, *Old Testament Ethics for the People of God* (Secunderabad: OM Books, 2004).

32 See Jones, Sian & Sarah Pearce, eds., *Jewish Local Patriotism and Self-Identification in the Graeco-Roman Period*, JSPSS 31 (Sheffield Academic Press, 1998)

their perseverance on the face of adversities to reclaim their identity. Even while on exile, the Israelites tried to maintain their religious and cultural practices through worship and celebration of festivals. When they were able to return to their native land after a period of exile, they tried to re-establish themselves with their own cultural and religious identity as Ezra and Josiah's reforms indicate.

Conclusion

It is my hope and prayer that our deliberations the next two days will help us to explore a little more in detail these subjugated, contested and reclaimed identities in the biblical narratives and the integral relation of these identities in our rootedness in communities. May God bless us all!

2

Quest for Identity in Community Formation
Biblical Perspectives

Keynote Address
Identity and People of God in Biblical Tradition

Vanlalnghaka Ralte

It's a great honour and special privilege to give the keynote address in this Biennial Conference of the SBSI 2018 which selects its theme, "Quest for Identity in Community Formation: Biblical Perspective." I thank the Executive Committee of the SBSI for assigning me this important responsibility. However, I feel myself inadequate to take up the task and I know that I will not be able to do justice to this respectable assignment. I am convinced that we are going to have insightful papers from our resource persons which address the theme from different biblical-theological perspectives, and that the august gathering of biblical scholars would enrich us with their profound scholarships through the discussions and the other sessions during this Conference. Gleaning some insights drawn from the selected themes in this Conference let me share some preliminary reflections which we are going to engage deeper in the ensuing sessions.

Identity can be said as trait of a person that distinguished an individual or a group from the others. As a matter of definition, identity is a fusion of both what are inherent and acquired in a person, and it is build up in due course of time. The group that has a shared identity formed a community characterized by ethnic or racial, socio-religious, socio-cultural and socio-political distinctions. The identity of a community often developed out of the need of the members within the community and also as a response to the external forces that threatened the stability of the community life and sometimes the very existence of the community. The characteristic feature of the community is that it treasured shared values, beliefs, world views, aspirations and visions. These commonly shared characteristics of the community function as identity markers for the community members and locate others as outsiders or different or even unclean.

The Biblical traditions of both the Old Testament and the New Testament are truly interpretative history of the People of God in the old and new dispensations. They tell of the continuing quest for identity on the part of the People of God to form a distinctive community at each stage of God's salvation history characterized by some specific and extraordinary events like the call of Abraham, the Exodus, the consolidation of Israel as a nation through the instrumentality of monarchy, the return from Babylonian exile, the Christ event and, the origin and development of the Early Church. We see that in each of these epochs in the history of the people of God, characterization of identity and formation of the community had evolved in the contexts of inner tensions on the one hand and threats from overriding colonial Empires on the other. The art of constructing identity, therefore, served as the agent of continuity, resistance and renewal for the community of the people of God. The biblical accounts of search for identity in community formation have implications for Christian communities today who have found themselves entangled in the contexts of inner tensions within the faith communities and threats from modern forms of oppressive empires.

By the turn of the 20th century due to freedom struggle movements on the part of the so called 'third world' countries, the colonial imperial powers of the West had to withdraw themselves from countries which they previously held as colonies. Therefore, many nation-states were born and began to re-affirm and re-create their identities resulting in the formation of new communities in those respective regions. The emergence of these socio-political phenomena had given new horizons to develop contextual theologies and indigenous biblical hermeneutics including that of postcolonial reading, dalit reading and the emerging tribal reading of the Bible. As part of these new trends in biblical interpretation, renewed interest evolved in research on the quest for identity in community formation basing on the experience of People of God in biblical tradition.

One important area of interest in Old Testament is the patriarchal traditions in the book of Genesis (Gen 12 – 50) which began with the call of Abraham with a promise of the land and to be the progenitor of a great nation, and be blessed so that all the families of the earth will be blessed through him(Gen 12:1-3). The stories of the patriarch such as Abraham, Isaac, Jacob and Joseph can be seen as foundation of Israel's identity as a community that worshipped Yahweh under various names, such as, El Elyon (14:18-24); El Roi (16:13); El Shaddai (17:1; 43; 14;); El' olam (21:33). The cultic practice, however, was quite simple with animal sacrifice and the head of the clan/ community performing the rituals. It must be noted here that the evolution of the identity of the ancestral community took place in tandem with that of the Mesopotamia, Syria and Canaan. In patriarchal tradition, some of the key characteristics of identity markers are the land, genealogy, the promise of blessings and the worship of Yahweh. These become very significant for the patriarchal community in the context of nomadic life, where wealth and progeny was a sign of power and dignity, and polytheism was the religious norm.

Another area of interest is the struggle for re-affirming Israel's identity in the context of Post-Exilic Judaism as reflected in the books of 1&2 Chronicles. After the tragic experience of defeat, deportation, displacement and shaking religious and cultural foundations in the hands of the imperial Babylon and the more considerate Persian regime, the Chronicler tried to help the post-exilic community of Israel to reclaim their glorious past identity as God's covenant people, whom God had guided with mighty hand from Adam till their return from Babylonian exile, led the people by God's anointed kings, David and Solomon in particular. The detail genealogy is given as proof of true identity for the community of Israel. The significance of the Temple as the symbol of Israel's religiosity, and the importance of the priesthood has also been underlined. The re-affirmation of the community's identity when the life of the community was at it low ebb was of great importance. In the same way, prophet Ezekiel's affirmation of the exilic experience and the fact of being Abraham's descendants as a proof for a true community of Israel is both redeeming and revitalizing. Besides these, it is of special interest to see the importance of wisdom literature in shaping the character and devotional life of a person which positively contribute to the welfare of the community life, that is, to promote peace and justice in the community.

In the New Testament as reflected in the Gospel accounts, in the context of political hegemony of imperial Rome and Jewish legalistic religiosity characterized by Temple sacrificial system controlled by the High Priest and his associates, we see how Jesus called for a radical discipleship of new religious identity which demanded total allegiance and devotion to God, and to love others as oneself. The new identity also carried along a call for humility, honesty, justice, genuine openness and compassion to those in the margins of the society, and to take the Gospel message of God's salvation in Jesus Christ to the ends of the world and to make disciples of all nations. Thus the call for this new religious identity aimed at forming an inclusive community of People of God in the new dispensation, the 'new Israel' who will become 'light of the world' and 'salt of the earth' even in the midst of oppositions and suffering. Whatever shortcomings and misgivings may come on the way the disciples need not be discouraged or feel daunted because the Spirit of God dwelt in them and will always stand by their side to empower them, and that their reward from God is assured. This was a source of encouragement and support even for the Christians in the Early Church as they began to find themselves as a religious community detached from Judaism and distinct from polytheistic religious traditions of Greco-Roman world.

The Pauline letters clearly betray the complexities and dynamism in the life of the early Christian communities in Greco-Roman world. As the letters of Paul are contextual they address various problems and discuss diverse issues pertaining to the concerns of the local churches. For Paul, the identity of the believers should be marked by their unity 'in Christ' which is of prime importance for the Christian community, and this should be reflected in the ministry and mission of the community which is a partnership of equals. The identity of the believing community as Paul envisaged is inclusive, irrespective of race, gender and social status. For, "There is no longer Jew or Greek, there is no longer slave or free. There is no longer male or female; for all of you are in Christ" (Gal 3:28). Paul also clearly spelt out certain matters relation to the moral and ethical standard that is expected of the Christian believers. This is significant as the Pauline churches spread over the major cities of the then Greco-Roman world which was known for moral laxity and licentiousness. For Paul holiness should be the mark of Christian identity and thus any kind of sexual immorality is unacceptable for a believer. For Paul holiness also includes shunning idolatry including participation in the religious festivities of non-believers. Paul is also vocal in his rejection of 'other gospels', other than the Gospel of Jesus Christ, which insist on Jewish legalism or subject to principalities and powers.

The First Letter of Peter and the Book of Revelation reflect what is expected of the believers in the midst of sufferings and persecution. Endurance, courage and faith in the all powerful God have to be the identity that the believers should exhibit in such times of trials and tribulation. The evil forces, though powerful and mighty they may seem, are much inferior and weaker than the true and only God. Ultimately God will defeat and destroy the evil with all its might and power. Thus the community of People of God should wait for the final victory of God with hope and Joy.

The identity of the People of God as attested in biblical tradition has a living message for Christian Community today. I sincerely believe that the papers presented in this SBSI Biennial Conference and the input that we give through our discussions and reflections will challenge us to re-discover and affirm our true identity as people of God today especially in the context of the socio-religio-political upheavals in India today.

3

Quest for Identity in Community Formation
Ancestral Narratives for Model Communities in the Book of Genesis

K. Jesurathnam

I

Introduction

Ethnic identity was an important issue in the ancient times that is during the biblical times of ancient Israel as they are faced with many threats of such identity living in the midst of alien nations far away from their homelands. For anyone living in that alien context feeling of being a 'foreigner' is obvious and inevitable. Various groups lived with that experience in biblical times must have experienced the same. The contemporary situation is no different. In the present Indian context such feeling of alienation has been created by the majority rulers on the minority communities based on the caste, religion and other affiliations. Religious and ethnic identity is being profoundly challenged in our current age. Wherever religious life becomes a matter of debate today, the focus of attention quickly shifts to zones of conflict. Violence, hostility and hatred in the name of God or the sacred captures our attention. In the name of caste and creed violence is leashed out and takes new forms of oppression. It is a mean trait of our age that hate is so closely aligned with religious identity. Examples differ by degree, even as a pattern is strikingly homogenous: religion, caste and culture are used to stigmatize and even obliterate the constitutive aspects of a shared humanity.

Communities are seeking renewal in many different ways in our world today. These include: reinterpreting difficult texts, the healing of memories and overcoming past divisions. Understanding more fully the historicity of the texts and of the divisions helps us to think anew about the constructive meaning of the texts in today's world. Each of our religious communities draws on rich interpretative expertise (Midrash, linguistic analysis, hermeneutics), and in reflecting on the interpretative challenges together we mutually benefit from this expertise.

In the above light we need to ask a question: how will religions have a role in cultivating the human future on this planet? Renewal of religious identity in the twenty-first century will require new metaphors alongside authentic reclamations of our multiple identities, in order to interpret where mystery is spontaneously emerging tomorrow. In the twenty-first century, diverse religious identities intersect every day. The classical borders for religious identity are both more porous and more vulnerable. In the face of this fluidity, the formation of religious identity requires a cross-religious aim, which we see today in the religious reclamation of early mysticism within the respective traditions. The aim is to go to the roots and to the depths of faith in community and the faith instinct generally, in whatever socio-and cultural-religious contexts we find ourselves. In a return to reshaping religious cosmologies that account for our full humanity, all human beings must ask how their respective religious identities enrich or skew a vision of our shared humanity on this planet, and explore the possible horizons of a shared witness to inhabiting the world today.

In the light of our foregoing discussion the task of this presentation is to do the following: first, to understand and explicate the ethnic and identity issues in the history and lives of the ancestral[1] narratives in the Old Testament, particularly in the book of Genesis; second, to relate the contemporary discourse on identity with that of biblical accounts; third, to draw implications on the discussed subject to the present ecclesial and societal context in our contemporary India.

II

Ancestral Narratives in the Book of Genesis

The structure of Genesis 12-50 is made up of three cycles of stories. The first is primarily concerned with Abraham. It is found in Genesis 12-24. The second

1 The word ancestral is being modified from the usual description of Patriarchal narratives in the book of Genesis. Both the terms patriarchal and ancestral are interchangeably used in this presentation. Moreover the word 'ancestral' implies inclusive language whereby both the Patriarch and matriarch are taken together into consideration.

primarily concerns Jacob found in Genesis 25-36. The third primarily concerns Joseph found in Genesis 37-50.

The literary genre of this material might be called "legend." It concerns larger-than-life figures from Israel's distant past. There might be some historical kernel behind all these stories, but that is lost in centuries of oral transmission. We may call these figures eponymous ancestors of the Israelite people. By this we mean that they are legendary figures whose life and actions somehow represent show Israelites see themselves, what they feel they are and what their destinies are. Jacob, of the second cycle, is renamed "Israel," and so somehow embodies the Israelite psyche. Jacob's twelve sons have the same name as the twelve tribes of Israel. The most important of the sons correspond with the larger and most important of the tribes. So what Israel says about their ancestors is in fact what they say about themselves.

The theme of blessing that bubbles under the surface of the first eleven chapters of Genesis bursts forth in the patriarchal section. The literary structure of Genesis shows how the three features of God's blessing are each focused in turn in the three cycles of narrative. Thus Abraham's story highlights the blessing of descendants and a great nation. Jacob's account revolves around the blessing of the land, and Joseph's story centers on the blessing of being a blessing to all peoples on earth.

In each of the stories the tension develops between human and divine activity in respect to blessing. When Abraham and Sarah take the initiative to make the blessing come true, there is heartache and eternal consequence. Later God tests Abraham to see whether he trusts God completely with the blessing. The Jacob cycle is characterized by deceit as, over and over again, Jacob takes the blessing into his own hands. The astonishing outcome is that of all the three characters, Jacob experiences the material blessing most unquestionably. He has twelve sons who found the twelve tribes of Israel, he amasses property wherever he goes. He enjoys life in the Promised Land and later is buried there as well. Joseph, on the other hand, embodies the model of a steadfast and faithful response to God and his blessing. Despite this faithful response, Joseph experiences betrayal, imprisonment, neglect and perhaps even a sense of distance from God. The patriarchal narratives clearly illustrate that there is never a one-to-one relationship between human and divine involvement in blessing. Blessing begins with God and is carried on by God. Human participation and response is crucial, yes, but it is not the hinge on which God offers and sustains blessing.

God's plan is to bless people. God promises and fulfills the blessing according to that plan. However, just as that blessing cannot be manipulated by people, neither can it be rushed. From the human standpoint, at moments it may seem that the blessing has been bestowed on the wrong people, come to a standstill, or even disappeared altogether. Yet the book of Genesis confirms that the story of God's interaction with humanity is a story of blessing. At the same time the story of each ancestor also depicts their struggle for identity and settlement as they moved and sojourned in their pilgrimage. They had to survive in the midst of their multi-religious and multi-cultural contexts that threatened their identity and their very existence. Despite the theme of blessing is an overarching theme in the ancestral narratives in the book of Genesis, quest for identity as a people of God remains a recurring and flowing theme. Out of this struggle of the ancestors of ancient Israel, a hopeful community has emerged. We shall focus more on this issue in the following sections below.

III

Social Context of the Ancestors

In the middle decades of the 20th century based on the discoveries of archaeology, the scholars associated with this method took a generally positive view of the historical value of Genesis 12–50. They acknowledged that the patriarchal/ancestral narratives in their present form were composed no earlier than the United Kingdom of Israel and Judah (tenth century B.C.E.). Nevertheless, they argued that these materials were based on historically reliable traditions deriving from earlier periods. Excavations had provided extensive new data, including a substantial amount of written material. After studying these texts, many scholars were convinced that the biblical ancestral stories contained authentic details preserved from the time of their origin. It seemed reasonable, therefore, to suppose that there was a historical ancestral period and to hope that it might be identified.

The above point of view is associated most closely with the work of William F. Albright and his students John Bright and G. E. Wright who worked under the banner of "Baltimore School." Their conclusions are based on the following assertions found within the ancestral narratives:

Certain details in the biblical ancestral stories—including personal names, social customs, legal practices and aspects of lifestyle—correspond to known features of second-millennium culture in Mesopotamia, Syria and Canaan. Many of the same details, moreover, do not fit into the culture of the Israelite monarchy, the time when the stories were written down. In the judgment of Albright and those who shared his viewpoint, it seemed likely that these details preserved authentic elements of the civilization of the patriarchal period; by studying them and comparing them to surviving second-millennium materials.[2]

Outside the Bible, we should be able to determine the original historical context of the patriarchal traditions. Nevertheless, archaeology might be able

2 For more details on this and related issues see, John Bright, *A History of Israel*, 4th edition, (Louisville, Kentucky: Westminster John Knox Press, 2000).

to shed light on the general historical context of the patriarchal stories. And this is primarily what was claimed by Albright and his students. They argued that the general cultural milieu of the patriarchal stories—as indicated by the details of social, economic and legal customs mentioned in the Bible—could best be identified with an early period and, more particularly, with the early second millennium B.C[3]

The reconstruction of patriarchal history achieved by Albright, Speiser and others has had far-reaching consequences. With all uncertainties in the accuracy of archaeological data the problems persist to establish the conclusions in an absolute manner.

IV

Extra-Biblical Input on the Ancestral Social Context

We must now turn our attention to the information that brings the close affinity of ancestral narratives in terms of their culture and customs based on Mari and Nuzi texts.

The names of the ancestors and relatives of Abraham in Ge. 11, include those of Haran, Nahor, Serug, and Peleg. These appear as names of cities in ancient records, particularly from Mari, a little farther down the Euphrates. Same of the vital clues may have been provided in the Mari to understand patriarchs in the Bible. Following are the vital points:

First, both patriarchal and Mari societies are "dimorphic". For instance, in Genesis some events reflect this such as: the frequent custom of camping in the vicinity of towns (Gen 12:6-9, 13:12-18, 33:18-20, 35:16-21, 37: 12-17); the occasional practice of agriculture (Gen 26:12f); the case of social and economic exchange with towns people (Gen 21:25-34; 23: 1-20, 26:17-33; 33:18-20); and the fact that Abraham, Lot and Isaac even dwell in the towns for various periods of time as 'resident aliens' (Heb. *gēr*, Gen. 23:4 cf; Yasab to dwell Gen 12:10). Perhaps the episode is best clarified by the notion of a dimorphic society are the separation of Abraham and Lot and Lot's taking up residence within the orbit of the Canaanite towns (Gen 13:8-13, 19:1-4). Lot was sitting in the gate simply means that he dwelt near the gate outside the town, as Mari tribes people are sometimes described as doing; the contrasting yet complementary vocations of Jacob and Esau (Gen 25: 27-34); and particularly the relation of Jacob to the Shechemites (Gen 33: 18, 34:31).

Second, in both dimorphic societies the groups representing the village pastoral morpheme are virtually identical. The tribal people of both Mari and the tribes of Genesis are pastoralists, i.e., sheep-breeders who move their encampments periodically in search of water and pasturage. In Israel this pastoral life is further characterized by the semi-nomadic life of shepherds

3 Ibid.

who live in tents and move with their flocks, sometimes over considerable distances seeking traditional and sometimes disputed pastures and well. (Gen 3:5-11, 18: 1-8, 21:25-31, 24:62-67, 26:1-33, 29-31 chs; 33:12-17, 36:6-8).

Third, both societies in question are tribally organized.

Fourth, the social institutions of the two-tribal societies might be compared, especially patrimony, the custom of census taking, and the prominent place given to genealogies.

In recent years, many attempts have been made at explaining elements in the patriarchal stories from personal names and from information about customs and legal practices known to us from this northern Mesopotamian are particularly from Mari (around 1700 BCE) and from Nuzi (further to the east, belonging to about 1500 to 1350 BCE) some vital points are follows:

First, the names in the patriarchal narratives fit perfectly in a class known to have been current in both Mesopotamia and Palestine in the second millennium, specifically among the Amorite element of the population. For eg: the names of the patriarchs themselves, "Jacob" occurs in an eighteenth century text from Chagar Bazar upper Mesopotamia (*Ya'Qubel*), as the name of the Hyksos chief (Ya'Qub-'al), and as a Palestinian, place name in fifteenth-century list of Thutmosis III. The name "Abram" (Abraham) is know from Babylonian texts of the first Dynasty and possibly from the Execration Texts. The word "Nahor" occurs in the Mari texts as the name of the town (Nakhur) in the vicinity of Haran (as in Gen 24:10).

Second, Patriachal customs against the background of the second millennium: the Nuzi texts which reflect the customary law of a predominantly. Hurrian population in the East-Tigris region in the fifteenth century are useful to get some clues for the patriarchal narratives and their surroundings. One such evidence can be traced for example:

i) From the story of Abraham's fear (Gen 15:1-4) that his slave Eleazar would be his heir becomes understandable in the light of slave adoption as practiced at Nuzi. Childless couples would adopt a son who would serve them as long as they lived and inherit on their death. But, should natural son be born, the adopted son would have to yield the right of inheritance.
ii) Sarah gave her slave Hagar to Abraham as a concubine (Gen 16:1-4), so at Nuzi a marriage contract obliged the wife, of childless, to provide her husband with a substitute. Should son be born of such a union, the expulsion of the slave wife and her child was forbidden which explains Abraham's reluctance to send Hagar and Ishmael away (ch. 21:10f).
iii) In Laban-Jacob stories, Nuzi texts are especially illuminating. The adoption of Jacob into Laban's household, the condition laid on him

to take no other wives other than Laban's daughters (Gen. 31), the resentment of Leah and Rachel against Laban (Gen. 31:15), and finally, Rachel's theft of Laban's gods (M. Greenberg argues: that possession of the gods conveyed title to headship in the family[4]); all are paralleled by Nuzian customs.

One may argue that such customs are not only limited to Nuzi texts, i.e., to the Hurrian population, but in general they are wide spread in the entire Palestinian area, but the fact remains only such parallels are found in Genesis accounts are not related to the other stories of the Bible. But we need to recognize the fact that the information available to link the Hurrian customs and patriarchal stories is not adequate.[5] However the fact remains that the ancestral narratives grew in the midst of contemporary cultures and although we do not have adequate proof, we may plausibly argue that the biblical ancestors would have struggled to establish their identity amidst such complex socio-cultural milieu. It seems most plausible to argue that they lived as sojourners in all their dwellings as they moved from place to place in search of their identity until they become a nation on their own right.

V

Syrian and Canaanite Background

An urban culture flourished in Syria and Canaan during the Early Bronze Age, which spanned much of the third millennium B.C.E. During the last quarter of the third millennium, however, this civilization collapsed and was replaced by a predominantly nonurban, pastoral culture. The factors that produced this change are not fully understood. The third dynasty of the city of Ur held sway in Mesopotamia at the time, and the records of the Ur III rulers complain of chronic trouble with nonurban peoples who were laying claim to lands previously controlled by the city. Scholars long supposed, therefore, that a chief factor in the urban collapse was an invasion—or at least a massive immigration—of nomadic peoples from the desert fringes of the region. These peoples, called *Amurru*—that is, "Westerners" or "Amorites"—in the Mesopotamian sources, gradually gained ascendancy in the settled portions of both Syria-Canaan and Mesopotamia, so that in the early second millennium they took the leadership in reestablishing urban centers.

The theory that an invasion or immigration of Amorites was responsible for the radical cultural changes that characterized the transition from the Early to Middle Bronze Age is sometimes called "the Amorite hypothesis." A corollary

---

4 M. Greenberg, "Another look at Rachel's Theft of Teraphim," *Journal of Biblical Literature* 81 (1962), pp. 239-248.

5 Kondasingu Jesurathnam, *Introduction to the Old Testament: Tracing the History, Culture and Scripture of Ancient Israel* (New Delhi: Christian World Imprints, 2018), pp. 36-38.

of this hypothesis identifies the biblical patriarchs as Amorites. Albright associated Abraham's wanderings with the Amorite movements and dated the Abraham phase of the patriarchal period to the end of the third millennium. He called this period, which he dated to 2100–1900 B.C.E., Middle Bronze I (MB I), since it represented a break from the preceding Early Bronze Age and was characterized by the arrival of the people who would assume cultural leadership later in the Middle Bronze Age. The succeeding period, which Albright called MB II A, was an age of unwilled villages in Syria and Canaan. The strong 12th Dynasty kings of Egypt encouraged the gradual development of a system of city-states in Syria and Canaan. Then, as Egypt began to weaken at the end of this period, the new urban centers entered a period of independence, prosperity and high cultural attainment. Albright identified this period, which he called MB II B, as the time of the patriarch Jacob. This was the Old Babylonian period in Mesopotamia, when Hammurabi and his successors ruled. In Syria it is sometimes called "the age of Mari," after a city on the Upper Euphrates that attained a position of ascendancy in Syria and western Mesopotamia at the time. The life and history of Mari are recorded in a major cuneiform archive found at the site, called Tell Hariri, on the Syrian side of the modern Syro-Iraqi frontier. Local leadership for the process of reurbanization came from the previously nomadic Amorite population. We know this because the new ruling dynasties in the city-states of Syria and Mesopotamia have characteristically Amorite names. There remained, however, a substantial nomadic population, which was also Amorite. The royal archives of Mari provide ample illustration of the coexistence of the two groups.[6]

VI

Family in the Context of Identity

At the outset of the ancestral narratives, we find a brief speech of the deity. In that address, God directs Abraham to leave the land in which he had been dwelling and to travel to another land. Following that command, the deity promises to Abraham that he will become a great nation and that "through you all the families of the earth shall be blessed" (Gen 12:3).[7] This is a rich

6 Hendel, Ronald S., McCarter, P. Kyle, Jr.. "The Patriarchal Age: Abraham, Isaac and Jacob." *Ancient Israel*, 1999.http://www.basarchive.org/bswbBrowse.asp?PubID=BSBKAI&Volume=0&Issue=0&ArticleID =1&UserID=2(accessed 8/19/2008)

7 For a more detailed discussion on this and related matters see, David L. Petersen, "Genesis and Family Values," *Journal of Biblical Literature* 124:1 (2005), pp. 5-23. Or, "through you all the families of the earth will bless themselves." Cf. other instances in which a comparable formula is used—in the *niphal* 18:18; 28:14; in the *hithpael,* 22:18; 26:4. Waltke and O'Connor emphasize "the passive import" of the verb (*IBHS* 23.6.4a). For a discussion, see Erhard Blum, *Die Komposition der Vätergeschichte* (WMANT 57; Neukirchen-Vluyn: Neukirchener Verlag, 1984). 350–53; Patrick Miller, "Syntax and

and provocative statement. In three other texts (18:18; 22:18; 26:4), we hear that those others who will be blessed are "nations" (*gôyîm*). In Gen 12:3 (and 28:14), however, the author uses familial language—the noun *mišpāḥot*, which is often translated "clan." Here, at a point where the deity has chosen to interact directly with the lineage of Terah, the biblical author wants readers to know that those outside that lineage have not been ignored. Moreover, they are to be thought of as family, the broader family of humanity. Other parts of that broader family are to share in Israel's blessing. This sort of explanation in the biblical text provides an identity to Abraham who has come from an "alien" land with another distant identity which is far away from the people of Israel in terms of their geographical location. We may argue that the family values kept intact within Abraham's pilgrim journey made and brought his identity within the community more strong than all other avenues.

The family values and their dynamics continue to reflect in the stories of other ancestors like Isaac, Jacob and Joseph stories. These values continue in the situations of possible conflict between Abraham – Lot, Jacob – Laban and Jacob – Esau. However the conflicts between these individuals resolved amicably within the context of the family. Thus all the ancestral narratives in one way or another have been captivated by the idea that they are able to maintain their community and family identity thus moved on successfully in their life journey.

VII

Religious Identity of the Ancestors

The religion of ancestors has been vital in the formation of the community identity in the case of all the individual ancestor's lives.

At the outset it must be said that to deduce the nature of the patriarchal religion from the Genesis narrative is not easy. According to Yahwist source (J) the God of the patriarchs was none other than Yahweh. But elsewhere in Exod 6.2f, it is stated that though it was really Yahweh who had appeared to the patriarchs, he had not been known to them that name. The other strand of thought (E and P) avoid mention of Yahweh until they come to Moses, and speak of the patriarchal deity simply "God" (Elohim). All accounts agree, however, that the patriarchs worshipped God under various names; *El Shaddai* (Ex 6: 7, Gen 17:1, 43:14 etc.); *El 'Elyon* (Gen 14:18-24); *El'olam* (Gen 21:33); *El Roi* (Gen 16:13 cf. *Yahweh Yir'eh*, (Gen. 22 1.4), *El Bethel* (Gen 31: 13, 35: 7).

Theology in Genesis XII 3a," *VT* 34 (1984): 472–76; Claus Westermann, *Genesis 12–36* (Minneapolis: Augsburg, 1985), 151–52; Keith Grüneberg, *Abraham, Blessing, and the Nations: A Philological and Exegetical Study of Genesis 12:3 in Its Narrative Context* (BZAW 332; Berlin: de Gruyter, 2003).

The God of the Patriarchs: In Genesis narratives each patriarch is represented as undertaking by a free and personal choice the worship of his God to whom he thereafter entrusted himself. Each patriarch seems to have a clan God, these are: The God of Abraham *('elohe Abraham* eg.; Gen. 28:13, 31:42, 53); the kinsman of Isaac (*Pahad yishaq*: Ch 31: 42, 53); and the champion of (might one) Jacob *('abir ya 'qob*: ch. 49:24). The God was the patron deity of the clan. This is illustrated in Gen. 31: 36-55 where Jacob swears by the Kinsman of

Isaac, and Laban by the God of Nahor; i.e., each swears by the God of his father's clan.

Although it is impossible to describe the religion of the patriarchs in detail, owing to gaps in our knowledge, it was clearly of a type at home in the world of the day. We may note that the central cult in Ur was Sin cult (moon cult), thus we may suppose that the family of Abraham had once been devotees of Sin. But later Abraham might have moved from Ur due to economic factor, and also due to their personal experience. Thus, the patriarchal religion was a clan religion, in which the clan was quite really the family of the patron God.

The cult of the ancestors is depicted as exceedingly simple, as one would expect it to be. At its center was animal sacrifice, as among all the Semites; but this was performed without organized clergy, and whatever place, by the hand of the clan father himself. As the patriarchs moved into Palestine they came into contact with various shrines; Shechem, Bethel, Beer-Sheba, etc., there is no doubt their cults were practiced and perpetuated in identification with the cults already at home at those places. The patriarchal cult, however, was never a local one, but always the cult of the ancestral deity of the clan. In this way they inherited and practiced a great cultural and religious heritage as part of their cult.

VIII

Identity Transformation of the Ancestors in Genesis

The ancestral narratives in the book of Genesis reflect the theme of identity formation and transformation as the ancestors underwent different realities/ situations in their lives. The identity transformation of Abram and Sarai is seen in Genesis 17 where Abram becomes the beneficiary of a covenant with God and receives the promise of offspring and land. This is a transformation in Abram's occupation, which God signifies with a new name: Abram becomes Abraham, who will be the father of a multitude of nations (17:4). At God's command, Abraham inaugurates the practice of circumcision, a transformation in body. Sarai's identity is disrupted along the same lines. God renames her Sarah, which does not lexically signify a new occupation; however, as with Abraham, God now announces that nations and kings will come from her

(17:15–16).[8] There is no corresponding female circumcision, but Sarah is promised a change in body: she will become pregnant, a transformation so remarkable that Abraham falls down laughing (17:17).

Jacob experiences a transformation in identity in Genesis 32. At the Jabbok ford Jacob wrestles with a divine being all night, and in the morning is renamed Israel (32:29). The name signifies a change in occupation. Jacob was a man of constant strife; he cannot even flee for his life from Esau without being assaulted by a divine being. Now, says his combatant, Jacob is a victor.[9] The divine being leaves Jacob with an injury, a change in body so much a part of Jacob's identity that it justifies a dietary restriction in the author's own time (32:33).[10] The change in Jacob's name is repeated in Genesis 35, at Bethel. God renames him Israel, tells him that nations and kings will issue from him, and assigns the land to his descendants (32:9–12). As with Abraham, Jacob's new identity is linked with the divine promise of land and offspring.

Identity is a major theme of the story of Joseph, where its transformation is gradual, equivocal, and incomplete. The brothers' mistaking Joseph's identity gives the climax its dramatic weight, and even readers may finally wonder, who is Joseph? Has the victimized Hebrew dreamer truly become a ruthless Egyptian bureaucrat? His journey is one of great change. In bodily terms, the cloak that visually identifies him is stolen and bloodied; he receives a haircut and a change of clothes when brought before Pharaoh; Pharaoh bestows upon Joseph his signet ring, fine clothes, and a gold chain. Whether it is these physical affects or the effects of time, Joseph's brothers do not recognize him when they next meet. Pharaoh makes Joseph Egyptian in name as well as appearance, dubbing him Zaphenath-Paneah (Gen 41:45).6 Joseph seems to acknowledge his own identity transformation with the naming of his son Manasseh, declaring that he has forgotten his hardships and his father's house (41:51).7 This could amount to a change in group membership and a transformation into the Egyptian "other," the man Joseph's brothers believe him to be. But Joseph never truly abandons his Hebrew identity, and his story ends with recognition and reconciliation. His transformation into an Egyptian is incomplete.[11]

There are several characters in Genesis whose identities seem to change temporarily. In each case, the agent is not God, but another character, and the purpose is deception. Abraham twice passes Sarah off as his sister, to fool the Egyptians and then the Philistines (Genesis 12; 20); Isaac does the

---

8 For more details on this and related points see, Ryan Stephen Higgins, "You Will Become My People: Pentateuchal Attitudes Toward Identity Transformation," Unpublished paper.

9 Ibid.

10 Some would call this as an etiology for a dietary restriction of a hip socket bone.

11 See for more details Higgins, "You will become."

same with Rebekah in Philistia (Genesis 26); and Rebekah turns Jacob into Esau to trick Isaac (Genesis 27).8 These identity assumptions are a different phenomenon the transformations that produce Abraham, Sarah, and Israel. But they are similar to the transformation of Joseph: his identity does not fully and permanently change, and he deceitfully hides his true identity from his brothers. God does not even appear to be the agent: Joseph's brothers expel him from his group, and Pharaoh promotes and renames him. However, Joseph insists that God is responsible for his journey, from pit to palace: "it was not you who sent me here, but God" (45:8), "God has made me lord of all Egypt" (45:9), "although you intended me harm, God intended it for good" (50:20). Even though Pharaoh replaces his Hebrew name, Joseph attributes his sense of lost identity to God, saying at the naming of Manasseh, "God has made me forget" (41:51).

The above discussion reveals that identity change has happened in the context of community even when an individual alone is involved in the process. This community could be within a family setting or among neighbours or even in an alien context. But the fact remains that the identity changes the destiny and way of life of the one who has undergone the process for better or for worse.

IX

Issues of Identity in our Contemporary Global and Indian Context: Implications from the Ancestral Narratives

In the global and Indian context we face many issues of identity that needs our urgent attention for the good of every individual as well as community in the world.

God and Neighbour: A first challenge and issue of identity for us is a twofold transcendence: toward God and toward our neighbor. Any type of personal discernment concerning our religious identity is more than an adventure. It is a journey, but it is not simply a journey. It is the path that God provides for us. The journey symbol is dominant in our religious traditions. Our traditions begin with the story of an act of faith expressed by a journey when God said to Abraham, "Go from your country." The journey out of ourselves allows us to meet God and to meet others. Closeness with God brings us closer to others. Put simply, this is love of God and love of neighbor. In this process closeness is a key word: be near. We need to explore this common understanding from our traditions in light of our special relationships with one another founded on faith of Abraham.

Structures and Institutions: A second challenge and issue of identity is to realize that we run into the risk if we allow our identity to depend too much on comfortable structures. True, structures serve their purposes, sometimes accomplishing what they set out to do, but then preserving them too rigidly becomes full-time work and creativity is lost. Besides, new generations may require adjustments to structure. In India in the last several decades unprecedented changes have taken place in the community formation in our ecclesial context. Several ecumenical bodies have been formulated by our ancestors for effective cooperation between various religious denominations and even within the same denomination. By and large these structures in due course have become rigid and their initial vision and purpose have been lost. Strict lines of demarcation appears today that led these bodies dominated by structure rather than the love of God.

We honor those pioneers who served not by preserving their old structures but by building on their achievements and meeting present needs. Too many of our co-religionists are so loyal to present institutional structures that they are prevented from experiencing God's grace. We are not suggesting that structures be thrown away completely but adjusted so as to be both faithful to what we believe and helpful to those who participate. In this process of mutual enlightenment and enrichment takes place suggesting that we are co-pilgrims with Abraham and other ancestors in our journey for identity and the formation of communities of God.[12] This attitude will help us be creative even when we are expected to operate within our given structures.

Abrahamic character: A third challenge and issue in our quest for identity and community formation is to face squarely how we each claim an Abrahamic character. We understand ourselves as a people who hear God and act. In the prayer of the church, morning and evening prayer, hymns from the Gospel of Luke are recited each day, the Song of Zechariah (the Benedictus, Luke 1:68–79) in the morning and the Canticle of Mary (the Magnificat, Luke 1:46–55) in the evening. Both mention Abraham: "Our father Abraham" and "the promise he made to our fathers, to Abraham and his descendants." And the liturgy each day refers to "the sacrifice of Abraham, our father in faith."

In addition, we see the polyvalent nature of Abraham and other ancestors of ancient Israel to the models of community identity whereby they represent an inclusive community with sober family values that are to be integrated to our present social and ecclesial life. This way of critical imagination helps us to imbibe the character of Abraham. The value of amicable settlement, negotiation, accommodation, and integration are all part of the process of community building and formation that is required in our contemporary Indian

12 In this connection I would like to draw our attention to the recent attempt made by the Church of South India to initiate and discuss on the theme: "Rethinking Ecclesia: Towards a borderless Church," where in a strong call is given towards rethinking our structures of various churches. This initiative calls us to think creatively and constructively how to remain borderless while retaining our structures and borders.

society. Then the so called Abrahamic "haggling" with God for the salvation of Sodom and Gomorrah even there are few righteous individuals.[13]

Companionship in Our Journey: The fourth challenge and issue that needs to be taken with utmost care in our cotemporary church and society in our quest for the identity in forming God communities on this earth is to look on our lives as spiritual journeys and to see how we are all companions on the journey. Abraham and other ancestors journeyed without any inhibitions and expectations and as they moved forward in their pilgrimage they discovered new yet very amazing things. There are increasing numbers of people identifying less and less with religious institutions and defining themselves as spiritual seekers. This is coupled with a renewed interest in spiritual practices within Christianity. For example, many religious orders have come to understand that their future depends on teaching lay people how to live their charism.

Fewer young people identify with religious communities, and there is an increasing number of "nones" or non-affiliated. Whether these are trends or not remains to be seen. By this we are not recommending centers of atheism and secularism in India. It only means how our society is in the process of transformation seeking common goals in living together as one community of God's creation. There are sober attempts at the integration of the communities as for instance, through the practice of Yoga and other borrowed forms of spiritual practice are more popular than ever. A debate rages in some circles on whether or not one needs to know something about Hinduism to practice yoga as a spiritual way of life. This means for us that spiritual hunger remains stronger than ever. We can certainly understand ourselves by what we believe, but more significant is what we do as people of faith. Our faith should give us joy, and joy should define our companionship with one another and with all. Abraham believed in God and he was considered as righteous in the midst and among all.

Challenge of Religious Fundamentalism: The fifth challenge with which we need to grapple within the Indian context in our search for identity and community formation is the question of religious exclusivism and fundamentalism. Recent times India stands on the hooks of this problem as we all are aware of the change in the current political scenario. The Hindutva forces harp on the national and religious unity on the basis of cultural and religious homogenization that majority of Indians are (should be) Hindus. This ideology creates tremendous pressure among the religious minorities and questions their identity seriously. Although there is a strong voice against

---

13 Patrick J. Ryan S.J., "The Faith of Abraham: Bond or Barrier?," in *Origins: CNS Documentary Service* 41, 5 (9 June 2011), 73, note 20. Also see Jon D. Levenson, *Inheriting Abraham: The Legacy of the Patriarch in Judaism, Christianity, and Islam* (Princeton: Princeton University Press, 2012).

such vested interest political agenda orchestrated by the Hindu majority, the Hindutva forces are gradually gaining a strong ground over the years. Mohan Razu affirms that the threat of religious fundamentalism is looming large for the religious minorities with the consolidation of the religious fundamentalist Hindutva forces. He writes:

> The Hindutva forces, in order to consolidate its social control, launched a process of standardization of Hindu law to categorize and exclude all those who could not be considered on the grounds of Christian, Muslim, and other religious minorities. In addition, the Hindutva hegemony has launched the census as a categorization device wherein the lower rungs of the social ladder, i.e., castes and communities, are given the option to clearly identify themselves as one or the other. They are posing as a homogenous 'Hindu' community by pretending that they have transcended the caste divides so that the other identities such as the Dalits and the Tribals who practice their own particular religious beliefs be brought under the category of 'Hindu.'[14]

In the midst of such a threat how do we talk about the communities that emulate equality and justice as hallmarks of God communities? We need to be aware of the dangers that confront us and perhaps develop a tolerant attitude towards people of other faiths rather than being aggressive to them. These days we hear about constant attacks on the churches, reports of vandalism on Christian communities, atrocities against the minorities etc are routine part of the daily news reports. In such disturbing situations what will be our attitude towards the people of other faiths? The church by and large lives like an exclusive community in this world. But as a theologically trained community we have the responsibility to build inclusive communities in this world without giving up our own identity. This is an urgent task in our quest for identity in forming the new and inclusive and tolerant communities. Ancestors in the book of Genesis have faced many aspects of religious and ethnic threats yet they remained as tolerant and inclusive communities in their best possible manner.

Prophetic Vitality: The sixth issue and concern in our quest for identity in community formation is the issue of justice of God. The prophetic ministry in Israel by and large concentrates on the practice of justice in all walks of the people's life in their daily living. No one should discriminate any member of the society. All the sections, particularly the marginalized groups are to be treated with fairness. This is the way in which the practice of justice is to be demonstrated in the Israelite society. Brueggemann is right in saying that "this

14 I. John Mohan Razu, Parliamentary Elections 2014: Battle for the Ballot – "unity in uniformity or unity in diversity," An informal paper written in February 2014.

prophetic accent to be that all members of the community, rich and poor, urban and rural, wise and foolish, powerful and marginalized, are bound to each other in a common historical and social enterprise. Every member, by virtue of membership in the community, has entitlement that cannot be abrogated. Thus "widow, orphan, alien" are ciphers for those most vulnerable and powerless and marginated in a patriarchal society, who are without legal recourse or economic leverage. They are entitled and must be given their share."[15]

Prophetic vision and conviction is now required to dismantle and destroy caste. Reflecting on the Prophetic text of Isaiah 40:4 Razu writes:

> Caste system brought unevenness, asymmetries, valleys and mountains, rugged and rough terrains. Caste is strongly entrenched and enmeshed in Indian psyche as well as in our systems and structures both in the society, church and theological institutions … As part of … ministerial training, conscious efforts should be made by the pedagogues and the pupils towards annihilating caste, and also to get involved in theefforts of lifting up the valley i.e. the terrains or the rough and rugged uneven valley rather than becoming perpetrators of the caste.[16]

In a technologically savvy and advanced twenty first century Indian church and society it is sad that caste broods over like an 'evil-spirit' all over the daily affairs of the people. In the Indian church and society ones identity is defined mostly by ones caste and the caste configurations always work better and are even rooted stronger than all other affiliations. It can only be rooted out with a strong prophetic emphasis and this must be continued in the new generations yet to emerge. Thus the theological vitality of the prophetic message must be taken seriously in all walks of our life in the Indian church and society. This would inaugurate a new era of our identity consciousness that we are God children with the kingdom values of justice, peace, equality and the integrity of creation whereby we form the new communities with a marked distinction and difference. The words of James Massey on the new community in our quest for identity may be used in this context. Massey states:

> I only want to add that the Church in India has to become a community of believers in the Jesus' model. This means that the members of all the Church denominations have to become 'Christian' in the real sense of the word, which will pave way for them to build a 'transformed community' or a 'new community' (world), to which they belong. This dual transformation (according

15 Walter Brueggemann, *Theology of the Old Testament: Testimony, Dispute, Advocacy*. (Minneapolis: Fortress Press, 1997), p. 645..

16 Razu, "Unity in Uniformity." p. 11.

> to Moses' model and Jesus' model) automatically will take care of the problem of various subaltern/oppressed groups (including that of the Dalits), and together they will succeed in forming a new community in which there will be no Dalits or non-Dalits, Tribals or non-Tribals, Adivasi or non-Adivasis. In that community all men and women will be seen as human beings created in the image of God. This is what we are looking for in the future. Towards the fulfillment of this vision both the 'cultural expressions' of Theology and the 'subaltern expressions' of Theology have to play a very crucial role.[17]

While this looks like a utopian reality this must be the dream of all those who aspire for God's kingdom on this earth. Let this vision of new humanity be engraved in our minds and consciousness all the days of our life on this earth in order that our quest for identity and community formation will come to fruition.

X

Conclusion

On the basis our foregoing discussion on the subject of quest for identity in community formation in the context of ancestral narratives in the book of Genesis we now make the following concluding remarks:

First, ancestral narratives while lacking any historical certainty do carry vitality in terms of their community and family value systems where the ancestors have tremendously gone through a social and community formation in order to define their firm identity in their religio-cultural and socio-economic matrices.

Second, the quest for identity was at times dreadful in the case of ancestors as they moved from place to place and lived among various cultures and ethnic communities.

Third, the ancestral narratives disclose clear signs of identity formation and transformation as co-pilgrims along with their neighbors that altered their course of life.

Fourth, the ancestral narratives do invoke in us the contemporary challenges in our quest for identity and community formation. This will be in the form of emulating the character of Abraham as we co-pilgrim with our neighbors on this earth. In the light of the challenges of religious fundamentalism and prophetic vitality we work towards companionship with our fellow human beings and nature so that we move towards the ideal and

17 James Massey, "Theology for a New Community: Looking ahead," in *Theology for a New Community: Dalit Consciousness with a symbolic universe and meaning systems* Eds. T. K. John and James Massey (New Delhi: Centre for Dalit and Subaltern Studies, 2013), p. 320.

reality of new community where all barriers and borders in terms of caste, gender, community, color, class and creed will be nullified.

Fifth, we are obligated to look into our faith journey in the light of the ancestral narratives in the book of Genesis since these ancestors do inspire us today as we consciously live within the transformative mission of God for liberation and emancipation of all in this world. We conclude that we can achieve this as God's mission since we are surrounded by God's amazing presence. The words of Psalmist in Psalm 139:7-10 are affirmative on this:

> *7. Where can I go from your spirit? Or where can I flee from your presence? 8. If I ascend to heaven you are there. If I make my bed in Sheol you are there. 9. If I take the wings of the morning and settle at the farthest limits of sea, 10. even there your hand shall lead me, and your right hand will hold me fast.*

4

The Chronicler's Blueprint for Israel's Identity in Community Formation Reflections from 1 Chronicles 1:1-2 Chronicles 9:31

Jose Varickasseril, SDB

Introduction

Quest for identity in community formation – a relevant theme has been chosen for our reflection during this gathering of theologians and biblical scholars.[1] There is no doubt that the *identity* of individuals and communities is at the heart of the various books of the Bible to a lesser or a greater degree. However, given the nature of the Historical books[2] they occupy primacy of place when investigating Israel's interest in discovering her identity in community formation. We are considering here only two of the historical books, namely, 1 & 2 Chronicles (although not in their entirety) to understand the above-mentioned theme.

1 The SBSI Biennial seminar was held at Aizawl Theological College (ATC) from 23 to 25 October 2018. This paper was presented during this seminar at Aizawl (Mizoram, India).

2 We are dividing the historical books into four categories irrespective of whether they are canonical or deutero-canonical. We categorize them as follows: 1) Joshua to 2 Kings, with the book of Ruth to be placed in the fourth category, 2) 1 & 2 Chronicles along with Ezra and Nehemiah 3) Ruth, Tobit, Judith and Esther, 4) 1 and 2 Maccabees. We are placing Ruth which is a novel along with Tobit, Judith and Esther since they share much in common as far as the literary type is concerned.

The two books of Chronicles are divided into three neat sections, as follows: (1) An Introduction (1 Chro 1:1-9:44), (2) The monarchy under David and Solomon (1 Chro 10:1-2 Chro 9:31), and (3) History of the 20 Kings of Judah from Rehoboam till the time of Zedekiah (2 Chro 10:1-36:23).[3] Our interest in this paper is only the first two parts, namely, 1:1- 2 Chronicles 9:31. Given the constraints of time and space, we want to see in a limited away how the author of the books of Chronicles strives to present the identity of Israel in community formation. Already at the outset, we would like to mention that the protagonists in this era are mainly David and Solomon on account of the vision that they had – a vision centred around and pivoting on the presence of the divine in their midst, symbolically depicted in the ark and the Temple. It goes without saying that they did not work as isolated individuals in presenting the unique identity of the community. They worked in unison with others and in particular with the priests and Levites. The time of David and Solomon is the golden age and their worldview is a blue print for the community to exist despite the inevitable vicissitudes of life.

1. Preliminaries

We begin by offering a few preliminaries as a prelude to our discussion. They serve to place in correct perspective the topic that we intend to examine, namely, how the Chronicler has given to the readers a blueprint for Israel's Identity in Community Formation.

A few details on the person of the Chronicler who wrote 1-2 Chronicles

The anonymous author of the two volumes (1 & 2 Chronicles) is referred to as the Chronicler. Some attribute the authorship to Ezra the scribe.[4] He lived (with a fairly reasonable amount of certainty) between 539-333 BC. According to Japhet, "the book was essentially composed by a single author, with a

---

3 For more details on the structure of 1 & 2 Chronicles, see Sara Japhet, "Chronicles, Books of", in *Encyclopaedia Judaica, Second Edition,* Volume 4 (Detroit: Thomson Gale, 2007) 695.

4 There are scholars who are of the opinion that Ezra (and Nehemiah) had a hand in the final editing of these volumes. As biblical scholarship stands at the moment, this supposition is not verifiable. Some are even of the opinion that the book was composed in the 4th century BC after the time of Ezra and Nehemiah. For details see Sara Japhet, "Chronicles, Books of", in *Encyclopaedia Judaica, Second Edition,* Volume 4 (Detroit: Thomson Gale, 2007) 703; Those who attribute authorship to Ezra do so primarily because the last verses of 2 Chronicles (2 Chro 36:22-23) and the opening lines of Ezra (Ezra 1:1-4) are similar in content. For details, See also "Chronicles", in John M'Clintock and James Strong, *Cyclopædia of Biblical, Theological and Ecclesiastical* Literature , Volume II – C, D (New York: Harper & Brothers Publishers, 1883) 287.

comprehensive outlook, clear aims, and a characteristic language and style".[5] As far as Israel is concerned the Persian period was a significant moment.[6] The Babylonian hegemony was replaced with the benevolent Persian presence for Israelites living in the diaspora. King Cyrus of Persia gave freedom to those who were in exile (in Babylon) to get back to their homeland. Many returned to Jerusalem although not all at the same time. The Chronicler tries to understand and interpret for the returnees the present scenario in the light of their glorious history going back in particular to the days of David, the man after God's heart, and his son Solomon. The author is deeply prayerful and religious. He was God-oriented and his focus was clear. In all probability, he must have been a priest or a Levite who was employed in the service of the Temple (539-332 BC).[7]

An explanatory note on the title of the two books of Chronicles

The Hebrew title of the book of Chronicles is possibly derived from 1 Chro 27:24. The meaning of the Hebrew title (*dibrē hayyāmīm*) is chronicle of events, happenings of the days, records of days or times.[8] This Hebrew title (*dibrē hayyāmīm*) is found in several biblical books (see 1 Kings 14:19, 29; Esther 2:23; 10:2; Neh 12:23 and as indicated above in 1 Chro 27:24).[9] However, those who translated the Hebrew text into Greek modified the title. The LXX calls the book as *paraleipomena* (things left out or history of events that were omitted in the books of 1, 2 Samuel and 1 & 2 Kings). The LXX also divided into two volumes an originally single volume work (in the Masoretic text). In the Hebrew Bible, it is placed as the last of the books of the Writings (*Kethubim*) whereas the LXX placed the book among the historical books. The Vulgate followed the LXX arrangement. Jerome referred to these two volumes as *chronicon* of the whole divine history from which we have the popular title, *the books of Chronicles*.[10] It is good to keep in mind that Benzinger calls the Chronicler as a Midrashist and not a historian. He does it so since there is a

---

5 Sara Japhet, "Chronicles, Books of", in *Encyclopaedia Judaica,* Second Edition, Volume 4 (Detroit: Thomson Gale, 2007) 703.

6 See "1 Chronicles", in *Lutheran Study Bible,* New Revised Standard Version (Minneapolis: Augsburg Fortress, 2009) 638.

7 See the notes on 1 Chro 21:1-22:1 in *E S V Study Bible*, English Standard Version (Wheaton, Illinois: Crossway, 2008) 697.

8 Jacob M. Myers, *1 Chronicles*, The Anchor Bible (Garden City, New York: Doubleday & Company, 1965) xvi.

9 For more details see Sara Japhet, "Chronicles, Books of", in *Encyclopaedia Judaica,* Second Edition, Volume 4 (Detroit: Thomson Gale, 2007) 695-696.

10 See "Chronicles", in John M'Clintock and James Strong, *Cyclopædia of Biblical, Theological and Ecclesiastical* Literature, Volume II – C, D (New York: Harper & Brothers Publishers, 1883) 286.

need to make a distinction between writing of history in the Old Testament books which are perceived as theological history that is quite different from our modern day understanding of history as a scientific discipline in a strict sense.[11] It is good to keep in mind that the main source of the chronicler is Deuteronomy to 2 Kings. He also availed himself of other existing sources. He sifted his sources and made a selection according to his purpose while writing a theological history of the nation of Israel.[12]

The historical setting and the aim of the Chronicler

To appreciate ever better the value of these two 'neglected books', one needs to look at the historical milieu.[13] There were several waves of deportation (in 605, 597, 587 and 582) when a portion of the upper echelon of the Judean kingdom was bundled off to Mesopotamia. The Babylonians left behind a decimated community and destroyed the infrastructure in the land of Israel.[14]

These two books composed during the Persian rule (somewhere between 539-332 BC) offer a history of the people of God spanning the time from the creation of the world through the end of the Babylonian exile and King Cyrus' permission for the people to return to their homeland.[15] Although not everyone was eager to return to Israel from the land of exile some did return in 538 due to the benign policy of Cyrus II. Others returned in the years that followed. In fact the temple was rebuilt in 516 BC. Later Ezra the scribe came (458 BC) and after some time Nehemiah too arrived on the land of Israel (445 BC).[16] Among the reasons for writing these two volumes we need to mention that the euphoria following the Decree of King Cyrus gave way to discouragement as the returnees faced the daunting challenge of rebuilding homes and cities and rebuilding the temple.[17] The Samaritans who were living in the land claimed to be the true Israel. The stark reality that they faced on return shook their tenuous

---

11 See Jacob M. Myers, *1 Chronicles*, The Anchor Bible (Garden City, New York: Doubleday & Company, 1965) xviii.

12 Jacob M. Myers, *1 Chronicles*, The Anchor Bible (Garden City, New York: Doubleday & Company, 1965) Lxii-lxiii. The Chronicler had recourse to Ezra-Nehemiah and other existing oral traditions. He also had access to the archives of the temple.

13 Jacob M. Myers, *1 Chronicles*, The Anchor Bible (Garden City, New York: Doubleday & Company, 1965) xv.

14 Mark J. Boda, *1-2 Chronicles*, Cornerstone Biblical Commentary (Carol Stream, Illinois: Tyndale House Publishers, 2010) 8.

15 See Daniel Durken, *The New Collegeville Bible Commentary: Old Testament* (Bangalore: TPI, 2018 / Collegeville: The Liturgical Press, 2015) 586.

16 See "1-2 Chronicles", in *E S V Study Bible*, English Standard Version (Wheaton, Illinois: Crossway, 2008) 698.

17 See Simon Sherwin, "1 Chronicles", in *Zondervan Illustrated Bible Backgrounds Commentary*, John H. Walton, Ed., (Grand Rapids: Zondervan, 2009) 224.

faith.[18] Therefore the Chronicler attempted to instil confidence in the hearts of the returnees. If the earlier historical books (Joshua – 2 Kings) answered the question, "why are we here in exile", then the Chronicler with his two volumes (1, 2 Chronicles) sought to assist the community to trace their glorious past in order to deal with the present. At the same time he aimed at offering a plan and a vision for the future. He tried to unravel the meaning of God's promises to David.[19] This explains how and why the Chronicler is much more interested in David's religious and cultic influence than in his life as a political figure.[20]

The Chronicler had in mind the spiritual and social renewal of the community that was slowly getting over the shock of the exile on their return to the home land.[21] Despite the tragedy of the erstwhile years, the present generation was "duty-bound to thank, praise, glorify, honor, exalt, extol, and bless him who did for our forefathers and for us all these miracles."[22] It could be added that he had a homiletic intent as well when reshaping the traditions received.[23] Hence he recounted the past in a unique manner keeping in mind the need of the present times. For the Chronicler, recalling the *mirabilia Dei* (the miraculous deeds of God) was of particular significance.[24] Duke, quoting Japhet, says that the purpose of this book is not just to give the negative consequences of the exile, but more important, to present a more comprehensive system that accounted for both good and evil events.[25]

The content and salient features of the books of Chronicles

The readers who follow the narrative of the Chronicler notice various literary genres in the narrative.[26] The more important among them are the following:

---

18 See "1 Chronicles", in *The Mission of God: Study Bible,* E. D. Stetzer and Philip Nation, Eds. (Nashville: Holman Bible Publishers, 1999 / 2012) 393.

19 See "1 Chronicles", in *Lutheran Study Bible,* New Revised Standard Version (Minneapolis: Augsburg Fortress, 2009) 638.

20 See "The First Book of Chronicles", in *The Catholic Study* Bible, Third Edition (Oxford: University Press, 1970 / 2010) 475.

21 See "1-2 Chronicles", in *E S V Study Bible*, English Standard Version (Wheaton, Illinois: Crossway, 2008) 698.

22 Scott W. Hahn, *The Kingdom of God as Liturgical Empire: A Theological Commentary on 1-2 Chronicles* (Grand Rapids: Baker Academic, 2012) 9.

23 Scott W. Hahn, *The Kingdom of God as Liturgical Empire: A Theological Commentary on 1-2 Chronicles* (Grand Rapids: Baker Academic, 2012)13.

24 Scott W. Hahn, *The Kingdom of God as Liturgical Empire: A Theological Commentary on 1-2 Chronicles* (Grand Rapids: Baker Academic, 2012)12.

25 See R. K. Duke, "Chronicles, Books of", in *Dictionary of the Old Testament Historical Books,* Bill T. Arnold and H. G. M. Williamson, Eds. (Downers Grove: IVP Academic, 2005)171.

26 For a good presentation on genres and other aspects of the books of Chronicles, see S. J. Schultz, "Chronicles, Books of", in *The Zondervan Encyclopedia of the Bible,* Merrill C.

genealogies, straight historical narratives, official correspondence, legislation and legislative history, private prayers and ritual practices, speeches, homilies, poetry, prophecies, inventories, summaries of events (such as the lists of the victories), Psalms, poetries, Levitical sermons, etc. (see also 1 Chro 16:8-46).[27] Examining the contents of the two volumes, one notices that the books are to a great extent a family history – all tied by blood and bound by divine-human covenant in a special kinship with God.[28]

While delineating the contents of the two volumes, it is apt to say that here one finds a theological history from Adam to the late sixth century BC. It goes without saying that it is not so much factual history but an interpretative history. The author shows the action of God in the affairs of men and of the community of Israel in a unique manner.[29] The presentation of the kings (David and Solomon in particular) is unique. They are leaders in political and religious spheres; they co-operate with the Levites, priests and prophets for keeping the nation loyal to God.[30] Whereas monarchy is rather negatively presented in the Deuteronomistic history (1 Samuel to 2 Kings), here instead, there is a more positive tone with David's era as the best. As in some other books of the Bible, exogamy (marrying outside the family or the tribe) is not condemned.[31] The Chronicler has no difficulty with intermarriages (see 1 Chro 2:17; 2:34-35; 3:2; 4:21-22).[32] God appears as mighty in power, the transcendent divinity and as sustainer of the world.[33] There is special interest in Judah. Significantly

---

Tenney, Gen. Ed. (Grand Rapids: Zondervan, 2009) Volume 1, 838- 846.

27 Scott W. Hahn, *The Kingdom of God as Liturgical Empire: A Theological Commentary on 1-2 Chronicles* (Grand Rapids: Baker Academic, 2012)12. For the literary forms used in 1, 2 Chronicles see also J. A. Thompson, *1, 2 Chronicles,* The New American Commentary, New International Version, Volume 9 (Nashville: Broadman & Holman Publishers, 1994) 25-28.

28 Scott W. Hahn, *The Kingdom of God as Liturgical Empire: A Theological Commentary on 1-2 Chronicles* (Grand Rapids: Baker Academic, 2012)13.

29 See *The International Student Bible for Catholics,* New American Bible (Nashville: Thomas Nelson Publishers, 1999) 348.

30 Daniel Durken, *The New Collegeville Bible Commentary: Old Testament* (Bangalore: TPI, 2018 / Collegeville: The Liturgical Press, 2015) 586.

31 Daniel Durken, *The New Collegeville Bible Commentary: Old Testament* (Bangalore: TPI, 2018 / Collegeville: The Liturgical Press, 2015) 590.

32 It was a way to expand the population of Judah. For more details, see Daniel Durken, *The New Collegeville Bible Commentary: Old Testament* (Bangalore: TPI, 2018 / Collegeville: The Liturgical Press, 2015) 591.

33 Daniel Durken, *The New Collegeville Bible Commentary: Old Testament* (Bangalore: TPI, 2018 / Collegeville: The Liturgical Press, 2015) 586.

there are about 100 verses designed to bring the tribe of Judah into prominence (2:3-4:23).[34]

The historian who wrote at a time of disorientation and uncertainty in the life of Israel shows that the exile is not the end of Israel's story.[35] He intends to show that God's plans cannot be thwarted. There is a new future for their land and for themselves. The Chronicler has a covenantal worldview. He invites Israel to have a "one flesh and bone" relationship with God.[36] He seeks to assure the readers that God's promise will not be broken (1 Chro 16:15; see also 2 Chro 13:5; 21:7). In this context, the memory of God's dealings with Israel plays a major role. The Chronicler has sought to incorporate history into Scripture – a process which was maintained and nurtured by transmission, recitation and education.[37]

The most important theme in 1 Chronicles is the contribution David in the life of Israel. His contribution pivots around his spiritual impact in the life of Israel. He made the necessary preparations for the building of the temple and entrusted the responsibility of the construction to his son Solomon who would be aided by a large team (see especially 1 Chro 28:20-21). We shall descend into some details about David's contribution since he has the larger share in carving out and presenting an identity for the community of Israel with a particular religious focus.[38]

David as a Religious Protagonist in the Chronicler's History

In the history of Israel, the era of David is the Golden age.[39] The Chronicler has structured his work with great care. After the genealogy, eleven chapters describe David's reign (10-20); the rest (1 Chro 21-29) is about preparations for the building of the Temple and all the needed arrangements in connection with the construction which would be done after his death. Among those who entered into his service (in all departments connected with the governance

34 Daniel Durken, *The New Collegeville Bible Commentary: Old Testament* (Bangalore: TPI, 2018 / Collegeville: The Liturgical Press, 2015) 590.

35 "1-2 Chronicles", *in E S V Study Bible*, English Standard Version (Wheaton, Illinois: Crossway, 2008) 699.

36 Scott W. Hahn, *The Kingdom of God as Liturgical Empire: A Theological Commentary on 1-2 Chronicles* (Grand Rapids: Baker Academic, 2012) 4.

37 As quoted by Scott Han from Stefan Reif, see Scott W. Hahn, *The Kingdom of God as Liturgical Empire: A Theological Commentary on 1-2 Chronicles* (Grand Rapids: Baker Academic, 2012) 2.

38 For a terse but good introduction on the books of Chronicles, see Roddy Braun, *1 Chronicles,* Word Biblical Commentary, 14 (Waco, Texas: Word Book Publishers, 1986) xvii-xlv.

39 Jacob M. Myers, *1 Chronicles*, The Anchor Bible (Garden City, NY: Doubleday & Company, 1965) xlii.

of the nation) David had the choicest and most valiant representatives of the tribes of Israel (12:1-23).[40]

The weaknesses of David are to a great extent overlooked by the Chronicler but for rare exceptions.[41] He comes across as a man of action, a poet, a tender lover, a generous foe, a stern dispenser of justice, a loyal friend, and one blessed by God. On account of David, the tribe of Judah too obtains special attention.[42] Certain personal details of his life (by way of an example, David has 19 wives and concubines[43] and numerous sons – see 1 Chro 3:1-9)[44] are given in order to show that fertility and posterity are signs of God's blessings as opposed to barrenness or sterility. He is not weak, vengeful, or indecisive as depicted in 1 Kings.[45] He is the faithful successor to the unfaithful Saul from the tribe of Benjamin! He is a leader who is zealous for God and one who brought peace. He is presented as a symbol of hope for the exiles who returned.[46] David did not lead the rebels who gathered around him against Saul. He fled from him into the Philistine territory only for the sake of self-preservation.[47] He is zealous for God's honour. He is talented and brave, and at his best represents an ideal of Israelite kingship.[48]

---

40 Edward Lewis Curtis and Albert Alonzo Madsen, *The Books of Chronicles,* ICC (Edinburgh: T & T Clark, 1910 / 1952) 194.

41 For details on what is omitted by the Chronicler when re-writing the history found in 1 & 2 Samuel and 1 & 2 Kings, see Sara Japhet, "Chronicles, Books of", in *Encyclopaedia Judaica,* Second Edition, Volume 4 (Detroit: Thomson Gale, 2007) 697. For the principal omissions and for the additions that are peculiar in Chronicles (related to David as well as to Solomon), see "Chronicles", in John M'Clintock and James Strong, *Cyclopædia of Biblical, Theological and Ecclesiastical* Literature , Volume II – C, D (New York: Harper & Brothers Publishers, 1883) 289.

42 See Eugene H. Merrill, *1 Chronicles,* in The Bible Knowledge Commentary: Old Testament, John F. Walvoord and Roy B. Zuck, Eds. (Hyderabad: Authentic, 2013) 590.

43 See S.L. McKenzie, "David's Family", in *Dictionary of the Old Testament Historical Books,* Bill T. Arnold and H. G. M. Williamson, Eds. (Downers Grove: IVP Academic, 2005) 212-213.

44 See S.L. McKenzie, "David's Family", in *Dictionary of the Old Testament Historical Books,* Bill T. Arnold and H. G. M. Williamson, Eds. (Downers Grove: IVP Academic, 2005) 214.

45 See P. E. Satterthwaite, "David", in *Dictionary of the Old Testament Historical Books,* Bill T. Arnold and H. G. M. Williamson, Eds. (Downers Grove: IVP Academic, 2005) 201.

46 See P. E. Satterthwaite, "David", in *Dictionary of the Old Testament Historical Books,* Bill T. Arnold and H. G. M. Williamson, Eds. (Downers Grove: IVP Academic, 2005) 205.

47 See P. E. Satterthwaite, "David", in *Dictionary of the Old Testament Historical Books,* Bill T. Arnold and H. G. M. Williamson, Eds. (Downers Grove: IVP Academic, 2005)199.

48 See P. E. Satterthwaite, "David", in *Dictionary of the Old Testament Historical Books,* Bill T. Arnold and H. G. M. Williamson, Eds. (Downers Grove: IVP Academic, 2005) 201.

David's spiritual vision at the heart of Israel's identity as a community

The Chronicler in his first volume narrative gives an extensive genealogy. This is offered as a prelude to the activities of David. God gives David victory in his battles. He puts his empire on a secure basis by bringing about prosperity, peace and wellbeing. Then David embarks on his ambitious project of building a house for God. He does not do it singlehanded; he will involve everyone possible in this project. We go into a few details on these aspects since it is irreplaceably linked to the theme under consideration.

The significance of the genealogy

The genealogy in 1 Chronicles is extensive (1 Chro 1:1-9:44). A genealogy is about the descent of a person or a group of persons. It can be written or it can be handed down by way of mouth. It is a family history or a record and can be presented in ascending (backward) or descending order (from earlier times to present day). Not all the details are given when offering a genealogy. A biblical genealogy serves many a purpose. We recall some of the functions of genealogy here:[49]

1) a social function (when dealing with a community, it is meant to establish community relationship between groups and for organizing and ranking society)
2) a legitimizing function (it is required for kingship, succession to leadership and for enhancing of status, etc.)
3) a theological function (to establish the continuity of the covenant people)
4) a historical function (providing information of the past to understand the present),
5) a literary function (for narrative purposes)
6) schematic function (to divide the history of the world into cycles of epochs)
7) a military function (to classify people for the purpose of clan involvement in conscription for government service)
8) a religious function (to decide who was qualified to act as priests, perform functions related to worship; for keeping the faith pure and to resist pagan influences)

49 For more details on the purpose of genealogy, see J.H. Walton, "Genealogies", in *Dictionary of the Old Testament Historical Books,* Bill T. Arnold and H. G. M. Williamson, Eds. (Downers Grove: IVP Academic, 2005) 313; see also Scott W. Hahn, *The Kingdom of God as Liturgical Empire: A Theological Commentary on 1-2 Chronicles* (Grand Rapids: Baker Academic, 2012) 9-27; Roddy Braun, *1 Chronicles,* Word Biblical Commentary, 14 (Waco, Texas: Word Book Publishers, 1986) 1-8.

9) a national function (in the genealogy of the Chronicler, there is greater interest in Judah since the editor wants to glorify David and the tribe of Levy).
10) a cultural and an aesthetic function (the author connects the readers with various aspects of culture and civilization like city building, tent dwelling, metal working herding, playing of musical instruments, etc.).
11) a juridical function (for deciding about inheritance rights and land allotments, the amount of taxes and contributions to be made to the state or to the temple).
12) an identification function (it is meant to give a sense of identity within a nation; to show a people's original unity, identity, continuity)[50]

In the Chronicler's history, when presenting the genealogical lists, there is an important reference to the return from exile and the resettlement in the land of Israel. The group that was returning consisted also of "the priests, the Levites, and the temple servants" (1 Chro 9:1-2). The genealogy focuses on David, the political history during his reign, and the priestly and Levitical religious institutions.[51] It is inclusive in nature as can be deduced from the fact that several non-Israelite groups are mentioned.[52] Many groups are going to worship Yahweh as mentioned in Proto Isaiah (see Isa 2:2-4) and his contemporary Micah (Mi 4:1-3).

The focus on the divine during the kingship of David

David is presented as a *man of* God by the Chronicler (2 Chro 8:14). That is an ideal way of presenting all what David stood for. The Chronicler removes all dichotomies between the secular and the spiritual. If there is any preference at all for any particular realm when viewing history, it is for the spiritual dimension since David had the insight and wisdom to discover the importance of the religious aspect in keeping the people united as one people serving the same God in the same holy place. David acts as king and chief priest.[53] He blesses the people. He feeds the people (1 Chro 16:3). The focus on the spiritual can be noticed from the emphasis given to the following: worship, sacrifice, prayer, the priesthood, the preoccupation with the ark, the interest in

50 There are several genealogical lists in the books of Genesis, Numbers, Ezra, Nehemiah, Ruth, Judith, etc.

51 See Eugene H. Merrill, *1 Chronicles,* in *The Bible Knowledge Commentary: Old Testament*, John F. Walvoord and Roy B. Zuck, Eds. (Hyderabad: Authentic, 2013) 590.

52 Scott W. Hahn, *The Kingdom of God as Liturgical Empire: A Theological Commentary on 1-2 Chronicles* (Grand Rapids: Baker Academic, 2012) 35.

53 Scott W. Hahn, *The Kingdom of God as Liturgical Empire: A Theological Commentary on 1-2 Chronicles* (Grand Rapids: Baker Academic, 2012) 57, 61.

the temple and the liturgical functions. The land of Israel is a liturgical empire that offers sacrifice to the living God that the author of the books of Chronicles presents.[54] He points out David's wisdom in making God as the fulcrum of the nation.

The Chronicler indicates the religious ethos of the nation during David's kingship

It is to the credit of the Chronicler that he has shown the significance of the Davidic covenant as the enduring basis of Israel's life and hope. The Davidic covenant is expressed in two institutions, namely the monarchy and the temple. They are mutually related (17:10-14).[55]

David was a conqueror, a statesman and an organizer. By subduing the inimical nations around him, he ensured economic wellbeing and political security in the land. This set the stage for ushering in a religious ethos and culture for the community. David constantly reminded the people that it was God who was guiding the destiny of the nation. Below we mention a few more details connected with the ark and the Temple which embody God's presence among the people. We will also refer to those connected to the handling of the sacred, namely, the ark, as well as those involved in the service of the Temple.

The ark as the harbinger of the temple

The ark is 3¾ feet long and 2¼ feet wide and high. The ark contained the 2 tablets of stone on which was inscribed the laws of God. The ark was kept in the tabernacle; it symbolized the presence of God.[56] Although the Chronicler mentions only the depositing of the law in the ark, en passant we want to mention that according to other biblical texts, the ark contained the following: the tablets (see also Deut 10:5), a copy of the Law (Deut 31:26), a pot of manna (Exo 16:33-34), Aaron's rod (Num 17:10).[57] The Chronicler will remind the readers yet again that the ark is holy (2 Chro 35:3).

The shifting of the ark with all pomp and solemnity is described in detail (see 1 Chro 15). The importance given to the way that the sacred is to be handled is stressed by the narrator. The King realized the folly of the first attempt to shift the ark (without paying heed to the norms of holiness) which brought

54 Scott W. Hahn, *The Kingdom of God as Liturgical Empire: A Theological Commentary on 1-2 Chronicles* (Grand Rapids: Baker Academic, 2012) 23.

55 See "1-2 Chronicles", in *E S V Study Bible*, English Standard Version (Wheaton, Illinois: Crossway, 2008) 697.

56 See Simon Sherwin, "1 Chronicles", in *Zondervan Illustrated Bible Backgrounds* Commentary, John H. Walton, Ed. (Grand Rapids: Zondervan, 2009) 248.

57 The author of the Letter to the Hebrews mentions the several sacred objects that were kept in the tent, called the Holy of Holies. They were the following: a golden urn with the manna, Aaron's rod, the tables of the covenant (see Heb 9:3-4).

about failure and disastrous consequences – the death of Uzzah (1 Chro 13). Non-compliance with the Levitical Law was the reason for the disaster. Now instead, David brought up the ark with due ecclesiastical state and ceremony.[58] The long-drawn ark narrative (see 1 Chro 15:1-29) is important since the ark is the harbinger of the temple and the symbol of God's presence (17:1).[59] Solomon gave the same veneration to the Ark as David his father did. In this context an aside given by the Chronicler is important. He says that Solomon shifted Pharaoh's daughter (that is, his own wife) to a residence away from the temple precincts for where the ark stood is a holy place (2 Chro 8:11).

The choice of a place for community worship

The tabernacle of the Lord and the altar of the burnt offering, which Moses had made in the wilderness were at that time at the high place in Gibeon (1 Chro 21:29). For David the choice of a suitable place where a temple could be constructed was important. In this connection, the blunder made by David in taking the census had also its advantages. It proved to be providential if one may say so.[60] The plot of land belonging to Ornan was acquired by David to build an altar (1 Chro 21:18-25). It eventually became the place where the temple would be constructed. Given this context, the temple site is important since it reminds one of God's mercy and forgiveness.[61] The temple will be built where David repented and offered sacrifice.[62]

One can speak of the unusual attention given to the temple and the worship there.[63] The preparations took on large proportions. Although it was Solomon who eventually built the temple, the credit for the concept of a house for God goes to David.[64] The plans were prepared by David as in days of old when Moses had designed the sanctuary (see Exo 25-31 and 35-40). He commanded everyone to give Solomon all support in realizing the plan.

58 Edward Lewis Curtis and Albert Alonzo Madsen, *The Books of Chronicles,* ICC (Edinburgh: T & T Clark, 1910 / 1952) 211.

59 See "1-2 Chronicles", in *E S V Study Bible*, English Standard Version (Wheaton, Illinois: Crossway, 2008) 700.

60 For more details on the choice of the spot where the Temple was to be built, namely, where God appeared to David, that is, the threshing floor of Ornan, see Sara Japhet, "Chronicles, Books of", in *Encyclopaedia Judaica,* Second Edition, Volume 4 (Detroit: Thomson Gale, 2007) 702.

61 See the notes on 1 Chro 21:1-22:1 in *E S V Study Bible*, English Standard Version Wheaton, Illinois: Crossway, 2008) 732.

62 See "1-2 Chronicles", in *E S V Study Bible*, English Standard Version (Wheaton, Illinois: Crossway, 2008) 699.

63 See Eugene H. Merrill, *1 Chronicles,* in *The Bible Knowledge Commentary: Old Testament*, John F. Walvoord and Roy B. Zuck, Eds. (Hyderabad: Authentic, 2013) 590.

64 Edward Lewis Curtis and Albert Alonzo Madsen, *The Books of Chronicles,* ICC (Edinburgh: T & T Clark, 1910 / 1952) 244.

Solomon was directed by David himself to conduct himself piously in order to secure prosperity (1 Chro 28:9).[65]

It must be added that David provided everything possible for the construction of the temple (see especially 22 and 29). Solomon and his successors would have to ensure that worship would be done with all propriety (2 Chro 13). Similarly they were to see that the temple was well maintained (2 Chro 24). The purification was deemed essential in case of any defilement (2 Chro 29; 34).

David's personnel for the religious sphere and the preparations for building the temple

The temple is meant not only for Israel but also for all nations. It was at the same time the means by which Israel demonstrated their exclusive and wholehearted relationship with God.[66] Along with David there was a special team consisting mainly of the priests and the Levites who promoted and supervised the correct forms of seeking Yahweh. The meticulous care in planning for the construction of the temple (along with the sacredness attached to the ark) and the establishment of worship, among other things, serve to present David as a model of faith, obedience and devotion to God.[67] It was to remain as the hub of all aspects of the life of the community. As indicated above the preparations were important as in days of old when Moses was given the blueprint for the construction of the tabernacle and as when Ezekiel was given instructions for the reconstruction and administration of the temple after its destruction by the Babylonians in 586 BC (see Ezek 40-48). Yahweh's dwelling place is considered as of utmost importance. Hence the Chronicler gives all details including the architectural plans, the furniture, the functionaries, the location, the orientation, the trappings, etc.[68] One may take note of the importance of the temple also from the fact that Josephus speaks about in a rather lengthy way.[69]

When Israel became a nation, a central shrine became a necessity. It is the gathering-point for all the people and a symbol of their unity in the

65 Edward Lewis Curtis and Albert Alonzo Madsen, *The Books of Chronicles,* ICC (Edinburgh: T & T Clark, 1910 / 1952) 244-245.

66 R. K. Duke, "Chronicles, Books of", in *Dictionary of the Old Testament Historical Books,* Bill T. Arnold and H. G. M. Williamson, Eds. (Downers Grove: IVP Academic, 2005) 177.

67 See "1 Chronicles", in *Lutheran Study Bible,* New Revised Standard Version (Minneapolis: Augsburg Fortress, 2009) 639.

68 See Simon Sherwin, "1 Chronicles", in *Zondervan Illustrated Bible Backgrounds* Commentary, John H. Walton, Ed. (Grand Rapids: Zondervan, 2009) 276-277.

69 See "Jewish Antiquities, 7.14.1-2", in *The Complete Works of Josephus,* translated by William Whiston, Commentary by Paul L. Maier (Grand Rapids: Kregel Publications, 1999).

worship of their God.[70] To seek Yahweh mans to orient one's life towards God in active faith and obedience, to be diligent in fulfilling the commands of the Mosaic Law, to oppose idolatry, and especially to support and participate in the authorized worship of the temple (see 1 Chro 10:13; 13:3; 15:13; 16:10; 22:19; 28:9).[71] The temple was the rallying point for the people since it was the symbol par excellence of God's presence. Everything therein or connected with it indicated his presence – the ark of the covenant, the very city of Jerusalem, the sacrificial system with all the ceremonies involved, the officiating priests, their Levitical assistants, the musicians and most of all the Davidic king who would sit on the throne.[72]

The importance of Chapter 22 where David made known to his son his pet project of building the temple (1 Chro 22:2-19) cannot be overemphasized. David told Solomon how he was specially chosen by God in view of the construction of the temple. He told him of the material that was already collected in view of the construction of the Temple. He also assured him that everyone in Israel would assist him in the execution of the project. Similarly the speech of David in chapter 28 (of 1 Chro) is of crucial importance. It revolves mainly around three themes: the building of the Temple, the divine election of Solomon, and an appeal to keep God's commandments.[73] The choice of Solomon, repeatedly mentioned, is particularly important here (see 1 Chro 28:5, 6, 10; 29:1).

The personal investment of David in view of the eventual construction of the temple is important. As Japhet has rightly pointed out, "Great wealth is one sign of God's blessing. David dedicated his affluence to the building of the Temple (1 Chro 22:3-4, 14-16; 29:2-5) and thus died 'full of days, riches and honour' (1 Chron. 29.28)".[74] David with far-reaching vision and wisdom deployed the necessary personnel not only for the construction of the Temple but also took measures to meet all exigencies related to its full operation once it was completed.[75] After David accomplished what he had in mind as per design of the Lord, he died in good old age, full of days, riches and honour (1 Chro

70 During the trek in the desert, the Jews had the tabernacle. After the settlement, David along with Solomon furnished the need to remind them of God's abiding and providential presence by building the Temple. For more details, see R.J. McKelvey, "Temple", in *New Bible* Dictionary, Third Edition, I.H. Marshall et al. (Hyderabad: Authentic, 2011) 1156.

71 See "1-2 Chronicles", in *E S V Study Bible*, English Standard Version (Wheaton, Illinois: Crossway, 2008) 698.

72 See R. K. Duke, "Chronicles, Books of", in *Dictionary of the Old Testament Historical Books,* Bill T. Arnold and H. G. M. Williamson, Eds. (Downers Grove: IVP Academic, 2005) 177.

73 Sara Japhet, *I & II Chronicles,* Old Testament Library (London: SCM Press, 1993) 486.

74 Sara Japhet, *I & II Chronicles,* Old Testament Library (London: SCM Press, 1993) 639.

75 Sara Japhet, *I & II Chronicles,* Old Testament Library (London: SCM Press, 1993) 500.

29:26-28). He had a long life resembling that of Abraham (Gen 25:8), Isaac (Gen 35:29), Moses (Deut 34:5-8), Gideon (Judges 8:32), Job (Job 42:17), Judith (Judith 16:21-25), Tobit (Tobit 14:2) and Tobias (Tob 14:14).

The prominent role of the Levites and priests during David's reign

The Levites and the priests are mentioned on several occasions in the books of Chronicles.[76] Already in the *genealogical* section, a huge list of items indicating the duties of the Levites are given (see 1 Chro 9:26-34). At various moments, the Chronicler points out the prominent role of the Levites in the temple (see 1 Chro 23).[77] They were deputed to supervise the liturgical services.[78] They invoke, thank and praise the Lord God (1 Chro 16:4-6). It is possible that some of them even composed Psalms; Asaph in fact is credited with the composition of 12 Psalms (see Ps 50; 73-83). Further they had the responsibility for the temple precincts and the sacred vessels; they prepared the food for the offerings; they were in charge of music and prayers of praise during the sacrifice.[79] They offered the praise through songs accompanied by a variety of musical instruments (see 1 Chro 6:31-47; 9:33; 13:8; 15:16-19; 15:28; 16:4-7; 16:37-38; 23:3-6; 25:1-31; 2 Chro 5:4, 13). They also served as officers, judges and gate keepers (1 Chro 25-26).[80] Before a permanent place was made to shelter the ark, they were deputed to carry it with all the sacredness possible. They continued to serve in various capacities after that as per directive of David. They were expected to carry out various types of duties like service in the house of Yahweh, care of courts and rooms, purification of the holy things, preparation of bread for the offering. They were duty-bound to appear before Yahweh regularly every morning and evening to give praise and thanks (1 Chro 23:28-31; see also 28:31). Among the various forms of liturgical duties, singing and playing of instruments had priority of place (1 Chro 25:1-7). Keeping record (making an inventory) was also entrusted to scribe Shemaiah who was at the same time a Levite (1 Chro 24:6).

The Chronicler has taken pains to go into details about the clans of the Levites: the Gershonites (23:7-11), the Kohathites (23:12-20), the Merarites (23:21-23) with their ancestry are listed. There were as many as 38,000

76 The Levites are mentioned about 86 times and the priests are mentioned about 82 times in 1 & 2 Chronicles. This indicates the importance that is given to them by the Chronicler.

77 Sara Japhet, "Chronicles, Books of", in *Encyclopaedia Judaica,* Second Edition, Volume 4 (Detroit: Thomson Gale, 2007) 702.

78 See *The International Student Bible for Catholics,* New American Bible (Nashville: Thomas Nelson Publishers, 1999) 348.

79 See the notes on 1 Chronicles 21:1-22:1 in *E S V Study Bible*, English Standard Version (Wheaton, Illinois: Crossway, 2008) 735.

80 Daniel Durken, *The New Collegeville Bible Commentary: Old Testament* (Bangalore: TPI, 2018 / Collegeville: The Liturgical Press, 2015) 607.

Levites for the various functions (23:21f). Those above 30 years (1 Chro 23:3) and those above 20 years (1 Chro 23:26-27) were recruited depending upon the nature of the functions that would be allotted to each. No slipshod performance of the sacred functions was tolerated. They knew that there would be punishment for relaxation of any rules related to their sacred function as demanded by Moses in days of old (see Lev 10:1-7; Num 3:4). The Chronicler also mentions that the Levites were subject to priests.[81]

The role of the Priests in the realm of holiness is conveyed in lucid terms by the Chronicler. As mentioned above, there are several moments in the running text when the Chronicler underlines the functions of the priests or refers to them. Primarily they are officers of the holy place and officers of the divine presence (1 Chro 24:1-5). They are to be available for all services in the house of the Lord (1 Chro 28:21). David's organization of the priests is presented by the Chronicler in great details (1 Chro 24:1-19). While it was the duty of the Levites to carry the ark as well as the Tent of meeting (see 2 Chro 5:5), it was the privilege of the Priests to carry it into the Holy of Holies or into the Debir of the Temple (2 Chro 5:7). They were also deputed to mixing the spiced ointments (1 Chro 9:30). They were in charge of offering sacrifices before the Lord, minister to him and bless his name (1 Chro 23:13). The priests (along with the Levites) also functioned as prophets (2 Chro 20:14, 20). Holiness is to issue forth from priesthood. Hence they were to be models of holiness as well.[82] It is not improbable that the priests are to be agents, heralds and harbingers of salvation as implied in the prayer of Solomon – "let thy priests O Lord God be clothed with salvation" (2 Chro 6:42; see also Psalm 132:8-10). Although the Levites are supposed to assist the priests (2 Chro 8:14) still it should be added that the Levites overshadow them with the greater prominence that they enjoyed (see 1 Chro 29:34).

The role of the prophets in the Chronicler's presentation

1 Chronicles contains many a reference to the prophets. Samuel is mentioned at the beginning of David's reign (1 Chro 11:3; see also 26:28). Prophet Nathan's role is given in greater detail (1 Chro 17). Gad the seer figures in the text (1 Chro 21:9). Heman the king's seer is mentioned (1 Chro 25:4-7). Names of three prophets are mentioned again at the end of the first volume – Samuel, Nathan and Gad (1 Chro 29:29) whose works were among sources for the Chronicler in his project of reproducing his history. Before concluding

81 See R. K. Duke, "Chronicles, Books of", in *Dictionary of the Old Testament Historical Books,* Bill T. Arnold and H. G. M. Williamson, Eds. (Downers Grove: IVP Academic, 2005) 173; see also Sara Japhet, "Chronicles, Books of", in *Encyclopaedia Judaica,* Second Edition, Volume 4 (Detroit: Thomson Gale, 2007) 697.

82 Scott W. Hahn, *The Kingdom of God as Liturgical Empire: A Theological Commentary on 1-2 Chronicles* (Grand Rapids: Baker Academic, 2012) 37.

the reign of Solomon there is yet another mention of Nathan, Ahijah and Iddo (2 Chro 9:29). We would like to recall what Japhet has said about the role of the prophets as can be deduced from the Chronicler's account. She says: "An important place in the book is devoted to the prophets. They are held to be writers of history, and in each generation there is a prophet who records the events of the period. They also stand as God's emissaries, who in each generation, appear before the king and the people, transmit the word of God to them, rebuke them for their deeds, warn them of God's wrath, and encourage faith in God and repentance … Levites and priests also served as prophets when inspired by God (2 Chro 20:14, 20)".[83]

David involved everyone in the smooth running of the God-focused empire

The religious realm functions smoothly when other aspects of the kingdom at the economic, social and political levels are taken care of. David ensured that he had a team of well-organized army personnel, tribal chiefs to monitor their own tribes, and overseers for taking care of every department in the land as well as an intelligentsia who acted as his counselors (1 Chro 27:1-34).

2. Solomon Executes the Plans of David

Solomon had a peaceful accession to the throne. The Chronicler has omitted many of the things that could tarnish his image. The peaceful ascension to the throne (as opposed to the description in 1 Kings 1-2) is designed to present him in a favourable light and as the undisputed successor to David. The failings of Solomon towards the end of his life (as mentioned in 1 Kings 11:1-40) are largely passed over in silence. His greatness is presented with a special focus on three topics: worship, wisdom and wealth (2 Chro 1:1-17). The main block of material, when highlighting his contribution, is in the area of the building of the temple and the dedication speeches and dedication ceremony on its completion (2 Chro 2:1-7:22 and 8:12-16). There are two more chapters about his achievements, maritime and nautical activities, the visit of the Queen of Sheba and about his splendour [and finally his death] (2 Chro 8:1-11 and 8:17-9:31).[84]

David had the wisdom and the ability to convince Solomon that the work entrusted to him was the plan of the Lord himself. This is explicitly stated in the text (see 1 Chro 28:19). David had also infused into him courage for the gargantuan and ambitious project of building a beautiful temple full of

---

83 Sara Japhet, "Chronicles, Books of", in *Encyclopaedia Judaica,* Second Edition, Volume 4 (Detroit: Thomson Gale, 2007) 702.

84 For details see, J. A. Thompson, *1, 2 Chronicles,* The New American Commentary, New International Version, Volume 9 (Nashville: Broadman & Holman Publishers, 1994) 201.

splendour (see 1 Chro 22:13-18; 28:20-21). Solomon continued the work of David in the religious aspects of the kingdom with particular commitment. In this context it is significant that the Chronicler tells the readers that he began his tenure as the King of Israel by seeking God (2 Chro 1:1-5).

Peace was essential to embark upon such a tremendous task as the building of the temple. David had ushered in an era of peace through conquests and consolidation of the empire (see especially 1 Chron 11-12 and 18-20). The Chronicler reminds the readers that Solomon prospered and all Israel obeyed him and everyone pledged their allegiance to him (1 Chro 29:22-25; see also 23:1). It is to the credit of David that he had the astuteness to retire to the background. He had Solomon anointed as prince of the Lord and had him seated on the *throne of the Lord* and Zadok was given to him as priest (1 Chro 29:22). The political and religious spheres had to merge if the community was to reach its desired goal.

Solomon builds, furnishes and dedicates the temple

The building the temple was the first and primary preoccupation of Solomon. The huge number of people that he employed shows the importance of the enterprise (see 2 Chro 2:1-2). Solomon had the wisdom to obtain the skill and expertise of Hiram the King of Tyre (2 Chro 2:1-16). He also co-opted into the work of construction many foreigners living in the land when building the temple (2 Chro 2:17-18). He made it clear that the purpose of the temple was for honoring the Lord (2 Chro 2:1) and as such it had to be a house of splendour. Hence he used the best of material for the temple (2 Chro 3:4-5:1). It is significant that the site chosen for the temple was the plot of land bought by David from Ornan (known as Araunah in 2 Samuel 24), the Jebusite (see 1 Chro 21:7-30; 2 Chro 3:1).

The shifting of the ark with the two tablets to the inner sanctuary of the temple

Solomon was aware of the demands made by God when handling anything sacred. Therefore the moving of the ark took place on a suitable occasion, during the feast of the Tabernacles (2 Chro 5:3). The priests who were Levites (2 Chro 5:5; see also 7:6; 8:14-15) brought the ark. It contained the two tablets.[85] Thus the Chronicler also informs the readers that there are Levitical priests (see also Deut 17:9 and Joshua 3:3).[86] He says that only the priests enter the inner sanctuary (2 Chro 5:7). They had consecrated themselves prior to

85 For whatever reason, the rod of Aaron and the jar of manna (mentioned in Exodus 16:32-34 and Numbers 17:10-11 and Hebrews 9:4) are not mentioned here!

86 J. A. Thompson, *1, 2 Chronicles,* The New American Commentary, New International Version, Volume 9 (Nashville: Broadman & Holman Publishers, 1994) 223.

carrying the ark on the poles (2 Chro 5:11). The Levites who were musicians dressed in fine linen played cymbals, harps and lyres and the priests sounded the trumpets (2 Chro 5:12). Music was important in worship.[87] Its purpose was to give praise and thanks to the Lord (2 Chro 5:13).

The dedication speech and prayer on completion of the temple (2 Chronicles 6:1-42)

Solomon felt a sense of gratitude that the will of God and the wish of his father David had been carried out (see also 2 Chro 7:11; 8:16). The Chronicler has given the contents of the prayer of Solomon which also demonstrate that he is a man of God – loyal to the Monotheistic God of Israel. The prayer focuses on the glory of God; the temple is for all.[88] The prayer underscores at several moments the mercy of God and his willingness to forgive a people who do go astray on account of their weakness.[89] The prayer does have a Deuteronomistic touch about it reminding the audience who are privy to the prayer that prosperity and protection from God are conditional to their loyalty, fidelity and the true worship that they are bound to render in the temple (see also 2 Chro 7:14-22).[90] The Chronicler has given special attention to the *whole* assembly of Israel (2 Chro 6:3) which is of special significance.[91] The prayer contains also a special note of sensitivity for the foreigners who will come to the land of Israel (2 Chro 6:32-33).

The cloud mentioned by the narrator (2 Chro 5:13-14) and the fire (2 Chro 7:1-3) are symbolic of God's presence and his gracious acceptance of the prayer raised to God by Solomon. The enormous numbers mentioned here (and elsewhere by the narrator) when offering cattle, sheep and goats (see 1 Chro 29:21 and 2 Chro 7:4-5; see also 29:32-36 and 35:7-9 for the large number of sacrifices during the time of Hezekiah and Josiah respectively) indicate bounteous gratitude towards God who is the source and origin of all good. As correctly pointed out by Japhet, the large numbers of animals slaughtered are a concrete expression of the grandeur of the event.[92] Sacrifice

---

87 For more details on liturgical music, see also Sara Japhet, *I & II Chronicles,* Old Testament Library (London: SCM Press, 1993) 611.

88 See Raymond B. Dillard, *2 Chronicles,* Word Biblical Commentary, 15 (Waco, Texas: Word Book Publishers, 1987) 52-53.

89 For more details on mercy and forgiveness as a Leit motif in the books of Chronicles, see Sara Japhet, *I & II Chronicles,* Old Testament Library (London: SCM Press, 1993) 594.

90 For an excellent presentation on the Deuteronomistic elements in the prayer of Solomon in 2 Chron 6:1-42, see Sara Japhet, *I & II Chronicles,* Old Testament Library (London: SCM Press, 1993) 587-605.

91 J. A. Thompson, *1, 2 Chronicles,* The New American Commentary, New International Version, Volume 9 (Nashville: Broadman & Holman Publishers, 1994) 227.

92 Sara Japhet, *I & II Chronicles,* Old Testament Library (London: SCM Press, 1993) 513.

is in fact the primary function that is being carried out in the Temple.[93] The Chronicler also brings to the attention of the readers that the worshiping community experiences joy and gladness (2 Chro 7:10). The worship does not come to a close with the dedication of the temple. The Chronicler informs the readers that daily sacrifices are taking place. Sabbaths, New Moons and the three annual feasts – Feast of the unleavened Bread, the feast of the Weeks and the Feast of the Tabernacles – are regular features (2 Chro 8:12-14). Solomon, although he is not of the tribe of Levi, yet he offers sacrifice on a regular basis (see 2 Chro 7:7 and 8:12-13).

At this juncture there is a glowing tribute paid to David! As mentioned earlier, he is referred to as the *man of God* (2 Chro 8:14). This certainly fits in although the Chronicler is speaking about Solomon in this section of the second volume. For it was David, the man of God, who had motivated Solomon to carry out the gigantic task entrusted to him. Solomon had learnt in the school of his father how to honour his God.

It is highly significant that of the 9 chapters that deal with Solomon (2 Chron 1-9), 6 chapters are pivoting around the construction and dedication of the temple.[94] The Chronicler is more interested in the wealth of Solomon than in his wisdom. This is because of the investment required in the completion of the project given to him by David his father. As with David, so too here, when narrating the reign of Solomon the emphasis is on the religious sphere. Rightly does Japhet say that the aim of the Chronicler is to present Solomon's reign as complementing and continuing the reign of David.[95]

After the dedication of the temple, the narrator returns to the theme of Solomon's wisdom and wealth. Before speaking about his death, he gives special attention to the visit of the queen of Sheba. The Chronicler brings to a close the forty year long reign of Solomon (970-931 BC), the space of time similar to that of David (1010-970 BC), without commenting on the last years of his reign when he went astray as mentioned in 2 Kings as well as by Ben Sira (Sir 47:19-22). Solomon, before being gathered to his fathers, rose to the occasion by accomplishing what his father had entrusted him with as we referred to above (1 Chronicles 28:1-21). He was successful in bringing to completion the project of building the temple since he remained faithful to the directives of his father David, namely, knowing and serving God (1 Chro 28:9-

93 For the importance of the sacrifice offered in the Temple (2 Chro 6:12-22), see also Sara Japhet, *I & II Chronicles,* Old Testament Library (London: SCM Press, 1993) 614.

94 For more details see, Sara Japhet, "Chronicles, Books of", in *Encyclopaedia Judaica,* Second Edition, Volume 4 (Detroit: Thomson Gale, 2007) 698.

95 Sara Japhet, "Chronicles, Books of", in *Encyclopaedia Judaica,* Second Edition, Volume 4 (Detroit: Thomson Gale, 2007) 698.

10). The main focus of the prayer (of David) was that the people maintain ever faithfully the spiritual perfection that they had attained (1 Chro 29:18-19).[96]

The Quest for Identity Reaches its Desired Goal

After taking note of the role played by David and his team, as well as the task accomplished by Solomon, namely, the building of the temple, one is in a position to become aware of the Chronicler's strategy in offering a spiritual vision for the community of Israel. With the theological themes that he has delineated in his theological history as well as through his vision for the community, the Chronicler keeps the community united and close to God. We want to recapture the main trends in this connection.

The theology in the Chronicler's history

There is a concern to connect the community in Jerusalem with its historical, geographical and religious roots.[97] Religious heritage is crucial in presenting the vision that the Chronicler tries to project. To be more specific although the Chronicler is narrating history from prehistoric times till the exile, his main interest is in *the religious life* of Israel.[98] The presence of God among his people and the means to become aware of this reality are crucial.[99] Other themes of the two volumes are the following: the people, the kingship, the temple and worship, retribution, mercy and repentance.[100] It must be added that the tribe of David, viz., the tribe of Judah and her trusting obedience to God are also highlighted.[101]

Evidently the themes presented in the course of the narrative project the theology of the Chronicler. Still we want to mention here the salient features of his theology. They can be viewed under the following titles: the concept of God, worship, Israel as God's people, the prophets, Torah and Messianism. By way of explication, the Chronicler has highlighted in particular the following:

---

96 See Sara Japhet, *I & II Chronicles,* Old Testament Library (London: SCM Press, 1993) 511.

97 See "1 Chronicles", in *Lutheran Study Bible,* New Revised Standard Version (Minneapolis: Augsburg Fortress, 2009) 639.

98 See J. E. Goldingay, "Chronicles, Books of", in *New Bible* Dictionary, Third Edition, I.H. Marshall et al. (Hyderabad: Authentic, 2011) 185.

99 "The Two Books of the Chronicles", in *The Didache Bible with Commentaries based on the Catechism of the Catholic Church,* Ignatius Bible Edition (Downers Grove: Midwest Theological Forum, 2014) 430.

100 See H.G.M. Williamson, *1 and 2 Chronicles,* The New Century Bible Commentary (Grand Rapids: Wm. B. Eerdmans Publishing Company, 1982) 24-33.

101 See J. E. Goldingay, "Chronicles, Books of", in *New Bible Dictionary*, Third Edition, I.H. Marshall et al. (Hyderabad: Authentic, 2011) 185-186.

1) The concept of God (the God of Israel is an active God who is interested in the life of Israel); he judges Israel and nations; he is present and transcendent; he is a holy God; the Lord uses the nations to announce his will and purpose. God is also Father (1 Chro 29:10); Israel, whose life is like a shadow (1 Chro 29:15) is totally dependent upon God for everything.[102] The author wants to stress the covenantal tie that exists between God and the people.[103]
2) The role of worship with the sanctuary in Jerusalem; God and the King (David) are on intimate terms. As Moses received the blueprint for the tabernacle, David received the plan for the temple from the Lord (1 Chro 22:1; 28:19).
3) The priests and Levites have unique roles. There is an extensive organization of the personnel employed for various tasks.[104] The Levites were in charge of the tabernacle, while the priestly family of Kohath was in charge of the ark and the appurtenances for worship (the table of the presence bread, lamp-stand, altars, etc). They were the bearers of the ark (1 Chro 15:15). They were also entrusted with duties as singers (1 Chro 15:16-22), porters (15:23). They were cult functionaries and for the most part under the direction of the priests (1 Chro 23:27-32). They were royal functionaries (1 Chro 26:20-30). They performed the role of judges (2 Chro 19:8, 11) and of prophets (2 Chro 20:14f).
4) Homage to God must find expression in the different types of offerings like burnt offerings and communion sacrifices (1 Chro 16:1-2, 40) and meal offerings (1 Chro 21:23; 2 Chro 2:3-6). Moreover what is most important in the mind of David is expressed in his prayer in the closing chapter – the thoughts and hearts of Israel should be directed to God, which itself is God's gift and for which she needs constantly the divine help (1 Chro 29:18).[105]
5) The prophets' roles are well delineated. They are involved in the life of Judah (1 Chro 17:3; 25:3-5).[106] They rebuked deviations. They held the Kings in line and pronounced judgement upon the kingdom. They announced return from exile. Some were considered as seers

102 For a detailed presentation on the prayer of David in 1 Chro 29, see Sara Japhet, *I & II Chronicles,* Old Testament Library (London: SCM Press, 1993) 502-517.

103 Sara Japhet, "Chronicles, Books of", in *Encyclopaedia Judaica,* Second Edition, Volume 4 (Detroit: Thomson Gale, 2007) 701.

104 Jacob M. Myers, *1 Chronicles*, The Anchor Bible (Garden City, New York: Doubleday & Company, 1965) LXVIII.

105 Sara Japhet, *I & II Chronicles,* Old Testament Library (London: SCM Press, 1993) 511.

106 Jacob M. Myers, *1 Chronicles*, The Anchor Bible (Garden City, New York: Doubleday & Company, 1965) LXXVII.

of the King. They are regarded without exception as men of God who deliver with undaunted courage God's message.

6) Giving glory to the Lord was crucial on account of the enduring love of God for the community, the tribe of Judah, and the family of David (16:29).
7) The bringing of the ark into Jerusalem[107] with the accompanying liturgy,[108] and the preparations that were made for the construction of the temple are not only a constant reminiscence for the community of its extraordinary spiritual heritage[109] but also proposes to focus on David as the great spiritual leader.[110]
8) Contributions for the construction of the temple were made not only by the King but also by the leaders and the entire populace. It had to be done joyously for that is a sign that one's heart is surely present in the act of giving.[111]
9) David is presented as a man of God and as one who is on good terms with God and as one who consults God (1 Chro 14:8-17; 17:16; 2 Chro 8:14).

The Chronicler shares his vision for Israel by focusing on the common identity of the people

The Chronicler has succeeded in sharing his vision which is God-centred and people-oriented. He has made it amply clear that Israel's prosperity and success were the result of God's blessings. The blessings were dependent upon the people's homage and obeisance. Hence at a time when the temple lay in ruins, it was important to return to the days of King David (the Golden age in the life of Israel) when he, the religious King, planned the construction of the temple. As in the days of old, during the present time as well, the re-building of the temple should be a new beginning in the life of Israel. For a time Israel was guilty of not having sought Yahweh. The Chronicler reminded the community of the restoration that seeking Yahweh consisted in the following: one turns to

107 Josephus also narrates the importance of the ark. For details, see "Jewish Antiquities, 7.4.1-4", in *The Complete Works of Josephus,* translated by William Whiston, Commentary by Paul L. Maier (Grand Rapids: Kregel Publications, 1999).

108 Daniel Durken, *The New Collegeville Bible Commentary: Old Testament* (Bangalore: TPI, 2018 / Collegeville: The Liturgical Press, 2015) 600.

109 *The Nelson Study Bible*, NKJV, Earl D. Radmacher, Ed. (Nashville: Thomas Nelson Publishers, 1997) 659

110 *The Nelson Study Bible*, NKJV, Earl D. Radmacher, Ed. (Nashville: Thomas Nelson Publishers, 1997) 659.

111 Sara Japhet, *I & II Chronicles,* Old Testament Library (London: SCM Press, 1993) 509.

him; trusts in him; prays to him; praises and worships him and joins hands with co-worshippers in uprightness of heart.[112]

The Chronicler in no ambiguous terms told the community of Israel that Yahweh rewards those who trust in him (1 Chro 4:10; 5:20-22) and punishes those who are unfaithful (1 Chro 5:25-26). When a king seeks Yahweh through establishing the proper temple rituals, as well as through sincerity in prayer and worship, then he and the nation are blessed with victory, peace, successful building projects, and unity among the peoples.[113] Those who seek God will have large families (1 Chro 14:3-7), success in the projects undertaken (1 Chro 14:1), riches and honour (1 Chro 14:1-2), military strength and success (1 Chro 5:20-22; 14:8-16; 18:1-20:8) and peace in the land (1 Chro 22:18; 23:25).[114] The readers reach a logical conclusion that seeking Yahweh (see 1 Chro 21:1-10; 22:6-19; 28:9) is crucial for obtaining God's blessings.

Conclusion

The temple is the place where God's name, eyes and heart are present (2 Chro 7:12-16). God himself made known this when he spoke to Solomon through a vision. The Chronicler who compiled his history several years after the destruction of the temple gives an explanation for the destruction of the temple as well. It was because the successors of Solomon had not taken to heart the warning given by God, namely, they went after other gods (2 Chro 7:7-22). In the mind of the Chronicler apostasy, idolatry, the neglect and abuse of the temple and its institutions, despising the words of prophets, and egregious violence, etc. are all expressions of an abandonment of Yahweh (1 Chro 28:9). Defeat and despoiling by foreign enemies (1 Chro 10:1-7), sickness and death (1 Chro 2:3; 10:10-13) and loss of land and the subsequent exile (1 Chro 5:25-26; 9:1) are all ways in which God punishes his people for their infidelity.[115] Serving God loyally is not an option for the people. Seeking for an identity in any place other than in the temple or wanting an existence devoid of God's presence is unthinkable.

In achieving the design of God for the people, the involvement of the entire community and at the same time, respecting diversity of roles are

---

112 See R. K. Duke, "Chronicles, Books of", in *Dictionary of the Old Testament Historical Books,* Bill T. Arnold and H. G. M. Williamson, Eds. (Downers Grove: IVP Academic, 2005) 171-172.

113 See R. K. Duke, "Chronicles, Books of", in *Dictionary of the Old Testament Historical Books,* Bill T. Arnold and H. G. M. Williamson, Eds. (Downers Grove: IVP Academic, 2005) 173.

114 See 1-2 Chronicles, in *E S V Study Bible*, English Standard Version (Wheaton, Illinois: Crossway, 2008) 698.

115 See 1-2 Chronicles, in *E S V Study Bible*, English Standard Version (Wheaton, Illinois: Crossway, 2008) 698.

nonnegotiable. The King, the priests, the Levites, and all the people work in unison. The Chronicler takes pains to present David as one totally relying upon God (1 Chro 17:16-27). The mysterious workings of the divine are visible in David the religious monarch. Joyful worship, not political intrigue and infighting are King David's final legacy as the Chronicler retells the story of days gone by for the Jewish community.[116]

For realizing the blueprint for Israel's Identity in community formation, it is necessary to avoid any form of dichotomy between the secular and the spiritual in the life of the nation. Authority is to be at the service of God and the people. Everyone will give his share in the task of coordination while paying homage to the Lord. What the Chronicler is more interested in is the reestablishing of the stability and permanence that existed in the community during the time of David and the years immediately following his death. He focuses on the tie between the people and their God on which depended also divine recompense. In this context, fidelity to the law and sincere worship with attention to the details were important.[117]

The purpose of the temple is to establish a new level of intimacy with God.[118] This explains the "full articulated cultic system" that is described in the two volumes of the Chronicler.[119] The description of an elaborate, colourful, joyful liturgy among other things aims at presenting the God of Israel as someone very close to his people.[120] The future of the community is assured provided they serve the living God who dwells in the temple.[121] The present plight is due to the forsaking of Yahweh. Sincere worship in the temple is among the ideal methods for seeking Yahweh. The community must read their present from God's perspective.[122] The prayer in the closing chapter (1 Chro

116 Danel Durken, *The New Collegeville Bible Commentary: Old Testament* (Bangalore: TPI, 2018 / Collegeville: The Liturgical Press, 2015) 610.

117 Sara Japhet, "Chronicles, Books of", in *Encyclopaedia Judaica,* Second Edition, Volume 4 (Detroit: Thomson Gale, 2007) 701.

118 "1 Chronicles", in *The Mission of God: Study Bible,* E D Stetzer and Philip Nation, Eds. (Nashville: Holman Bible Publishers, 1999 / 2012) 393.

119 See R. K. Duke, "Chronicles, Books of", in *Dictionary of the Old Testament Historical Books,* Bill T. Arnold and H. G. M. Williamson, Eds. (Downers Grove: IVP Academic, 2005) 173.

120 "The Two Books of the Chronicles", in *The Didache Bible with Commentaries Based on the Catechism of the Catholic Church,* Ignatius Bible Edition (Downers Grove: Midwest Theological Forum, 2014) 430.

121 See *The International Student Bible for Catholics,* New American Bible (Nashville: Thomas Nelson Publishers, 1999) 348; see also " The First Book of Chronicles", in *Little Rock Catholic Study Bible, Catherine Upchurch, Gen. Ed.* (Bangalore: Claretian Publications, 2011 / Collegeville: Liturgical Press, 2011) 655.

122 Scott W. Hahn, *The Kingdom of God as Liturgical Empire: A Theological Commentary on 1-2 Chronicles* (Grand Rapids: Baker Academic, 2012) 6.

29) has a particular significance. David is asking the Lord to keep the people strong in spirituality.[123] All the tribes of Israel should remain as one people. The fortyfold occurrence of "all Israel" in the books of Chronicles shows an inclusive concern that should not be lost sight of.[124]

Ben Sira, when singing the praises of David, rightly gave greater attention to the religious aspects in the life of David (see Sir 47:2-11). The author of Maccabees instead underscored the mercy of David (1 Mac 2:57) for he had experienced the abundant mercy of God in his life. Man and woman who are created in the *divine image* will be able to realize their potentiality only if they are able to blend well the spiritual and the secular, with priority always for the former. Not to have had the books of Chronicles as part of Scripture or to ignore them is to lose the spiritual vision and God-orientation that David tried to inculcate in the community of Israel.

---

123 Daniel Durken, *The New Collegeville Bible Commentary: Old Testament* (Bangalore: TPI, 2018 / Collegeville: The Liturgical Press, 2015) 609-610.

124 See "1 Chronicles", in *Lutheran Study Bible,* New Revised Standard Version (Minneapolis: Augsburg Fortress, 2009) 638.

5

The Role of Human Being in Identity Formation in Wisdom and Poetry

Tekayaba

Hebrew Scripture deals with the formation of the identity of the People of God known as the Hebrews,[1] Israel[2] and the Jews.[3] In relation to the identity formation of the people of God issues are dealt; who is God? Who are the people? And what is and what should be the relationship among them? These quarries are analyzed in relation to divine and human, human and human, human and creation relationship. In wisdom and poetry the issue is dealt in two

1 Abraham was called a Hebrew from Genesis 14 following, the children of Jacob were called as Hebrews from Exo. 1-2. Basically the term Hebrew describes the nameless, faceless, landless, speechless and religious-less mass of sojourning people who were not fit into any categories that makes a title. Naveen Rao, *Life and Faith of the People of God*, BD/BCS Study Material: OT (Kolkata: SCEPTER, 2013), 11. C.f., N.P. Lamkhe, *The Israelites in History and Tradition* (SPCK: London, 1998), 57-62.

2 Since God's covenant with Abraham and their journey to the promised Land the term Israel was used to refer to this group of people who left their slavery and were moving towards the goal of becoming a nation. After monarchy the term was applied to the ten tribes of Northern Kingdom. Thus the term denotes a geographical location as well as a group of people who were a community and later become a nation. Naveen Rao, *Life and Faith of the People of God*, 12.

3 After the people of Judah, *yehuda*, the Southern Kingdom returned from Babylonian exile the people were known by the term *yehudi*, Jews. Naveen Rao, *Life and Faith of the People of God*, 12.

ways[4]: Firstly, the sources are cross-cultural in nature. Cross-cultural nature is projected by quoting non-Israelite personalities and their wisdom: "The words of Agur son of Jakeh of Massa" (Proverbs 30:1); "the words of Lemuel, king of Massa" (Proverbs 31: 1); none of the friends of Job appear to be Hebrew: Eliphaz, Bildad, Zophar and Elihu. (ii) Secondly, the sources are focused more on individual capabilities on how one should and should not live. The sages and teachers are more concerned with individual matters of life: How can we live life to its fullest and best? How can we discern the meaning of life? Rankin states,[5] Wisdom Literature recognizes God's interest in individual life and human responsibility based on reasoning, intellect and freedom. The study will focus on human being as creatures capable of discerning the right from wrong in creating right identity of things created.

The sages hold, "God founded the earth by Wisdom; by understanding established the heavens; and by knowledge the deep broke forth and the clouds drop down the dew" (Prov 3: 19-20), and wants the people to discover it within individual search and initiation. Wisdom and Poetry is rational rather than supernatural therefore the teaching is, we learn from observation, experience and reflection. Wisdom sages believe and teach that God created human mind with ability to notice and interpret and these gifts enables an individual to understand. Gerhard von Rad states, "experience presupposes a prior knowledge of myself; indeed it can become experience only if I can fit it into the existing context of my understanding of myself and the world."[6]

Every creation is created with certain purposes and functions which describes the identity of why things are created. G. von Rad in his book "Wisdom in Israel" affirms, the main step to look into in the wisdom literature is "to understand reality".[7] They deal on, how, when, and why certain actions are to be performed and certain insights to be appropriated to fulfill the purpose of one's creation and identity (cf. Prov 15:23; 25:11 etc). Wisdom literature is shaped and founded on human's participation in the acts of justice which defines the propose of one's identity of creation.

4 Don F. Morgan, *Between Text and Community: The Writings in Canonical Interpretation* (Minneapolis: Fortress Press, 1990), 41; Carol S. Grizzard, "The Scope of Theology in Wisdom Literature," in *An Introduction to Wisdom Literature and the Psalms. Festschrift Marvin E. Tate*, Editors, H. Wayne Ballard, Jr and W. Dennis Tucker, Jr. (Georgia: Mercer University Press, 2000): 197.

5 O.S. Rankin, *Israel's Wisdom Literature*, 35f.

6 Gerhard van Rad, *Wisdom in Israel,* translated by James. D. Martin (Nashville: Abingdon Press, 1972), 3.

7 By "understanding reality" G. Von Rad means to state, theology that is concerned in understanding that is oriented towards individual. Gerhard Von Rad, *Wisdom in Israel,* 6.

According to William P. Brown,[8] wisdom literature assists in the formation of identity, character, and shaping of worldview with instructions and warnings for individual and society. In Proverbs the teaching is portrayed as parent-child or teacher-student relationship. In Ecclesiastes *Qoheleth* the teacher instructs the hearers what he has experienced. In Job, he and his friends debate on what is life and how life is to be lived in righteousness. Safeguarding one's identity is one the main issue dealt in wisdom literature while explaining the purposes of creation.

1. The Role of Wisdom in Identity Formation

Wisdom and Creation share universalism; God creates, sustains and bless the humanity while wisdom shapes, designs and life-enhancing which undergirds order and reality.[9] The world was grounded in the "confidence concerning human ability to perceive and grasp the nature of reality."[10] Human's reasoning power, to perceive and understand is portrayed as the very essence of identity formation. Wisdom here means; understanding reality, the meaning in life, the way of coping, the way to success, the discovery of the orders of creation and conformity to them.[11]

In wisdom literature one's identity is to be formulated within the chaotic order of life.[12] The present identity is defined by those in power, and the failure to recognize and confront to this world realities result in misfortune, misery and chaos. In this process fighting for rights and justice is the right principle through which one's identity can be defined. Hebrew word צַדִּיק *tsdiq* goes beyond the very term "to judge" which can also mean "to arrange," "to put in order."[13] The word צֶדֶק *tsdq* "justice" thus means "order/righteousness",

8 William P. Brown, *Character in Crisis: A Fresh Approach to the Wisdom Literature of the Old Testament*, (Grand Rapids: Eerdmans, 1996) in James Crenshaw, "Unsolved Issues in Wisdom Literature," *An Introduction to Wisdom Literature and the Psalms. Festschrift Marvin E. Tate*, 218.

9 Westermann viewed, wisdom literature portrays humans to be the creatures created by God with possibilities and limits that are indigenous to their creatureliness. Humanity as creatures gifted with organs of sense to know, perceive and to sustenance. Claus Westermann, *Blessing in the Bible and the Life of the Church*. (Philadelphia: Westminster, 1978), 37ff; Claus Westermann, *Wurzeln der Weisheit. Die altesten Spruche Israels und Anderer Volker* (Gottingen: Vandenhoeck & Ruprecht, 1990), 93-99.

10 Ronald E. Clement, *Wisdom in Theology* (Grand rapids: Eerdmans, 1992), 47.

11 Dianne Bergant, *Israel's Wisdom Literature: A Liberation-Critical Reading*, 12.

12 Leo G. Perdue, *Wisdom and Creation: The Theology of the Wisdom Literature*, 80, 90.

13 Generally "Justice and Judgment" are phrases used in association with court, charged, sentenced, or acquitted. But "Justice" too can mean bringing things into order and proper arrangement. Claus Westermann, *Hand Book to the Old Testament* (London: ISPCK, 1969), 96; J.P. Miranda, *Marx and the Bible: A Critique of the Philosophy of Oppression* (Maryknoll: Orbis 1974), 111f; David J. Reimer, **qdc** *NIDOTTE* vol. 3 : 744-769.

the one who engaged in creating order is known as צְדָקָה *tsdqh* who lives in harmony with God and society and experiences well-being in life. To hear the cry of the poor and the oppressed is the first act of Justice.[14] Justice is a characteristic essence of God, and to know God and to do justice are the same thing.[15]

Friedmann W. Golka views that the book of Proverbs describes the creation of human functions as a part of social criticism.[16] The book encourages utilizing wisdom in order to defuse conflicts and minimize social tensions to discern the true meaning of life in living.[17] The first social problem in relation to our present social scenario that comes in the book of Proverbs is in Proverbs 1-9, where wisdom is personifies as a female character which give rise to many feminist reading raising their voice against injustices in relation to the concept of creation of men and women as equal.[18] Human being and the creations exist with some inherent worth but they are suppressed and dominated by the rich and powerful subjectively.[19]

The sages' conception for maintaining social order through justice is the order that was established by God out of chaos at the first creation event and

---

14 "God hears the human crying and groaning from the place of struggles all over the world. … The cry of the rejected and discriminated people from the lands of racism; the cry of the mistreated and exploited from the lands of rapidly developing countries under dictatorship; the cry of the poor and alienated people from the lands of capitalism; and the cry of the imprisoned and rejected people from the land where one political ideology… is dominant and oppressive." Stephen Charles, *Christian Faith and Democracy* (New York: Association Press, 1939), 16.

15 Karen Lebacqz, *Justice in an Unjust World* (Minneapolis: Augsburg Publishing House, 1987), 72.

16 According to Friedemann W. Golka, the book of Proverbs chapters 10-29 portray God as the creator of both rich and poor and that they are brothers, they both have the same maker. This fact prohibits the exploitation of the poor and warns the rich against despising the lower strata of society. Since these chapters and teaching about creation is portrayed to teach in line with the social realities, the creation of human is viewed as a social criticism in its functioning in Proverbs. Friedemann W. Golka, *The Leopard Spots: Biblical and African Wisdom in Proverbs* (New York: T&T Clarke International, 1993), 119.

17 Peter Doll, *Menschenschopfung und Weltschopfung in der alttestamentlichen Weisheit* (Stuttgart, 1985), 29.

18 Claudis V. Camp, *Wisdom and the Feminine in the Book of Proverbs,* BLS 11 (Sheffield: Almond Press, 1985); Carol R. Fontain, *Traditional Saying in the Old Testament,* BLS 5 (Sheffield: Almond Press, 1982); Carol A. Newsom, "Women and the Discourse of Patriarchal Wisdom: A Study of Proverbs 1-9," in *Gender and Difference in Ancient Israel,* edited by Peggy L. Day (Minneapolis: Fortress Press, 1989); Athalya Brenner, editor, *A Feminist Companion to Wisdom Literature* (Sheffield: Sheffield Academic Press, 1995).

19 All created things have their own inherent worthiness and goodness of their own. Regardless of any instrumental or inherent value therefore, all creatures should be given the space to exercise such worth. Paul W. Taylor, *Respect for Nature: A Theology of Environmental Ethics* (Princeton: Princeton University Press, 1986), 75f.

leaves with humanity to maintain order in the cosmic realm (Gen 1:28-31; 2:15-16; Prov 14:31, 23:10-11, etc). Thus, to maintain social order, the sage teaches us to uphold justice within oneself, society and to all creation.

Identity formation advocates a theology for the well being of the whole humanity which is not only to the few privileged, rich and the powerful but for the whole will balance statements of order.[20] Scholars are of the view that bible reflects the perspective of the Israelite peasant,[21] ethnic, class, and gender biases which are the main obstacles towards the means of life.[22] Social structures are unjust when the counterpart power and decision-making is put in the few hands of the rich and powerful. Re-membrance of the issues of justice will lead to a new focus for forming a new community of commitments towards their own identities. Proverbs 16:10-16 describes the power of king to exercise righteousness within themselves and for others. The pedagogy of the text portrays the ability of human being to reason, know and understand the world and its order for life as well as the commission to master life and attain one's identity.

A person without self-mastery and integrity is a person without identity. The Hebrew word תֹּם *tom,* 'integrity' also means "wholeness" or "completeness". When applied to identity formation it conveys a sense of self-possession, or maturity. People of integrity are able to be responsible and loyal in human relationship, the arena wherein all the virtues of the wise are employed.[23] Human wisdom is the ability to imagine a righteous and beneficent order in the world[24] to shape and sustain just institutions, to enable the social order to exist in concert with creation, to engage in the moral life that is in harmony with the cosmos and society, and to experience well-being and success. The description of human and social reality existed within the socio-political configurations of a society. For the sages, order of creation was understood in terms of social order that is organized in just and humane ways with the interactions with human's life realities. For Von Rad, "The most

20 Friedemann W. Golka, *The Leopard Spots: Biblical and African Wisdom in Proverbs*, 121; Friedemann W. Golka, "Universalism and the Election in the Jews" *Theology* (July, 1987): 273-280.

21 R.N. Whybray, *Wealth and Poverty in the Book of Proverbs* (Sheffield: JSOT, 1990); R.N. Whybray, *The Composition of the Book of Proverbs* (Sheffield: JSOT, 1994).

22 Dianne Bergant, *Israel's Wisdom Literature: A Liberation-Critical Reading*, 105.

23 Such people seem to live from within, fed by inner springs known only to them. They have a profound honesty about themselves and the world, and they have the self-possession to act accordingly. Such people are particularly, nothing to lose. "The one who walks in integrity walks in safety" Prov 10:9. Kathleen M. O'Connor, *The Wisdom Literature,* 48-49.

24 D.J. McCarthy, "Be Sober and Watch," *The Way* 14 (1974): 167; Leo G. Perdue, *Wisdom and Creation: The Theology of the Wisdom Literature*, 326.

characteristics feature of her [Israel] understanding of reality lay in the fact that she believed man to stand in a quite specific, highly dynamic, existential relationship with his environment."[25] Human's identity is defined on how one live in accordance with the contest by coping one's daily life's experiences.

It is practically a common place in wisdom teachings to discover one's identity in the realm of experience and nature which are humanly initiated. Claus Westermann notes, to choose Wisdom to create one's identity is left with "your own best interest."[26] In wisdom literature, there is an inevitable relationship that exists between the kinds of lives people leads and the things that happen to them. Carlston has rightly observed, the truth of many sayings is only realized when they are fittingly applied.[27] Wisdom is thus a search of patterns for the purpose of living in shaping the identity of the creations.

2. Role of Individual in Identity Formation

Wisdom literature gives importance to individual among the created being to address the matter how one could contribute towards an individual and social identity. G. Von Rad, states that practical insight to formulate a wisdom theology is gained through individual experiences of life[28] emphasizing wisdom as primary human enterprise which stresses human freedom and the requisite responsibility to forge social and individual destiny. Human are called with personal responsibilities to accept challenges in determining the destiny of life. Wisdom literature concern towards individual may be that beginning from individual will fairly and in a better way open the concern and theology into a wider range as possible.

Naturally every individual and society faces challenges in life which distort the individual and social identity. Wisdom offers answers to the problems, dilemmas, and quarries in relation to social and individual issues and realities. To which the book of Proverbs offers guidance and education on how to live a life according to the requirement of society, law, and nature which are pragmatic and practical. The book takes a practical approach, stating those who follow wisdom will prosper and find meaning in life but those who do not will face disaster (1:32-33). The task of an individual in attaining Wisdom in proverbs is to know, choose and do the right things. People who follow and do

25 Gerhard von Rad, *Wisdom in Israel,* 301.

26 Claus Westermann, *Roots of Wisdom: The Oldest Proverbs of Israel and Other People,* translated by J. Daryl Charles (Louisville: Westminster/John Knox Press, 1995), 133.

27 C.E. Carlston, "Proverbs, Maxims, and the Historical Jesus," *JBL* 99 (1980): 87-105.

28 Gerhard Von Rad, *Old Testament Theology*, vol. 1 (New York: Harper & Raw, 1962), 418ff.

the righteous deeds were identified as righteous, wise and are in attune with the purpose of creation and existence.[29]

This concept and theology of individual righteousness in identity formation is seen in numerous instances in the book of Proverbs, especially in chapters 10-18. Human being are created with intellect and wisdom to discern how to cope chaos and deal with fellow beings, neighbours, society and cosmos. King's roles were to create a society of justice without discriminating and alienating the general people and the poor. Individual were instructed to create order and peace stating their purpose of creation. Performing justice, order and peace were the purpose God created human being in his own image and likeness and that is the soul identity of being human.

The book of Job endows with life's approaches and challenges directly and practically from his own life's experiences. The book deals with meaning of life, overcoming sufferings, faith affirmation, discovering joy, health and discerning wise living and identity formation. The teachings have a retrospective tendency basically with practical and empirical value and so one must have wisdom and an understanding in order to feel the beauty of its expressions embedded within the poems, dialogues, and narratives. The book of Job shows its portrayal of human centered in two ways.[30] Firstly, it was human who has to decide one's destiny and identity. Major section of the book from chapter 3 till 37 God does not appear and how God reacted to human's speeches and characters are not portrayed. The beginning part of the book expresses the uncertainties in the conversation between God and Satan, God allowing Satan to destroy Job's riches, family, and health which is explained by David Noel Freedman as, God does not know whether the accusations about Job are true.[31] Secondly, individual reflection and observations was the expected way to learn. All individual characters use observation to back up the point they make (cf. Job 4:7-11; 12:7-13:1; 18:5-21; 20:4-29; 36:24-33).

The book of Job after emphasizing on individual and self contemplative characters especially in chapters 3, 6-7, 9-10 stating suffering is a part of life. Suffering, pain and agony create chaos however in 7:1-2 Job compared the suffering life of human to the hard service of a hired labourer. Job however confirmed that there can be some rational for suffering, stating suffering can be a way of God testing human's loyalty defining suffering, coping, enduring suffering gives peace of mind, blessings and meaning to life.

29 C. Hassell Bullock, *An Introduction to the Old Testament Poetic Books*, 58.

30 Carol S. Grizzrd, "The Scope of Theology in Wisdom Literature" *An Introduction to Wisdom Literature and the Psalms*, 202.

31 David Noel Freedmann, "Is it Possible to Understand the Book of Job?" *Bible Review,* 4 (April, 1988): 31-33.

In the book of Ecclesiastes, Qoheleth is little optimistic yet skeptical in his teachings on life. The book deals with dilemma of human's life and its existence where Qoheleth the author contemplated and viewed life's situations through his own personal experiences. In the book Qoheleth begins with the inquiry of human's life and the reasons and advantages of being human and its existence. He begin by stating; "What advantage does human have in all their work which they does under the sun?" 1:3. He teaches that, no matter what kind of individual one may be, all will die; "How can the wise die just like fools? So I hated life, because what is done under the sun was grievous to me; for all is vanity and a chasing after wind" (2:16-17). Qoheleth has affirmed that there is no reason to think that human beings have any advantages over other created things and beings. Qoheleth follow the traditional wisdom teaching; it cannot go beyond what people can observe. This means he does not look for justice after death. This does not lead him, however to believe that there is no point in being wise (or human), because his observation have also taught him that living in accordance with wisdom leads to a better life.

He also observed many joys in life explained in chapters, 2:24-25; 5:18-19; 9:7-10; 11:8 etc. Qoheleth talks about individual's gain and finding meaning and joy in their toiling and earnings. Qoheleth defined life by searching education, wealth and fame. He asserted everything a person seek under the sun will only result meaningful when one let God judge, lead and bless one's deeds.

In his search and investigation on life's fate he concludes living the setback to individual life's dilemma. The search of Qoheleth ends by expresses, "For human goes to his eternal home while mourners go about in the street" 12:5c and thus one has to keep the commandments as individual's duty for God will bring every deeds into judgment whether good or evil, (12:13-14). Human being lies in the hand of God yet we are creatures created with intellect, reasoning power and wisdom which can create identity during our existence in the world and after.

Conclusion

Every nation and culture has its own traditional assets which plays vital role in identity formation by educating, guiding and shaping the youngsters into responsible and accountable citizens. Most importantly it helps in integrating the younger generation into the values and worldview and shape themselves into an respectable citizen as society require. Especially among the traditional societies this wisdom forms provide a source for discerning and decision making to the communities for de-fusing potential conflict situations and become better individuals. In such a way wisdom movements and literatures implements moral conduct as the primary and core concern for the formation of one's life.

Such a society and culture like ours today our contemporary society and culture need to find an anchorage for moral conduct. Our socio-cultural identity has lost its identity because there is hardly few who bothers about one's neighbours, society and culture, instead of love and unity only war and hatred among individuals, groups, religions, society and nation exists. One's rich tradition and culture has lost its identity and where everything is demoralized wisdom can be the best teacher to shape an individual. In such a context we need to recapture the pervasive power of our Christian faith, which includes and addresses all human experience within the wider circle of life. The basic element of what is morally permissible and what is not is based upon the individual's relationship to the community, world and to God. Because a healthy society is solely depended upon the individuals and their relationship and inter-linking with one another and with the creator. It is in the individual's philosophy of life and living style the society's identity at large is determined. Hence, for the well-being of the whole humanity an individual attitude towards other human and non-human being and society is very important. Knowing the fact and reality wisdom literature has beautifully explained this ideology by looking into the most important group of the creations which represents society or which functions the entire society in general.

6

Quest for Israelite Identity in the Exilic Prophets

B. Lalnunzira

Introduction

Human life is marked by a search for identity. An individual or a group seeks to explain who he/she is or who they are in relation to others. Social scientists believe that identity is shaped by self-concept and the tendency to favorably evaluate one's group while degrading other groups. In a situation where identity consciousness is highly salient, people evaluate their identity either by self-categorization or identification of others.[1] Ideologies, beliefs, and traditions are developed as part of social identification. The Hebrew Bible is considered as an outcome of social identification where Israel defined herself in relation to other communities. In their experiences of alienation, deportation, displacement and restoration, the people of Israel sought to define the true nature of their own community.

The issue of identity in relation to formation of a community in ancient Israel is significantly found in the exilic and early postexilic period. The period was marked by a search for identity among the communities of Israel. This paper attempts to explore how a quest for identity played a role in Israel's

1 For detail study of Social Identity Theories and the process involved in identity formation see Henri Tajfel, "Introduction," in *Social Identity and Intergroup Relations*, edited by Henri Tajfel (Cambridge: Cambridge University Press, 1982) and John C. Turner, "Some Current Issues in research on Social Identity and Self-Categorization Theories," in *Social Identity Context, Commitment, Content*, edited by Naomi Ellemers, Russel Spears and Bertijan Doosje (Malden, Massachusetts: Blackwell Publishers, 1999).

existence as a community in the exilic period and how prophetic literature responded the same. The book of Ezekiel will be taken as a test case to explore how a search for 'true Israel' was stimulated to restructure and refine cultural/religious and kinship-based standards of identity, responding to the conditions of exile that were endangering Israel's identity.

Identity and Community Defined

"Identity" is an ambiguous term, rarely defined in a precise way. However, it can be understood as a product of social or political action wherein a group defines itself as having a distinctive history, experiences, and social locations that endow its members with unique perspectives on social issues.[2] Identity is that which defines or distinguishes one or a group from other(s), – such as character, qualities, beliefs, personalities, ethnicity, nationhood, etc. An identity, whether personal or collective, depends on social processes whereby group values and norms define an individual and a group. A quest for identity plays a significant role in community formation where members of a community interact and relate to each other. A community may be defined as "a small or large social unit that has something in common, such as norms, religion, values, or identity." Sylvia Dale defines it as: "a body of people living in the same locality…Alternatively, a sense of identity and belonging shared among people living in the same locality… Also, the set of social relations found in a particular bounded area"[3] Hence, community is formed with a quest for identity in the existing socio-political and religious contexts. The Hebrew Bible could be considered as a literature (if not ideology) that seeks to construct a particular (Israelite) community in which a quest for identity is at the epicenter of Biblical writers and authors.

Methodological Consideration

In my analysis of quest for Identity in the formation of Israelite community in the exilic and early postexilic period, I hereby apply Michael Walzer's *Revolution of the Saints*. Michael Walzer discusses how rigorous ideologies are developed by groups of people who face uncertain situations, especially the situation of exile. He posits that the Puritan exiles, who constructed Puritan

---

2 Brubaker and Cooper argue that social sciences and humanities have surrendered the word "identity" and that it tends to mean too much, too little or nothing at all. Their idea is that the conceptual and theoretical work of identity might be better accomplished by other terms that offer less ambiguity. In their attempt to find alternative terms for "identity," they propose terms such as identification, categorization, self-understanding, social location, commonality, connectedness, and groupness. See Rogers Brubaker and Frederick Cooper, "Beyond "Identity," Theory and Society 29, no. 1 (Feb 2000): 1-47.

3 Sylvia Dale, *Controversies in Sociology. A Canadian Introduction* (Toronto: Copp, Clark and Pitman, 1990), 562.

ideology rooted in Calvinism, shaped radical politics that subsequently played a decisive role in the English revolution.[4] Walzer argues that the Calvinist idea of radical politics was developed through a difficult process of invention and experimentation of the Calvinist saints in the historical situations in which they appeared.[5] He argues that the Puritans (exiled from England during the rule of the Catholic monarch, Mary) who were intellectuals exiled from their former land, deeply felt the urge to remake the world in the image of their own rigorous, demanding religion.[6] The returning Marian exiles responded to the experience of their exile with their own demanding theology. This includes their self imposed authority and critique of existing social structures.

In his other article entitled "Puritanism as a Revolutionary Ideology," Walzer argues that Puritanism was a "response to disorder and fear, a way of organizing men (sic) to overcome the acute sense of chaos."[7] The returning Marian exiles responded to particular experiences of confusion, change, alienation and exile by creating their own ideology. He considers that the responses were in the form of discipline and political activity. One trait of their response was a response to their own fear, "fear in themselves of the 'unsettledness."[8] Another aspect of their response was political activity "whose immediate purpose was to regain control of a changing world; hence the great concern with method, discipline, and order, and the frequent uneasiness with novelty."[9] The Puritan response to their social world not only aimed at coping with personal and social problems, but it was an intense response to transforming society, "to create a holy commonwealth."[10] Walzer's theory offers insight into

---

4 See detail in Michael Walzer, *The Revolution of the Saints: A Study in the Origins of Radical Politics* (Cambridge: Massachusetts, Harvard University Press, 1965).

5 Walzer examines the French Huguenots and English Puritans as examples to demonstrate how Calvinism has a new form in Western society. According to him, French Protestantism (the Huguenots) took up Calvinist concept of resistance with a new language of conscience in their justified resistance against kings. On the other hand, the Puritans (Marian exiles) took up Calvinist alternative political community of the Christian commonwealth, and therefore deprived of all official functions shaping another radical political figures. See Walzer, *The Revolution of the Saints*, 66-113.

6 Walzer, *The Revolution of the Saints*, 97.

7 Michael Walzer, "Puritanism as a Revolutionary Ideology," in *Puritan New England: Essays on Religion, Society, and Culture*, eds. Alden T. Vaughan and Francis J. Bremer (New York: St. Martin's Press, 1977), 29. 19-41.

8 Walzer, "Puritanism as a Revolutionary Ideology," 32.

9 Walzer, "Puritanism as a Revolutionary Ideology," 35.

10 Walzer, "Puritanism as Revolutionary Ideology," 37. Cf. Walzer, *Revolution of the Saints*, 198. Kai T Erikson, who wrote about the Puritan of the Massachusetts Bay maintains that Puritanism of seventeenth-century Massachusetts and the fifteenth-century France shared the same fatalism. He writes: "In their confessions they insist they are worthless and contemptible, but in their professions they declare that it is their special privilege and

the study of the radical politics/ideology of the prophets and priestly groups of the exilic age. A quest for identity was evident in the time of national crisis of the Israelites who were traumatized by exilic catastrophe. Moreover, exilic experience impregnated with laxity of lifestyle, compromising attitude and religious syncretism of the community compelled a search for viable society. A quest for identity was an inexorable task of prophets and priests of the then period.

Exile and Identity Crisis

The sixth century BCE has often been described as a "creative age," as it was a period in which political and cultural changes took place on a global scale. This period was significant for the Israelites, who experienced the end of monarchy and the exile over its duration. This century is also labeled the "Exilic Age," due to the exile of groups of people to Babylonia and Egypt during the Neo-Babylonian and the early Persian period. Though not all biblical scholars agree with the actual events of Israel's deportation, exile and return, majority consensus is that Israelite communities were in exile in the land of Babylonia and Egypt following the fall of Judah at the hand of Babylonia.[11]

A cursory survey of the exilic and early postexilic age shows that this period was a period of a quest for identity for the Israelites as they were deported, displaced, and migrated due to imperial regime of Babylonia and Persia. Biblical and extra biblical sources reveal that a number of Judeans were deported to Babylonia in the early sixth century BCE. Evidence of the settlements of the Babylonian exiles can be found in the Murashu Tablets.[12]

---

obligation to challenge all the established tradition in Christendom." See Kai T. Erikson, *Wayward Puritans: A Study in the Sociology of Deviance* (Boston: Pearson Education, Inc. 2005), 50-51.

11 Traditionally, scholars claimed exile covering the period from 597-539 BCE (First deportation to Edict of Cyrus). For some scholars, 587 BCE (the final destruction of Jerusalem) is the beginning of the exilic age. The end of the exilic age for some is 515 BCE. I assume that the exilic age began in 597 BCE, the year Jerusalem was captured and the first group of deportees left Jerusalem for Babylon. It ended in 520 BCE when the rebuilding of the Jerusalem temple was undertaken at the decree of the Persian king Darius I. See Cf. Rainer Albertz, *Israel in Exile: The History and Literature of the Sixth Century BCE*, trans. David Green, SBL 3 (Atlanta: Society of Biblical Literature, 2003), 2. Thus Middlemas defines the exilic age as the "Templeless Age" (587-515) based on the books of Haggai, Zechariah 1-8, and the Holiness Code. See Jill Middlemas, The Templeless Age: An Introduction to the History, Literature, and Theology of the Exile (Louisville: Westminster John Knox Press, 2007). Also see John J. Ahn, *Exile as Forged Migrations: A Sociological, Literary, and Theological Appropriation on the Displacement and Resettlement of the Southern Kingdom of Judah,* BZAW 147 (Berlin: De Gruyter, 2011), 38, 40.

12 The 730 tablets belonging to the archives of the house of Murasu were discovered in May 1893 in a room at Nippur during the excavations sponsored by the University of

It is also evidently shown that a greater number of people remained in Judah during the same period.[13] A major decline in the population of Judah in the Neo-Babylonian and early Persian period is also acknowledged.[14] As shown in the book of 2 Kings 25:26 and Jer 44:1 groups of people migrated to Egypt for fear of Babylonian reprisal. Elephantine papyri demonstrate their continued stay, thereby forming an Egyptian-Jewish community in Egypt.[15]

According to available biblical and extra biblical sources, tremendous political and sociocultural changes led to intergroup conflicts in this period. Literature of the period reflects those changes with ideological discussions on group identification. During those periods, a pursuit for identity had become more apt due to intergroup conflicts and interrelationships of various groups. As found in the book of Ezekiel, a struggle for land ownership resulted to deep rift within the community (Ezek 11; 33). Jeremiah also criticized those prophets who claimed early return from Babylonia as he accused the exiles receiving consequence of religious apostasy (Jer 21; 27). Documents from Egypt reveals that the Jewish community in Egypt maintained Jewish identity by securing worship of Yahu. However, mixed marriage and syncretistic worship might

---

Pennsylvania. The tablets contain collections of names that include a large number of individual with Babylonian names, Persians, Medes, Egyptians and West Semites (including biblical personal names). See detailed study of the onomasticon of the Murasu tablets in Michael David Coogan, *West Semitic Personal Names in the Murasu Documents* (Missoula, Montana: Scholars Press, 1976).

13 Biblical evidences (2 Kings 25 & 26) and archaeological findings show this. For archaeological findings see Hans M. Barstad, History and the Hebrew Bible: Studies in Ancient Israelite and Ancient Near Eastern Historiography (Tubingen: Mohr Siebeck, 2008). Also Jeffrey R. Zorn. "Tell-en-Nasbeh and the Problem of the Material Culture of the Sixth Century," *Judah and the Judeans in the Neo-Babylonian Period*, 413-447; and Ephraim Stern, *Archaeology of the Land of the Bible Vol. II: The Assyrian, Babylonian, and Persian Periods (734-332 BCE)*, (New York: Doubleday, 2001), 312-327.

14 According to Lipschits, the decline of settled areas at the end of the Iron Age (7th century BCE) to the Persian period (5th century BCE) is as follows: Benjamin - 56.5%, Jerusalem environs 89.0%, Northern Judean Hills - 2.0%, Southern Judean Hills - 71.7%, The Shephelah - 66.7%, Beer-Sheba-Arad Valleys - 75.0%, Eastern Strip - 88.9%. Total decline = 72.3% See Oded Lipschits, "Demographic Changes in Judah between the Seventh and the Fifth Centuries B.C.E.," in Judah and the Judeans in the Neo-Babylonian Period, edited by Obed Lipschits and Joseph Blenkinsopp (Winona Lake, Ind: Eisenbrauns, 2003),356. See also Oded Lipschits, The Fall and Rise of Judah under Babylonian Rule (Winona Lake, Ind: Eisenbrauns, 2005).

15 The Elephantine Papyri are a group of papyrus documents and fragments written in Demotic Egyptian, Aramaic, Greek, Coptic, and Latin dating from the 5th century BCE originating at Elephantine, a site in Upper Egypt. They are classified as: Letters, Contracts, Literary Texts, Historical Texts, Accounts, and Lists. Of the Papyri, some of them, including Letters have generated interest in biblical studies. See Gary A. Herion, "Elephantine Papyri," in ABD Vol. 2, 445-455. Though they are late, they help in reconstructing the history of the Judean community in Egypt that may have been established in the 7th/6th centuries BCE.

have been noticed.[16] In the early postexilic period, mixed marriage was a crucial issue for the deportees as well as those remaining in the land of Judah in the sixth-fifth century BCE. Foreign wives and their children were separated and rejected (Ezra 10; Neh 13). Mixed marriage was condemned (Neh 13:23-29). A pertinent question was: "Who are the true Israel and what are the markers of true Israel?" In short group dynamics in the exilic and early post exilic period ensued a quest for identity among the communities of Israel.

Quest for Identity in Exilic Age

Charles E. Carter argues that a new ideology arose during the exilic age to explain the failure of the Judean kingdom and to endure the catastrophe of the exile in order to maintain the social identity of the Judean community.[17] Daniel L. Smith also views the exile as a creative event in Judean history in which the *golah* community sought to find meaning (through literature) in their survival strategy that characterizes community in the crisis of exile.[18] Dalit Rom-Shiloni ascribes many literary works during the 6th-5th century BCE as Babylonian exilic (group) ideologies. She argues that the conflicts between the Exiles and the people who remained in Judah "constructed and reconstructed group beliefs in the process of self-definition, and developed counter-definitions to delegitimize the others."[19] What is obvious from the above is that exile and

---

16 Bob Becking contends that the Yehudites in Elephantine were "the descendants of a branch or various branches, of the poly-Yahwism that existed in Judah before the Yahweh-alone movement." The names of deities associated with temples at Syne, such as Banit, the Queen of Heaven, Bethel and Nabu, support the probability of polytheistic worship. See documents in Bezalel Porten, *The Elephantine Papyri in English: Three Millennia of Cross-Cultural Continuity and Change* (Leiden: E.J. Brill, 1996),
These include names: Mordekai - which contains the name of the Babylonian deity Marduk (Ezra 2:2; Neh 7:7), Bilsan - which contains the name of Babylonian deity Bel (Ezra 2:2; Neh 7:7), Bigvai - a Semitic rendering of the Persian personal name (Ezra 2:2, 14; Neh 7:7, 19; 10:16), Elam - a name related to a territory in Iranian plateau (Ezra 2:7; Neh 7:12), and Azgad - a non–Semitic name (Ezra 2:12; Neh 7:17). See discussion in Bob Bekcing, "On the Identity of the 'Foreign Women in Ezra 9-10," in *Exile and Restoration Revisited: Essays on the Babylonian and Persian Periods in Memory of Peter R. Ackroyd* Library of Second Temple Studies 73, ed. Gary N. Knoppers and Lester L. Grabbe with Deirdre N. Fulton (New York: T&T Clark, 2009), 35-36.

17 See Charles E. Carter, "Ideology and Archaeology in the Neo-Babylonian Period," in Judah in the Judeans in the Neo-Babylonian Period, 318.

18 See Daniel L. Smith, *Religion of the Landless:* The Social Context of The Babylonian Exile (Bloomington, Ind: Meyer-Stone Books, 1989), 64-65.

19 See Dalit Rom-Shiloni, *Exclusive Inclusivity: Identity Conflicts Between the Exiles and the People who Remained (6th-5th Centuries BCE)* (New York: Bloomsbury, 2013). 23. See also Rom-Shiloni, "From Ezekiel to Ezra-Nehemiah: Shifts of Group Identities within Babylonian Exilic Ideology," in *Judah and the Judeans in the Achaemenid Period:*

exilic period was marked by a quest for identity among different groups of Israelite community who were displaced in different places.

Prophetic Quest for Identity in the Exilic Age

In response to the exilic experience concomitant with intergroup processes and conflicts, biblical literature developed as a strategy for social identification and negotiation. Scholars generally agree that much of the biblical literature was written, redacted, and compiled during this period. Steed Davidson rightly points out that "in a vacuum created by lack of institutions such as monarchy, prophets, and temple, biblical texts emerged to represent divine speech as survival mechanism."[20] During this time different groups tried to explain the catastrophe of the Babylonian destruction and exile and fostered an ideal vision for the new Israel or the true Israel. The Judeans in Babylonia, who were most threatened by the danger of loss of identity are probably most responsible for the innovation of religious and ritual elements. In their quest for identity of true Israel, they constructed boundaries as markers of identity. Group dynamics within the communities is reflected in the ideologies of different exilic literature, particularly of the prophetic literature.[21] Jeremiah, Ezekiel and Deutero-Isaiah are to be listed among others. In order to specify a quest for identity in community formation, special attention will be given to the book of Ezekiel in the following.

The Book of Ezekiel as a Quest for Identity

The book of Ezekiel has been accepted as written by the prophet Ezekiel, who also experienced the exilic catastrophe. It is generally agreed that the book received its final and fullest redaction sometime in the late exilic/early post-exilic period by a priestly school or schools, who ascribed the book to Ezekiel during the formation of Judean community after the exile.[22] It is

---

Negotiating Identity in an International Context, eds. Oded Lipschits, Gary Knoppers, and Manfred Oeming (Winona Lake, Ind: Eisenbrauns, 2011), 127-128.

20 Steed Vernyl Davidson, Empire and Exile: Postcolonial Readings of the Book of Jeremiah (New York: T&T Clark, 2011), 181-182.

21 Exilic literature(s) here designates a large corpus of biblical literature authored or edited during the exilic age. Some of the literatures were written in the exilic age but received their final forms in the Persian period. Scholars do no share consensus around the attribution of "exilic literature." See discussion in Rainer Albertz, Israel in Exile. Dalit Rom-Shiloni assigns Ezekiel, Deutero-Isaiah, Ezra-Nehemiah, Haggai, and Zechariah 1-8 as exilic literature. See Dalit Rom-Shiloni, "From Ezekiel to Ezra-Nehemiah: Shifts of Group Identities within Babylonian Exilic Ideology," in *Judah and the Judeans in the Achaemenid Period*, 127-128.

22 See the discussion of scholarship on the authorship of Ezekiel in Brian Neil Peterson, *Ezekiel in Context: Ezekiel's Message Understood in Its Historical Setting of Covenant Curses and Ancient Near Eastern Mythological Motifs* (Eugene, Oregon: Pickwick Publications,

plausible that the book of Ezekiel went through revisions, and that the present form demonstrates the heavy hand of the Babylonian exilic group, possibly Zadokite priests. The book's distinctiveness comes from its emphasis on purity/impurity.[23] There are several hints of a quest for Israelite identity in the book. The prophetic-priestly ideology of Ezekiel's author (s) might be best understood in the light of Walzer's theory of society or "revolution of the saints." As a result of exilic experiences, the book of Ezekiel ideologically fosters a community in which a search for (distinctive) identity is behind the literature.

First, we find experience of exile in their history as a basic criterion for Israelite identity. An explicit reference to the choice of Babylonian Exiles is found in Ezekiel 11:14-21. This oracle is a disputation speech directed against the Judahite community who remained in their homeland, as well as a thesis that affirms the choice of the exiles who were in Babylonia. The text appears to address the immediate situation after 597 BCE.[24] Ezekiel affirms Yahweh's choice of the exiles as his people, with whom his presence is to be felt as a sanctuary to them even though they are removed from their land (11:16). They will be gathered and restored (11:17) and he will give them the land of Israel (11:17). By contrasting the exilic group and the non-exiles, Ezekiel ramified his political and social arbitration in his quest for Israelite identity. Experience of exile characterizes identity of the true Israel.

Secondly, Ezekiel uses land rights on the basis of genealogy as a criterion for true community of Israel. The claims of descendants of Abraham and inheritance of the land had become an interpretative theological term that defines group identity in the time of exile. This is found in Ezekiel 33:21- 24 (Cf. 11:14-21; 36:1-5). The setting is post-587 BCE, as the picture of desolation "laid waste" points to a drastic destruction of Jerusalem.[25] In this oracle, we find the claim of the inhabitants of the 'waste places,' who claim possession of the land (33:24 Cf. 11:15). Emphasizing the genealogical bond between Abraham and the present community in Jerusalem, those who remained in

---

2012). Also see Meindert Dijkstra, "The Valley of Dry Bones: Coping with the Reality of the Exile in the Book of Ezekiel," in *The Crisis of Israelite Religion: Transformation of Religious Tradition in Exilic and Post-Exilic Times*, edited by Bob Becking and Marjo C.A. Korpel (Leiden: Brill, 1999), 114-133.

23 For an in depth study of the use of purity in relation to group identity see Lalnunzira Bungsut, *Purity and Group Identity in the Book of Ezekiel, PhD Dissertation* (Berkeley, California: Graduate Theological Union, 2016).

24 Zimmerli argues that the oracle undoubtedly goes back to the period when the Jerusalem sanctuary was still standing, before the year 587 BCE. See Walther Zimmerli, *Ezekiel 1*, translated by Ronald E. Clements, edited by Frank Moore Cross, Klaus Blatzer and Leonard Jay Greenspoon (Philadelphia: Fortress Press, 1979), 263.

25 Cf. Walther Zimmerli, *Ezekiel 2*, trans. James D. Martin, eds. Paul D. Hanson and Leonard Jay Greenspoon (Philadelphia: Fortress Press, 1983), 198.

the land, the text affirms rightful possession of the land to the descendants of Abraham (cf. Gen 15:7; 17:8; Exo 6:4). Ezekiel accuses those who claimed the land of disobeying purity rules and Deuteronomic teaching because they ate meat with blood, worshipped idol, and involved in murder, and adultery. This disobedience invalidated their claim. The case is clear for Ezekiel that ownership of the land is reserved for authentic descendants of Abraham. On the other hand, those who violated priestly purity rules and Deuteronomic moral teaching led the inhabitants of Judah unqualified to be called Israel. Ezekiel's judgment on landownership based on Abraham's descendants is a quest for true Israel during socio-economic turbulence.

Another identity marker for true community is cultic and moral purity/impurity. Many oracles denigrate Jerusalem (Judah) for her sinful conducts.[26] Among them, Ezekiel 22:1-31 contains a series of diatribes against Jerusalem and its inhabitants. The majority of critics agree that the oracle pertains to the Babylonian exiles and historical situation of 597 and 587 BCE.[27] The oracle may originally have come from the prophet Ezekiel or the Ezekiel's school may have logically arranged it in the late exilic or postexilic period.[28] The systematic presentation of the case against Jerusalem, and particularly her political leaders, suggests rulers such as Jehoiachim and Zedekiah, or perhaps Gedaliah and the Shaphanids.[29] Jerusalem, her rulers, and her inhabitants are charged for their cultic and moral sins. Rom-Shiloni rightly points out that Ezekiel's intensive references to Jerusalem (those who remained in Judah) and its fate are a response to both his immediate audience in exile and to the need to redefine the religio-national identity of the Exiles.[30] In short, for Ezekiel, purity is a criterion for inclusion in the community of Israel. In Walzer's term, Ezekiel sought "to create a holy commonwealth" by imposing radical socio-religious reform.

Finally, the clearest example of a quest for identity among the communities of Israel is found in 44:1-31. This passage represents an exclusive Zadokite

---

26 Clear examples of these types of oracles are found in Ezekiel 6:1-14; 7:1-27; 11:1-13; 16:1-43; 21:1-32; 22:1-31; 24:1-14.

27 See Leslie C. Allen, *Ezekiel 20-48: WBC Vol. 29* (Dallas: Word Books, 1990), 34; Peter Craigie, Ezekiel (Philadelphia: Westminster Press, 1983), 165.

28 Block argues that the logical arrangement may be occasioned by the need to address the postexilic community to explain the rationale for judgment on Jerusalem. See D.I. Block, The Book of Ezekiel Chapters 1-24 NICOT (Grand Rapids, Michigan: Eerdmans, 1998), 700.

29 Allen, Ezekiel 20-48, 36. G.A. Cook, A Critical and Exegetical Commentary on The Book of Ezekiel Vol. 1, ICC (Edinburgh: T&T Clark, 1937), 241.

30 Dalit Rom-Shiloni, "Ezekiel as the Voice of the Exiles and Constructor of Exilic Ideology," in HUCA LXXVI (Cincinnati: Hebrew Union College-Jewish Institute of Religion, 2006), 41-43.

view on other priestly families and foreigners. The text assumes its present form in the Persian period, probably during the reign of Darius I.[31] Israelite identity is defined by kinfolk and ethnicity. The second generation of Ezekiel's disciples (Zadokite lineage) downgraded other priestly families by claiming that the latter led Israel into sin during the pre-exilic period (Ezek 44:10, 12). This section protects the purity of worship by forbidding foreigners to worship in the temple (44:9), because mingling with foreign counterparts defiles the temple (44:6-9). Similar deliberations are also found in the book of Ezra and Nehemiah where we find ethnic and religious reform. From the perspective of Michael Walzer's "Revolution of the Saints," this view reflects a radical ideology of Zadokite priests, who out of their exilic experience and struggles fabricated their vision of a pure society.

Conclusion and Implication

From the above discussions, we can infer that a quest for identity is necessitated by intergroup relationships. In the context where society is in insecure conditions, boundaries are constructed to maintain group identity. As Walzer has pointed out, revolution of the saints was an indispensable task in the state of exile to maintain an ideal society. In other words, a quest for identity of the saints was resulted by a need to maintain society's cohesiveness and survival. A cursory survey of the situation during the Babylonian exile reveals that an identity crisis was one of the realities that marked the sixth century BCE. Out of intergroup processes, there emerged competition, categorization, and identification of self and others. Amidst fear of loss of identity resulted by deportation, displacement and relocation in the exilic period, 'who is the true Israel' was the main agendum of the exilic and early postexilic communities. Through their writings authors of the exilic and early postexilic period ramified their quest for Israelite identity. A search for identity also enhanced biased views and radical politics.

The author(s) of the book of Ezekiel championed group identification by enlisting various criteria. It is plausible that Ezekiel sought a rationale for explaining the exilic catastrophe and a vision for the new Israel. At the dawn of the restoration, when the exiles and the homelanders were in intergroup relationships, priestly author(s) of Ezekiel maintained a more stringent view on group membership. For the author (s) of Ezekiel, true Israel is defined by their experience of exile, their ancestry, moral and cultic purity and ethnicity. It is likely that the authors of Ezekiel, in their attempt to maintain the identity of Israel enforced a rigorous purity legislation that excludes some members of the community of Israel and other foreigners.

31 Cf. Steven Shawn Tuell, The Law of the Temple in Ezekiel 40-48, HSM 49 (Atlanta, Georgia: Scholars Press, 1992), 14.

The Indian Christian community also seeks to find her identity amidst various pressures from national agenda of pluralism, secularism, and Hindu fundamentalism, among others. Our Christian identity is in question. Churches in India are being tempted to compromise their identity amidst pluralism and a framework of one nation, one culture and one religion. She has to involve in strengthening and protecting her community in the quest for identity. In this search for Christian identity, a struggle for our rights such as citizenship, emphasis on our roots in India, and our experiences as part of the Indian community has to be strongly emphasized. Even within the Christian fold, identity crises have been noted which are being triggered by ethnicity, cultural differences, difference in ecclesial structures, disunity, etc. Churches have to stand in unity to promote our search for Christian identity.

Being geopolitically isolated from the mainland, the people of Northeast India have experienced instabilities and insecurities in politics and socio-economic systems. A quest for identity has been at an issue among different groups of the region. Experiences of alienation, subjugation, displacement, demarcation, and oppression of the Northeast Christians by mainline Indians could not be overlooked. Not only that, there are inter-tribal tensions in the region for freedom and land rights. Attitude towards the mainland Indians as well as towards other tribal groups has been very much affected by their experiences. Tribalism has been one way of searching for identity among Northeast Christian community. As Northeast Indians search for building up community, revolution has been experienced at various levels. As shown by the studies of Walzer and Prophetic response in Ezekiel, ideological innovations are the hallmark of a society in a transitional stage such as in migration or context change. The experiences of confusion, change, alienation and exile could heighten radical ideologies. We can rightly say that a quest for identity in Northeast India has been necessitated by circumstances However, as the Puritan saints and the priestly group of the exiles procured radical movements, we have to ponder how our quest for identity can be an impediment for a community. Instead our quest for identity should promote a healthy community.

7

The Matthean Community
Diverse, Complex and Overlapping

Zakali Shohe

Introduction

The intention of this essay is to show that the Matthean community is constituted not only by multiple identities, but that understanding how such a community is formed requires paying attention to how these multiple identities overlap[1].

---

1 Or what others call intersectionality. In the literature some have argued for an intersectionality approach to the study of identity in Galilee that has been an important contribution to studies of the gospels. In the recent years, along the line of intersectionality of identities in the ancient communities of Ancient Palestine and Galilee there are studies on region or people group. These studies show how different realities overlap and intersect and this is what I am also interested in. Hence, throughout the essay I am also employing some of the insights used by the intersectionalist in the field. To mention a few are, Joseph Geiger, "Language, Culture and Identity in Ancient Palestine," *Greek Romans and Roman Greeks* (ed. Erik Nis Ostenfeld; ASMA 3; Aarhus: University Press, 2002), 233-246; J. Zangenberg, H. W. Attridge & D. B. Martin (eds.), *Religion, Ethnicity, and Identity in Ancient Galilee* (Tübingen: Mohr Siebeck, 2007); D. R. Edwards & C. T. McCollough (eds.), *The Archeology of Difference: Gender, Ethnicity, Class and the "Other" in Antiquity: Studies in Honor of Eric M. Meyers* (Boston: ASOR, 2007); Halvor Moxnes, "Identity in Jesus' Galilee–From Ethnicity to Locative Intersectionality," *Biblical Interpretation* 18 (2010): 390-416; Halvor Moxnes, "Constructing the Galilee of Jesus in an Age of Ethnic Identity," in *Making of Christianity: Conflicts, Contexts and Constructions: Essays in Honor of Bengt Holmberg* (eds. Magnus Zetterholm & Samuel Byrskog; Winona Lake. IN: Eisenbrauns, 2012), 147-170.

To be sure because identity as a concept is both complex and complicated, this essay does not intend to discuss the concept in the abstract but rather, in relation to the context of the followers of Jesus, i.e., the Matthean community of Jesus. Of the time of Jesus scholars have long argued that in general social status, ethnicity, purity system, gender, illness and health often determined the identity of a person and the communities to which one belonged. Moreover, bounded space and place play an important role in constituting these communities especially in the context of social relations, referring not only to a physical or geographical location, but also to psychological, emotional, as well as social, cultural and economic boundaries. In effect, both community and identity bind people together as an affinity group with shared values and lifestyles, and shared space.

As I will suggest in this essay, in the Matthean community gender, status, health, purity rites and customs and ethnicity played important roles in the formation of both community and identity. The Matthean Jesus situates himself in the company of outcaste, like the tax collectors, sinners, sick, women, and other nations outside the boundary of "Israel"/"ethnic Jew." From the standpoint of the Jewish leaders these were people groups who were categorized as "outsiders" and "degraded" according to the Jewish laws and traditions. In such situation Jesus often challenged the Jewish leaders who claimed authority over the law and tradition and dominated their interpretation on the basis of their specific Jewish identity. In the encounters the Matthean Jesus responds the Jewish religious leaders by "standing with" the vulnerable groups in the society in line with the teaching of the prophets in the Old Testament and God's will in interpreting the Law.

The encounters between Jesus and the Jewish leaders suggest that the Matthean Jesus has a much broader understanding, if not framework, of what community and identity entailed. As I will show in this essay, the Matthean community of Jesus assumes not only diverse and multiple identities, but specifically enlarged such identities by deploying categories as the excluded-included, healthy, sick, insider and outsider. Additionally, such identities are constructed in relation to the overlap of ethnicity, socio-cultural, economic and also religious structures. Hence, identity refers to ways of life, belief, values, practices and behaviors in which members of the Matthean community as individuals and as a community are distinguished from other communities like the Jews, etc.

Focusing on the diverse, complex and overlapping identities for example, ethnicity, religion, class, virtues, gender can provide an alternative and broader reading on communities in the gospels in the light of hierarchy within people groups, power forces involved in interpretation, the insider-outsider, human values and ethnic groups. The overlapping of diverse and relevant categories becomes important in order to locate and protect the identity of the community of Jesus' followers in Matthew within the many movements and people groups during the time of Jesus.

In the light of the above general reflection first, the essay will briefly analyze the social structure in Matthew and the diverse identities in the Matthean community. Second, the essay will look at identity, Torah and tradition as the primary elements of formation in the Matthean context. Third, it seeks to articulate a hermeneutic that allows for an understanding that take into account the multiple identities in the formation of Matthean community.

The Society in Matthew: Diverse, Complex and Overlapping

The Gospel according to Matthew reflects a highly stratified society with wide gap between the rulers and the subordinates[2] and in such a context the Matthean Community is situated. There are the urban elite comprising of the rulers and governing classes on the top of the social structure. The urban elite class controlled the society. The ruling class and the governing classes in Palestine comprised of the procurators and their household, the Herodian household, and the state officials. There was also the retainer class who belonged to the upper class and supported the ruling class. From the narratives in Matthew this group includes the Pharisees, the Scribes, the Sadducees, the centurion, the tax collector.[3] In Matthew we find close association between the Pharisees and the chief priests (Mt 21:45; 27:62), so also the scribes who appear in leadership within Judaism (Mt 26:57, 59; 27:41) are in agreement

2 Saldarini, *Pharisees, Scribes and Sadducees*, 20-27, 39-45; D. Duling, "Matthew's plurisignificant "Son of David" in social-science perspective: Kinship, kingship, magic, and miracle," *Biblical Theology Bulletin* 22 (1992): 101 (Duling also points out the characteristics of an advanced agrarian society of the first century Mediterranean community). The discussion on the stratification of society in Matthew's gospel is dependent on In-Cheol Shin, "Matthew's Inclusive Community: A Narratological and Social Scientific Reading," A dissertation submitted in partial fulfillment of the requirements for the degree Philosophaie Doctor (PhD), University of Pretoria (2004), 130-139. https://repository.up.ac.za/bitstream/handle/2263/25000/Complete.pdf?sequence=9 (accessed on September 2, 2018).

3 D. Duling, "Matthew as marginal scribe in an advanced agrarian society," *Hervormde Teologiese Studies* 58 (2002): 528; Saldarini, *Pharisees, Scribes and Sadducees*, 161.
Top in the social structure as reflected in Matthew's gospel are: Herod (Mt 2:1), the Magi (Mt 2:1-12), the rulers of Judea (Mt 2:6), the chief priests (Mt 2:4; 16:21; 20:18; 21:15, 23, 45; 26:3, 14, 47, 51, 59; 27:1, 3, 6, 28:11), Archelaus (Mt 2:22), the King (Mt 10:18; 11:8; 18:23; 22:2, 5, 11, 13; 25:34, 40, 45), Herod the tetrarch and Philip (Mt 14:1, 3), Antipas (Mt 14:1, 9), the rulers of the Gentiles and high officials (Mt 20:25), the high priest Caiaphas (Mt 26:3, 57, 62, 63, 65). Still, on the high strata of the society, but below the ruling class are the others like the chief priests and the teachers of the Law (Mt 2:4; 20:18; 21:15-23, 45; 27:1-20, 41, 62; 28:11-12), a physician (Mt 9:12), and Pontius Pilate (Mt 27:2, 13, 15, 19).

with the elders and chief priests (Mt 16:21; 20:18) in revolting against Jesus. Most of those belonging in this group were not part of the followers of Jesus.

At the lower strata of the society were the urban non-elites like the merchants, the peasants, and the artisans. From within the urban non-elite class Jesus choose disciples to his inclusive ministry.[4] There are also references to urban non-elite among the followers of Jesus.[5]

Then we find in Matthew, the unclean and the degraded class who were treated inferior to the common people.[6] They were the landless, itinerant and a group with high death rate.[7] In his public ministry, the Matthean Jesus encountered and interacted with members from this level of social structure. It comprised of both Jews and other nations. To these people Jesus reached out and included them into the Kingdom community, although they were categorized by Jewish religious leaders as outside the purity system and exempted from public gatherings and places. The rural peasants were part of the lowest class, and comprised of the freeholders, tenants, day laborers and slaves. Jesus started his public ministry in these rural areas, among the members of the peasant class who constituted his followers.[8]

---

4 See Duling, "Matthew's plurisignificant "Son of David" in social-science perspective," 103; E. J. Vledder, *Conflict in the miracle stories: A socio-exegetical study of Matthew 8 and 9* (Sheffield: Sheffield Academic Press, 1997), 126.

5 The fishermen (Mt 4:18; 4:21; 13:48; 14:28,29; 15:15; 16:16,22,23) the city-dwellers (Mt 8:34; 11:20), a merchant (Mt 13:45), money exchangers (Mt 21:12).

6 See Duling, "Matthew's plurisignificant "Son of David" in social-science perspective," 102-103; Vledder, *Conflict in the miracle stories*," 128.
The unclean, degraded and dispensable classes were the sick (Mt 4:23, 24; 8:16; 9:12, 35; 10:8; 14:14, 35), the paralytic (Mt 4:24; 8:6; 9:2, 6), the demon-possessed (Mt 4:24; 8:16; 8:28-34; 12:12; 15:21-28), the epileptic (Mt 4:24; 17:15), the poor (Mt 5:3; 11:5; 19:21; 26:9, 11), the man with leprosy (Mt 8:2; 10:8; 11:5; 26:6), a sinner (Mt 9:10,11; 26:45), a bleeding woman (Mt 9:20-22), the blind men (Mt 9:27,28; 11:5; 12:22; 15:14,30-31; 20:30; 21:14), the man with the withered hand (Mt 12:10), the Canaanite woman and the demon-possessed woman (Mt 15:22), the eunuch (Mt 19:12), children (Mt 19:13), the tax collectors and the prostitutes (Mt 21:31-31), robbers/bandits (Mt 21:13; 27:38,44), and Barabbas (Mt 27:16,21). The centurion (Mt 8:5-13) and the tax collector (Mt 9:9-13) were a part of the retainer class; as far as Judaism was concerned they were unclean.

7 Saldarini, *Pharisees, Scribes and Sadducees,* 44.

8 Vledder, *Conflict in the miracle stories*," 128-129. The rural peasants in the Gospel of Matthew included: people (Mt 3:5; 8:27; 22:10; 13:27; 18:23-25; 20:27; 21:34, 36; 22:3-10; 24:45-50; 25:14-30), the crowds (Mt 5:1; 7:28-29; 8:1, 18; 9:8, 33, 36; 12:46; 13:2, 36; 14:13- 19; 15:10, 30-39; 17:14; 19:2; 20:29, 31; 21:8-11, 46; 22:33; 23:1), slaves/son (Mt 8:6, 8; 12:18; 14:12; 21:15), the larger disciples of Jesus (Mt 8:21- 25; 9:37; 10:1; 12:1, 9, 49; 13:10, 36; 14:15-18; 15:2, 12, 23, 32, 33, 37; 16:5, 13, 20, 24; 17:6, 10, 14, 19, 24; 18:1; 19:10; 14:23, 25; 20:17; 21:1-2, 6, 20; 23:1; 24:1, 3; 26:8, 19, 20, 36, 40; 26:56; 27:64; 28:7, 8, 16), the disciples of John the Baptist (Mt 9:14; 11:2,7; 14:12), those who were in the boat (Mt 14:33), tenants (Mt 21:35-41), the bystanders at the cross (Mt 27:39, 47) and Mary Magdalene (Mt 27:56; 28:1).

The above brief analysis reflects a stratified society with multi-layers/levels of structure in the Gospel according to Matthew. In the midst of the stratified society, the community of the followers of Jesus was no exception as a stratified community. It was a hierarchically structured community with majority belonging to the vulnerable groups. Thus, the Matthean community as a structured community comprised of diverse, complex and overlapping of identities from different walks of life. This is demonstrated with examples in the next section on –Identity, Torah and tradition.

As mentioned in the introduction studies have highlighted the overlapping of ethnic, class and gender and the models for understanding the complexities of region and roles in the ancient world. Along this line Joseph Geiger also comments, "Multiple and complex identities may have been almost the rule, rather than the exception, in a part of the world where Hellenization, the Roman conquest, the return from the Babylonian exile, and the crystallization of Jewish and of Samaritan identity, the turning of Aramaic into a lingua franca not confined to political and ethnic boundaries, and the geographic instability of the Nabateans and the Idumaeans, among other factors, call up the image of kaleidoscope rather than that of the mosaic."[9] Geiger points to multiple identities by observing diverse factors that transformed the Southern Levant in antiquity and Galilee as part of this region. No doubt Geiger's observation is confined to a geographical area, but this does not prevent one from applying to a community. This is because the study on identity of any region or territory concerns people-group and its inhabitants.

Studies on people groups or ethnic communities focus on the differences and distinctions between the groups and communities. The identity of any community is complex and can comprise of ethnic culture, religion, folk lore, music, mannerism, social principles and values, language, class, clan, caste distinctions and so on. As stated in the introduction, identity can thus comprise of multiple forms, factors and roles. Thus, in the context of different forms of identities, S. Jones suggest that "it is necessary to consider the intersection of different kinds of identity- ethnic, class, gender and so on – and the ways in which they become institutionalized in different societies."[10] As also seen in Matthew's gospel the different kinds of identities - the urban non-elite, women, unclean, other degraded groups, rural peasants, etc., should not be treated separately from each other, but as interrelated, i.e., in their diverse, complex and overlapping in the formation of a community. In such encounters human relationships, moral responsibilities and power structures are challenged, negotiated, interpreted and produced.

9 Geiger, "Language, Culture and Identity…," 242.

10 Jones, *The Archaeology of Ethnicity*, 85-86.

The diverse, complex and overlapping of identities in the study of communities and people groups provides us a fuller picture of a particular community. In considering the multiple identities from different walks of life, especially the vulnerable groups in the society helps in our understanding of the Matthean Jesus' controversies with the Pharisees on identity, law and tradition to which we now turn to.

Identity, Torah and Tradition

In the Gospel according to Matthew the reference to Torah, Jewish customs and traditions are referred to throughout the gospel.[11] There are sources that refer to Jesus upholding the Law (Q16: 17).[12] Other gospel writers also present Jesus as confirming and upholding the law (Mk 2:15-22; 7:1-23; Lk 2:22-24; 4:16; 22:39). Some even suggest that Jesus defended the biblical law against the Oral Tradition. In the Second Temple Period there are traces of inconsistencies in the interpretation of the Torah and tradition. In Qumran the authority for interpretation was based on divine inspiration and revelation. While, the later Rabbis points to human activity and exegesis in interpretation. The Halakic argument in Qumran is also not always in line with the tradition. Such developments in the interpretation of Torah and Tradition are traced during the time of Jesus.[13] One can thus presume that the Jewish Pharisaic leaders in Matthews's gospel interpreted the Law and Tradition in a way that suited their exclusivist narrow understanding of community and identity. For example, the narrative on washing hands before meals in Matthew 15:1-20 is an extra-biblical innovations. Of course, hand washing in the context of purity and impurity is rooted in scripture (Lev 15:11). So also, during the late Second Temple Judaism hand washing was practiced in the context of being cautious of different forms of impurity. However, the custom of hand washing before meals either appeared only after the time of Jesus or was not a practice until later (M. Ber 8:2).[14] Jesus in criticizing it opposed extra-biblical traditions from the Rabbinic initiative practiced by some extremist during the time of Jesus. In contrast Jesus upholds the scripture in the light of the teaching of the law and the prophets.

11 Some examples from the gospel are: Mt 5:17-20; 7:12; 11:13; 12:1-14; 15:6; 22:34-40; 23:1-26.

12 Although in the recent studies scholars (Francis Watson, Mark Goodacre, Werner Kahl) question the existence of "Q" (For the view of Watson, Goodacre and Kahl refer to, Mogens Müller & Heike Omerzu, *Gospel Interpretation and the Q-Hypothesis* (London: Bloomsbury T & T Clark, 2018).

13 Thomas Kazen, "Jesus' Interpretation of the Torah," 4-5. https://www.academia.edu/21663437/Jesus_interpretation_of_the_Torah_prepublication_version (accessed on September 25).

14 Kazen, "Jesus' Interpretation of the Torah," 7-8.

In Matthew the Jewish purification rites does not stop Jesus and the disciples from taking actions in contrast to the purity regulations. Some of the regulations include refraining from persons with skin diseases (Lv 13-14; Num 5:2), but in Matthew Jesus comes into direct contact with a leper (Mt 8:3). In such contact Jesus still was upholding the law by asking the Leper to show himself to a priest and to offer sacrifice. Another example is a regulation to refrain from contact with blood (Lv 25-30), but Jesus does not object the touch by the woman with the flow of blood (Mt 9:20-22), or avoid contact with the dead (Num 5:2; 19:11-13; Num 19:14), but Jesus touches a dead girl and heals her (Mt 9:25). Such contact demands a person to undergo purification rites (Num 19) failing which a person could be excommunicated from the community or barred from any gatherings or public places (Num 19:13, 20). Yet, the Matthean Jesus does not go through any purification rites, but he was doing what the prophets and the Jewish scripture commanded in reaching out and including the neglected- foreigners, orphans, widows, etc (Deu 24:17; 27:19; Isa 1:17, 23; 10:2).

The Jewish religious leaders, in Matthew's gospel, especially the Pharisees controlled the "space" for interpreting the law and tradition and built boundaries accordingly. They interpreted only those that suited their needs and agenda. By doing so they failed to take into account the whole Torah in line with the teachings of the prophets. They had dominated the interpretation of the law and tradition and had decided the limits of one's "space" for interpretation and dictated the "insider" and the "outsider." Their interpretation separated the pure - impure, holy/special - normal days, male – female, sick – healthy and so on. They were the forces of domination, the "insider" as of interpreters. The "outsiders" comprised of the Matthean community. For the Jews, the Torah and Jewish tradition, rites and place of worship, the synagogue was the identity marker for their exclusivism especially in their diaspora. Thus, the Jewish notion of identity and community is fairly a narrow identity. Torah, Jewish tradition and ways of life, ethnicity and circumcision circumscribe it.

The Torah was important for the people of God, as such; its interpretation was an important feature of division in Judaism. The different groups and sects within Judaism took care to study and interpret the Law.[15] Thus, Jesus and the Pharisees are also in conflict over the boundaries identifying a community and the criteria for the interpretation of customs and traditions. In such a context, the Matthean community as one of the offshoots of Jewish groups that had

15 For a full discussion with regard to the commandments in the Torah and the division between the positive and the negative commandments, see L. Morris, *The Gospel according to Matthew* (Eerdmans: Grand Rapids, 1992).

separated from the Synagogues was making attempts to establish its claims of the messiah and as an interpreter of the Law.[16]

The Matthean Jesus and the Matthean community are portrayed as frequently in conflict and conversation with the Jewish leaders and groups, basically the Pharisaic[17] group. In Matthew's gospel the Pharisees are portrayed as a dominant group and the gospel writers polemic with the Pharisees is reflected in the gospel (Mt 12; 15; 21-23). In contrast to the exclusive form of preserving identity based on Torah and tradition in the Jewish community, the Matthean community presents a broader interpretation of the Law and Tradition because it can include Jews, but it also includes the poor, excluded, sick, tax collectors, and other nations.[18] The claim for Jesus' identity as the messiah was also important for the Matthean community.

Jesus did not break or nullify the Torah despite being in conflict with leaders and teachers of the law. In stead Jesus' attitude towards the law is based on his unique authority in line with the teachings of the prophets (Mt 5:17-28; 12:1-14; 22:34-40). Scholars and commentators interpret Jesus as the fulfillment of the Scriptures and comments that Matthew explained the fulfillment theme extensively.[19] The fulfillment citations from the Old Testament aims to validate

---

16 P. Foster, *Community, Law and Mission in Matthew's Gospel* (WUNT, 2, Reihe 177; Tübingen: Mohr Siebeck, 2004), 28.

17 Without any attempt to go into details of the text, it is enough to mention that Matthew modifies Mark by inserting the Pharisees. E.g., The call of Levi in Mt. 9:9-13 & Mt 12:7=Mk 2:13-17; Healing a man with the withered hand in Mt 12:9-14=Mk. 3:1-6; Jesus and Beelzebub in Mt. 12:22-30=Mk. 3:22-27; Parable of the tenants in Mt 21:33-46=Mk 12:1-12; Paying tribute to Caesar in Mt 22:15-22=Mk 12:13-17; The Great Commandment in Mat. 22:34-40=Mk 12:28-34; Christ as David's son in Mt 22:41-46=Mk 2:35-37a. The role of the Jewish leaders in Matthew is considered as redactional to fit the theology of the gospel or to give emphasis on tradition. However, it is beyond the scope of this essay to go into details. Refer, A. J. Saldarini, *Pharisees, Scribes and Sadducees in Palestinian Society* (Edinburgh: T & T Clark, 1988), 157-158; Thomas C. Fraatz, "Social Conflict Theory and Matthew's Polemic against the Pharisees," (2010), 4. https://escholarship.org/uc/item/08g733kh (accessed on August 27, 2018).

18 Luz proposes that Matthean community's interpretation of the Law was to defend the Gentile mission (Ulrich Luz, *Matthew 1-7. A commentary* (Edinburgh: T & T Clark, 1990), 84. So also some propose that it is to resist the Judaist stand on exclusivism (A. J. Saldarini, *Matthew's Christian Jewish Community* (Chicago & London: University of Chicago), 1994; F. P. Viljoen, "Matthew's Sitz Im Leben and the Emphasis on the Torah," *Acts Theologica* 32/2 (2012): 267-268.

19 A few examples where the fulfillment theme is explicitly indicated are Matthew 1:22-23; 2:15-18; 2:23; 4:14-16; 8:17; 12:17-21; 13:35; 21:4-5; 26:56; 27:9. See, F. P. Viljoen, "Fulfillment in Matthew," *VERBUM ET ECCLESIA* 28/1 (2007), 314-320: (https://verbumetecclesia.org.za/index.php/ve/article /view/109/83) (accessed on 10/09/2018); W.D. Davies, & D. C. Allison, *Matthew 1-7* (International Critical Commentary (London & New York: T & T Clark, 2004), 1: 167; Richard B. Hays, "The Gospel of Matthew: Reconfigured Torah," *HTS Teologiese Studies / Theological Studies* 61/ 1-2 (2005): 165-

the identity of Jesus as the Messiah. This is grounded in the Jewish scripture. Thus, the attitude of Jesus towards the Law and the prophets is not rejection, but he upholds the law and the prophets by emphasizing on inclusion rather than, exclusion. In such approach of upholding an inclusive community we find overlapping of diverse identity- the urban non-elite, women, unclean, other degraded groups, rural peasants, etc., which become institutionalized in the Matthean community. For example, among the larger followers of Jesus is the woman who came to Jesus for her daughter's healing (Mt 15:21-28). Matthew mentions that she is a Canaanite woman (Mt 15:22) and in Mark it says she is born in the region of Phoenicia in Syria (Mk 7:26) As for her identity she is a Canaanite which means, a gentile from the standpoint of Jew, an outsider, a woman, which means lower than men in the Jewish society.

However, as a follower of Jesus she is not only a Canaanite, a woman, but becomes part of the community that upholds the teachings in the Law and the prophets to it's fullest. Another example from among the twelve who followed Jesus is Matthew (Mt 10:2) and Simon, the Canaanite (Mt 10:4). Matthew was a Jew, a publican i.e., a tax collector by profession and so was considered unclean from Jewish standpoint, but Jesus took him among his close disciples. As a disciple of Jesus Matthew is not only a Jew, but also a member among the close associate of Jesus that accepted Jesus' messiahship, and accepted the inclusive motif in the law and the teachings of the prophets. So also Simon was a Canaanite, but Jesus chose him as his close disciple. Thus, ethnically Simon is still a Canaanite who became a part of the community of the believers in Jesus as the Messiah.

Thus, the examples from Matthew show the interrelatedness of the diverse identities that overlaps in the formation of a community. In such encounters of multiple identities the exclusive nature of a community is challenged, negotiated and the inclusive nature of a community is produced.

Taking into consideration the multiple identities from different walks of life, especially the vulnerable groups in the society also helps in understanding the Matthean Jesus' emphasis on the ethical values of justice, mercy and faith in his controversies with the Pharisees on law and tradition.

The Need for Hermeneutic of Justice, Mercy and Faith in the Context of Diverse, Complex and Overlapping Identities

It is important at this point to develop a hermeneutic of Justice, mercy and faith because the Matthean community had a wider view of the notions of community and identity. The Matthean Jesus gives importance to the law and the prophets and thus emphasizes on the love commandments (Mt 22: 37-39 correspond to Deu 6:5, Lev 19:18) and on the teachings of the prophets

169. R. T. France, *Matthew evangelist and teacher* (New Testament Profiles; Downers Grove: Intervarsity Press. 1998), 167.

grounded on "justice, mercy and faith" (Mt 23:23-24). Jesus does not abolish the law neither he undermines the teachings of the prophets, but calls his followers to a higher righteousness that exceeds that of the Scribes and the Pharisees (Mt 5:17-48). Richard B. Hays refers to the "higher righteousness" as a matter of not only "outward example, but of inner dispositions and motivations." Hays further points out that throughout the gospel the Matthean Jesus proposes a "hermeneutical refocusing of the law in terms of justice, mercy and faith."[20] However, Hays develops only on the hermeneutic of mercy in reading the Gospel according to Matthew.

Francois Viljoen in his analysis on righteousness and identity formation in the Sermon on the Mount also states that the gospel writer assures his community that in following Jesus and accepting his teachings, they are not breaking away from the Torah but are "fulfilling it by bringing it to a higher standard of righteousness."[21] Thus, in Matthew Jesus calls his followers to do God's will in a way that moves beyond the ways of the scribes and the Pharisees (Mt 5:20, 48; 6:1-18). A call to move beyond the Scribes and Pharisees is grounded on the law and the prophets. Such call within the Matthean community grounded on "justice, mercy and faith" create "space" for diverse identity that overlaps in the context of community formation. Israel's scripture and tradition is a call for justice, mercy and faith and the Matthean Community emphasizes on these virtues to a great extend.

The motif of justice is given importance in Matthew with the constant reference to righteousness (Mt 5:3-7:21; 10; 13; 18; 24-25). Through the emphasis on the need for righteousness the Matthean community is reminded on the importance of right living before God and also with members of the community and the wider society. Matthew's gospel especially the Sermon on the Mount sketches a society of justice in contrast to the practices and the values of those who are not part of the Kingdom of God.[22] So also the text that emphasizes on the custom of hand washing before meals (Mt 15:1-20), is not a critique of the purity laws. Rather, the criticism is against washing hands when it is given more importance to or contrasted with social and economic justice, which are an important aspect in prophetic tradition (Isa 58).

Righteousness is broadened and used in a call of the demand where the disciples' righteousness should exceed that of Pharisees and the teachers of the

20 Richard B. Hays, "The Gospel of Matthew: Reconfigured Torah," 177-178. https://repository.up.ac.za/bitstream/handle/2263/13613/Hays_Gospel(2005).pdf (accessed on 10/10/2018).

21 F.P. Viljoen, 'The foundational statement in Matthew 5:17–20 on the continuing validity of the Law', *In die Skriflig* 45(2/3) (2011): 403-404. http://dx.doi.org/10.4102/ ids.v45i2&3.20 (accessed on September 11, 2018).

22 W. Carter, 'Matthew and the margins: A socio-political and religious reading', *Journal for the Study of the New Testament*. suppl. ser. 204, (2000): 128.

law (Mt 5:20). However, righteousness is not only a personal matter, but it is a social value, which concerns commitment and relationships. The righteous God is faithful to his covenant commandments and delivers the oppressed from the unjust society. So also, the believers are to remain faithful to the covenant requirements. Being faithful to God is carrying out God's work in the community and the wider society, i.e., standing for the oppressed and the needy in an unjust, selfish society. This understanding of the justice shapes the community of the followers of Jesus who come from diverse walks of life and also reflects the teachings of the prophets.

Further, the Matthean community must also practice mercy. The motif of mercy is highlighted in the gospel especially with the use of Hosea 6:6. In the Matthean Jesus' encounter with the Pharisees with regard to his company with the tax collectors and sinners (Mt 9:9-13), Hosea 6:6 is directed to the Pharisees to understand the God of mercy. Likewise, in the pericope of plucking grain on the Sabbath (Mt 12:1-8), where the Pharisees demand strict observance of the law at its face value and by overlooking human needs and values, the gospel writer refers back to Hosea 6:6. Prophet Hosea upholds the teaching of mercy over temple rituals. Another Sabbath controversy is the healing of a man with a withered hand (Mt 12:9-14).

In response to the question by the Pharisees whether it is lawful to heal on the Sabbath (Mt 12:10), Jesus responds in rhetoric by contrasting a human value and that of a sheep (Mt 12:12). In the controversy narratives on Sabbath traditions Jesus is not rejecting the Sabbath traditions, but the issue is the "overdevelopment of Sabbath legislation" by the pharisaic leaders.[23] The Sabbath is to be practiced in the context of God's command and here the command is stated as, "I desire mercy and not sacrifice (Mt 12:7 from Hosea 6:6). Along this line, Richard B. Hays identifies the motif of mercy as a hermeneutical lens for interpreting the Torah in Matthew. Hays goes on to comment that the Pharisees fail to provide a proper understanding of the law because they ignore the central aim as disclosed in Hosea, i.e., mercy.[24] Hays rightly observes that we need to take into consideration the motif of mercy which has an important place in the writings of the prophets as the lens for interpreting the entire Torah.

Finally, the faith of the Matthean community is grounded on Jesus as the Messiah. The question of Jesus' messianic identity brings about conflict between the Matthean Jesus and the Pharisees (Mt 12). Faith in Matthew is thus grounded on the authority of Jesus as the messiah. In the healing narratives,

---

23 Jonathan Burroughs, "Jesus and the Law, in the Gospel of Matthew," *Doctrine and* Life, 64/10 (December, 2014): 54. https://www.academia.edu/10370416/Jesus_and_the_Law_in_the_Gospel_of_Matthew._Doctrine_and_Life_64_10_December_2014_45-58 (accessed on September1, 2018).

24 Hays, "The Gospel of Matthew," 182.

i.e., the healing of the Roman officer's servant (Mt 8:10) and the paralytic (Mt 8:2) faith is referred to in the context of trusting in the authority of Jesus.[25] The authority and power from God that Jesus possessed was also acknowledged by those in authority like the centurion (Mt 8:5-13). In the gospel according to Matthew and Luke the authority of Jesus is specifically emphasized. The act of healing is not explained in detail but it only takes place with the utterance of Jesus, "go, as you believed let it be so unto you" (Mt 8:13; Lk 7:10). As a man in position, the centurion narrates his own authority to delegate works and command his subordinates. Such power and authority the centurion acknowledged that Jesus had received from God, to do the impossibility to make known the divine power of God. It is trusting in Jesus as the Son of God who brings justice in the lives of those denied justice and is merciful. Faith is then, doing the will of God and this applies even in the context of the interpretation of the Torah and the traditions. The Matthean community is not grounded on the Jewish rites of circumcision, but claims for faith working through justice and mercy, which is grounded in the Jewish commandment of love. Therefore, the Torah and the Prophets should be interpreted in the light of the love commandment- you shall love the Lord your God (Deu 6:5) and you shall love your neighbor as yourself (Lev 19:18), which in Matthew is the greatest commandment (Mt 22:34-40). Such understanding makes possible for the diverse communities to fit into the Matthean Community as a community of faith.

These three motifs, i.e., justice, mercy and faith are important motifs in the writings of the prophets and for the Matthean community understanding of the Law. The Hermeneutics of justice, mercy and faith goes beyond the closed exclusive community to include people from all walks of life and social standing. Thus, the motifs of justice, mercy and faith create space for the diverse, complex and overlapping of other ethnic nation, sick, excluded groups, sinner, impure from the standpoint of the Jewish religious leaders.

Conclusion

Thus, from the above analysis we can summarize that the Matthean community has a much broader understanding, if not framework, of community and identity by deploying such categories as the excluded-included, healthy, sick, insider and outsider. These diverse identities though complex overlap each other providing a fuller picture of the community, especially in the context of the teachings of the Law and the Prophets. The Matthean Jesus did not break or nullify the law and tradition, but his attitude is based on his unique authority

25 This stand is also observed by G. Bornkamm, "End-Expectation and the Church in Matthew," *Tradition and Interpretation in Matthew*: *The New Testament Library* (eds. G. Bornkamm, G. Barth & H. J. Held; Philadelphia: The Westminster Press, 1963), 28.

in line with God's will and the teachings in the Law and the Prophets. As such, the motif of justice, mercy and faith provides a fuller understanding of what community and identity entails.

8

Early Evidences on the Identity of Matthean Community

Laurence Culas

Introduction

It is generally accepted that Matthew addressed his Gospel to the Christian community in Antioch. There are various factors supporting this suggestion. First of all, the strategic location of Antioch remain significant. Antioch is the capital city of the Roman province of Syria. Located on major east-west and north-south trade routes, Antioch in the early first century was the Roman Empire's third-largest city, behind Rome and Alexandria. During the second century, the Gospel according to Matthew became the most commonly quoted gospel. The Gospel's widespread popularity was possible as it originated from the influential city, Antioch. Secondly, the earliest citations of the Gospel according to Matthew appear in writings associated with Syria and Antioch. The early second-century church leader Ignatius of Antioch refers to his letters material found only in Matthew. Another document from Syria, the *Didache* or Teaching, cites Matthew. Thirdly, Matthew alone refers to Jesus' fame spreading "throughout all Syria" (Mt 4:24), which is missing in the likely source passage in Mark 1:28. It is possible that the author of Matthew writes his own location and audience in the gospel narrative. Fourthly, Cephas or Peter was prominent in Antioch where Paul had a fight with him (cf. Gal 2:11-14). Peter is also prominent in Matthew: He is the first disciple to be called (Mt 4:18-20); the first in the list of disciples (Mt 10:2); imitates Jesus in walking on the water (Mt 14:28-32); confesses that Jesus is "Christ, the Son of the living God" (Mt 16:16); was designated as the rock on which Jesus will build his church (Mt 16:18); was given "the keys of the kingdom" (Mt 16:19); witnesses Transfiguration (Mt 17:1-8) and often becomes the spokesperson for the Twelve (Mt 15:15; 16:22; 18:21; 19:27). Peter's significant role in the gospel possibly reflects his importance in the church at Antioch.

Finally, there are significant resonances between the emphases in Matthew's Gospel and features of life in Antioch. In the early first century Antioch had a significant presence of Jews and Gentiles. Therefore Matthew draws extensively on Jewish scriptures. It debates upon Jewish practices and heightens the conflict between Jesus and Jewish leaders and synagogues (Mt 5:17-6:18; 23:1-39). Since Antioch had a significant Jewish population, such debates would be familiar. Matthew accommodates the Gentiles. Matthew points to the fact that the Good News is for the Gentiles as well. Matthew affirms Jesus as the hope of Gentiles (Mt 12 :21). Therefore, the above features assist us to assume that Matthew addressed the Gospel to a Christian community in Antioch, the Roman province of Syria.[1] This paper makes a modest attempt to bring out the early evidences on the identity of Matthean community in Antioch, analysing two reliable sources on the early history of the formation of Antiochene church: Acts of the Apostles and Paul's Letter to the Galatians. These two valuable early evidences of the Christian community in Antioch are analysed as they are given in the canonical order. This would facilitate us to arrive at the true historical picture.

I. Texts from Acts of the Apostles

Important elements about the emergence and nature of Christian community at Antioch are contained in the Acts of the Apostles, chapters 11-15.

A. Church in Antioch: Acts 11:19-26

Acts 11:19-26 gives witness about the presence of a Christian community at Antioch for the first time. Significant points of this text are the following:

1. Hellenist Christians in Antioch

Luke switches the attention from the church in Jerusalem to the church in Antioch. At this point, Luke, as part of his technique of simultaneity, picks up the thread of the Hellenists' story-cycle. In 6:1-6, Luke reported two groups

---

1 For a detailed discussion see, R.E. Brown and J.P. Meier, *Rome and Antioch: New Testament Cradles of Catholic Christianity*, New York, Paulist Press, 1983, 15-27; D. Senior, *What are They Saying about Matthew*, New York, Paulist Press, 1996, 15-27; W. Carter, *Matthew: Storyteller, Interpreter, Evangelist*, Peabody, Hendrickson, 1996, 15-33; D.C. Sim, *The Gospel of Matthew and Christian Judaism: The History and Social Setting of the Matthean Community*, Edinburgh, T & T Clark, 1998, 53-62.

of Jewish believers within the Jerusalem community: the Hellenists and the Hebrews. They clashed over the distribution of common goods. The disciples acknowledged the problem and suggested that the Hellenists choose seven of their own to fulfil this duty, while the disciples devoted themselves to prayer and to the ministry of the Word. Despite the inoffensive tenor of this conflict and the amicable nature of its resolution, the account of this dispute serves to introduce a series of further controversies and dramatic developments. The first among the Hellenists, Stephen, embarks on a ministry of preaching among the other Diaspora Jews in Jerusalem, resulting in his trial and execution on the charges of apostasy and blasphemy (Acts 6:8-8:1). His circle of supporters among the Hellenists are subsequently persecuted and dispersed (Acts 8:1-4), and Philip carries the Christian message to Samaria (Acts 8:4-40). At this point Luke describes how those who had been scattered following the death of Stephen carried the Christian message as far as Phoenicia, Cyprus and Antioch in Syria (Acts 11:19). In the ensuing verse, Luke relates that in Antioch the Hellenists focused initially on the Jewish community. But certain men from Cyprus and Cyrene eventually took the next step and approached the "Greeks" (Acts 11:20); in other words the Gentiles.

2. Promoters of mission to Gentiles in Antioch

Luke does not specifically name those who first initiated the mission to the Gentiles in Antioch. We might plausibly speculate that Nicolaus, the proselyte from Antioch and one of the seven named in Acts 6:5 as a leader of the Hellenists, played some role in this mission.[2] It can also be inferred that Lucius of Cyrene and Symeon Niger who are mentioned in Acts 13:1 participated in this mission.[3] These men being Hellenists would have preached a Law-free Gospel among the Gentiles in Antioch. This would explain the overwhelming success of the mission which Luke reports in Acts 11:21: "And the hand of the Lord was with them and a great number that believed turned to God."

3. Barnabas in Antioch

The Jerusalem church heard about the success of the Hellenists' mission among the Gentiles in Antioch. Barnabas was sent to Antioch as an envoy of the Jerusalem church (Acts 11:22-23). Barnabas was originally a well-known member of the Jerusalem church. He is a Levite (Acts 4:36). He sold a field and brought the money to the apostles to contribute to the common fund (Acts 4:37). Barnabas is from Cyprus (Acts 4:36). Later when he becomes a missionary along with Paul, they go first to Cyprus (Acts 13:1-4). Being

2 This possibility is raised by W.A. Meeks and R.L. Wilken, *Jews and Christians in Antioch in the First Four Centuries of the Common Era*, SBLSBS 13, Missoula, Scholars Press, 1978, 14.

3 E. Haenchen, *The Acts of the Apostles*, Philadelphia, Westminster Press, 1971, 370.

a Greek-speaking Cypriot, he probably belonged to the Hellenist faction. He most likely escaped the persecution and remained in Jerusalem with the Hebrews. He was perhaps a more moderate Hellenist and was acceptable to the apostles. Probably, he was sent by the Jerusalem church with the intention that Barnabas, being a former colleague of the Hellenists, would have more success in stemming the rising tide of the Law-free Hellenist mission as it gained further ground in Syria.[4] But Barnabas was apparently impressed by the success of the Gentile mission and he approved of it (Acts 11:23).

4. Paul in Antioch

Being impressed by what he saw (Acts 11:23-24), "Barnabas went to Tarsus to look for Saul (Paul) and when he had found him, he brought him to Antioch" (Acts 11:25-26). This becomes the occasion for the author of the Acts to bring Paul to Antioch. Paul was last mentioned in 9:30 where Luke began with the account of Paul's conversion and its aftermath (Acts 9:1-30). Luke recounts that Paul's conversion was effected by Jesus himself and Paul received the Holy Spirit (Acts 9:17) and he preached "Jesus is the Son of God" (Acts 9:20). Luke also lays the basis for the future activity of Barnabas with Paul by telling us that it was Barnabas who supported Saul against those in Jerusalem, who could not believe that the persecutor had now changed. Luke then postpones the activities of Paul by telling that he went back to Tarsus (Acts 9:30).[5] Luke reports the incident of Paul's conversion twice more in the lips of Paul in his speeches of self-defence (Acts 22:3-21; 26:2-23). In these accounts Paul links his vocation to evangelize the Gentiles with his conversion experience. Probably it was a result of his affiliation with the mission at Antioch among the Gentiles and later in his great missionary journeys that Paul worked out the full implication of his call to preach the Gospel among the Gentiles.[6]

4 D.C. Sim, *The Gospel of Matthew and Christian Judaism*, 74-75. But E. Haenchen, *The Acts of the Apostles*, 370-372, thinks that Barnabas would have been among the scattered Cypriot and Cyrenean Hellenists who began Gentile mission at Antioch. Hence, he is not an agent of Jerusalem church.

5 There is a famous discrepancy between this and Paul's own account in Gal 1:15-22. In Galatians he says that after the revelation he did not go up to Jerusalem to see the apostles but went immediately to Arabia. Then he returned to Damascus. After three years he went to Jerusalem for fifteen days. In Jerusalem he saw and conversed with Cepha (Peter) and James. Finally he went to Syria and Cilicia. Possibly, as R.E. Brown remarks, Paul's brief summary of what happened twenty years before is imprecise; probably the author of Acts had heard only a simplistic version. Cf. R.E. Brown, *Introduction to New Testament*, New York, Doubleday, 1997, 298.

6 H Räisänen, "Paul's Conversion and the Development of His View of the Law," *NTS* 37 (1987) 404-419; see also by the same author, *Paul and the Law*, Tübingen, Mohr, [2]1987, 251-63; *Jesus, Paul and Torah: Collected Essays*, JSNTSS 43, Sheffield, Sheffield Academic Press, 1992, 288-95.

5. Paul's relationship with Barnabas

Barnabas sought Paul in Tarsus to enlist his help with the Gentile mission at Antioch (Acts 11:25-26). The historicity of this episode depends heavily upon the historical worth of Barnabas' earlier association with Paul at Jerusalem in Acts 9:26-30. In that former episode (Acts 9:27) Barnabas offered his assistance and encouragement to the newly converted Paul, introducing Paul to the apostles and supporting Paul's cause. The story serves not only to present Barnabas as the champion of the newly converted Paul (Acts 9:27), but also to explain how Paul was forced to escape to Tarsus following a series of disputes with, and threats made on his life by certain Greek-speaking Jews in Jerusalem (Acts 9:29-30). Now Barnabas brings back Paul to Antioch from Tarsus. It was probably in Antioch that Barnabas and Paul became both good friends and convinced allies of the Gentile mission.[7] Paul did not return to Jerusalem until fourteen years later (Gal 2:1). During the intervening years he probably exercised his ministry in Antioch, where he quickly became a prominent figure and a leading proponent of the Law-free mission to the Gentiles.

6. Disciples were first called Christians at Antioch

The church at Antioch grew large as a result of its Gentile converts, distinctive enough to receive a new designation from the Gentiles. Thus the followers of church at Antioch were called Christians for the first time (Acts 11:26). The popular recognition of the movement at Antioch as "followers of the Χριστός" is significant. It testifies both to the success of the Gentile mission in Antioch and its emergence as an innovative religious movement that was considered by the wider, multicultural society in Antioch. It is unlikely that such a designation would have been devised earlier in Jerusalem. The Jerusalem community would have been perceived as no more than another Jewish sect.[8] Perhaps among their fellow Jews, the Christian-Jews at Jerusalem were even known commonly as the "Sect of the Nazarene," as Luke suggests in Acts 24:5. It is only later, when the Hellenists had severed their attachment to the Torah, and initiated a vigorous and successful Law-free mission among both Jews and Gentiles in Antioch, that such a term could arise.[9] Thus, while the Jerusalem church in the person of Peter was taking the first steps toward admitting

7 D.C. Sim, *The Gospel of Matthew and Christian Judaism*, 76.

8 Acts 24:14; 28:22; cf. 5:17; 15:5.

9 É. Trocmé observes that Χριστιανός is a political term (Latin suffix *–ianos*) that may have been used in a derisory fashion ("supporters of the oiled one") and thus indicates a first contact with pagans who, lacking any biblical background, did not fully comprehend the Jewish roots of the term Χριστός. Cf. É. Trocmé, *L'enfance du christianisme*, Paris, Noêsis, 1997, 32.

Gentiles (Acts 9:31-11:18), Antioch developed as a second great Christian centre, more vibrantly involved in mission.

B. Prophets and Teachers in Antioch: Acts 13:1-3

The next reliable piece of information about the Christian community at Antioch is found in Acts 13:1-3. Important elements of this passage are the following:

1. Presence of Leadership in Antioch

The list of "prophets and teachers" of the Antioch congregation comes from Luke's tradition. Five names are mentioned: Barnabas, Simeon who was called Niger, Lucius of Cyrene, Manaen (Menahem), who was a childhood companion of the tetrarch Herod Antipas, and Saul. Barnabas is named first as the head of the list while Saul is placed at the end.[10] "That a childhood companion of Herod should be a leader in the early days of the Antiochene church serves as a reminder that Christianity did not start as a slave religion and did not entirely lack members from the higher strata of society."[11] While we note a leadership made up of prophets and teachers in the early stages of Christian community, in the light of 1 Cor 12:28 we understand that, in the later stage the leadership in the Christian community was evolved with a structure made of apostles, prophets and teachers. The prophets and teachers of Acts 13:1 are attached to or associated with their mission centre at Antioch. They are quick to go out on a mission as the later verse indicates (Acts 13:3). They are not itinerants but teachers, apostles and prophets on a mission operating from the mission centre at Antioch.

2. Liturgical Service in Antioch

We are told that the Antiochene prophets and teachers were "worshipping the Lord and fasting" (Acts 13:2). What did the worship consist of? If it was Eucharistic celebration, in the absence of the twelve, who would have presided? The text of *Didache* depicting a situation where "spiritual leaders" of the community presided over the Eucharistic celebration (*Did* 9:1f.). That might have been the custom in the Christian communities. In the context of prayer and fasting, hands are laid on Barnabas and Saul. It is understood as a commissioning by the church of Antioch for a mission, which could be counted as the first Pauline mission journey and dated to 46-49 CE. Thus, the passage

10 Only during the mission activities, the name Paul is used consistently in place of Saul and the order of names are reversed to Paul and Barnabas (Acts 13:13, 43). In other words, during the mission the great proclaimer of the Gospel finds his identity and status. Cf. R.E. Brown, *Introduction to New Testament*, 303.

11 R.E. Brown and J.P. Meier, *Antioch and Rome*, 35.

remains as a testimony of the presence of leadership and liturgical service in the church of Antioch.

C. Council at Jerusalem: Acts 15:1-35

Another important piece of information about the Christian community in Antioch is seen in the presentation of developments at the Council of Jerusalem according to Luke. We divide this text into five for an enhanced analysis.

1. Prehistory (Acts 15:1-5)

The introductory words in verses 1-5 include competing accounts of the immediate impetus for the conference. A controversy started at Antioch where "some men came down from Judea and were teaching the brethren, unless you are circumcised according to the custom of Moses,[12] you cannot be saved" (Acts 15:1). In a serious discussion, Paul and Barnabas opposed the views of men from Judea.[13] Therefore, Paul, Barnabas and some others were appointed to go to Jerusalem to discuss this question with the Apostles and the Elders (Acts 15:2). Basically, it concerned a question of agreeing on the nature of the requirements to be imposed on Gentiles who adhered to Christ. Were they to obey the Law of Moses, and thus to be circumcised or, is it enough for them only to convert? For Paul and Barnabas, it seems that conversion was sufficient. But obviously it was not the case for those who are in Jerusalem and in Judea.

As Paul and Barnabas reached Jerusalem, they were welcomed by "the church and the apostles and the elders" (Acts 15:4). Paul, Barnabas and their companions gave an account of their mission among the Gentiles. But some believers who belonged to the sect of the Pharisees were persuaded that, to be saved, to be integrated into the people of God, "it is necessary to circumcise them and thus to charge them to keep the Law of Moses" (Acts 15:5). Thus we understand that the immediate reasons for the conference were the advent of Judaizing teachers in Antioch and the upsurge of Pharisaic sentiment in Jerusalem.

2. Peter's Speech (Acts 15:6-12)

As the apostles and the elders decided to examine the case (Acts 15:6) Peter spoke first (Acts 15:7-11).[14] This shows that Peter enjoyed a privileged position in the hierarchy of the earliest Christian community. According to

12 The circumcision prescribed by the Pentateuch came from Moses. However, the Jewish tradition traced the rite to Abraham, not to Moses (Gen 17:9-14; cf. Rom 4:9-12).

13 In the light of Acts 15:24 we understand that these people did not receive any mandate from the church of Jerusalem to express such a view.

14 It was his last speech in the Acts of the Apostles. Interestingly, it was the last appearance of Peter in Luke-Acts.

the traditional list of witnesses to the risen Christ, he was the first to receive such a revelation (1 Cor 15:5). This gave him a position of superiority over the other disciples. Moreover, after the ascension of the Risen Lord (Acts 1:6-11), Acts of the Apostles tells us Peter was the representative of the disciples and their appointed leader. His position of leadership can be seen in the election of the twelfth apostle (Acts 1:15), the interpretation of the miracle of Pentecost (Acts 2:14), the healing of the lame man (Acts 3:1), the defence of the Gospel against the authorities (Acts 4:8; 5:29), the exercise of church discipline (Acts 5:1-11), the inspection of the mission in Samaria (Acts 8:14-17) and the missionary activity in Lydda, Joppa and Caesarea, along with the conversion of the Gentile Cornelius (Acts 9:36-10:48). Paul travelled to Jerusalem after his conversion to meet Peter (Gal 1:18), acknowledging Peter as the leader of the Christian community in Jerusalem.

Therefore, the apostolic voice appropriately sounded first and his speech shows its literary origin and function in the fact that we grasp its allusions to the Cornelius story narrated in length in Acts 10-11.[15] Peter brings forth the events that happened at Caesarea (Acts 10:1). For Peter, the Cornelius event now belongs to the "classical" past, even at this relatively short temporal distance.[16] He shared the lesson he drew from that incident, more preciously, the truth that he was chosen by God to be an apostle for the Gentiles. Peter affirms with certitude, "God who knows the heart bore witness to them, giving them the Holy Spirit just as he did to us and he made no distinction between us and them, but cleansed their hearts by faith" (Acts 15:8-9; cf. Acts 10:20). In other words, God himself had removed the Law's distinction between clean and unclean people (cf. Acts 10:34-35) and this was revealed in Peter's vision (Acts 10:14-15).

Continuing his reasoning, Peter deduces that if God granted salvation to the Gentiles, who did not observe the Law, then observance of the Law was not necessary for salvation. Consequently, Peter adds that to impose Law on the future disciples of Christ is unjustified as it proved to be an unbearable yoke[17] to the Jews themselves.[18] It would be "making trial of God," which means to challenge the manifest will of God (Exod 17:2). With overwhelming enthusiasm for the cause of Gentiles, Peter concludes: "we believe that we shall be saved through the grace of the Lord Jesus, just as they will" (Acts 15:11). When Peter concluded his speech, the assembly kept silence (Acts

15 Cf. M. Dibelius, *Studies in Acts of the Apostles*, London, SCM Press, 1956, 94-95.

16 M. Dibelius, *Studies in Acts of the Apostles*, London, SCM Press, 1956, 94.

17 This view of the Law as unbearable yoke is neither Pauline nor mainstream Jewish; it is the perspective of Christians for whom the break with Judaism lies well in the past. Cf. H. Conzelmann, *Die Apostelgeschichte*, Tübingen, J.C.B. Mohr, ²1972, 91.

18 Acts 15:10; cf. 13:38-39; Gal 3:10-11, 19; Rom 2:17ff; 7:15-20.

15:12). Does this imply that the controversy which prompted Peter's speech was settled by the assembly? The continuation of the account shows that Paul and Barnabas shared the signs and the wonders[19] "God had done through them among the Gentiles" (Acts 15:12). Then James, the brother of the Lord, speaks.

3. James' Speech (Acts 15:13-21)

James, the brother of the Lord, accepts Peter's judgement from the divine action towards Cornelius (Acts 15:14). Thus James' argument shows the structural parallelism and complementarities of the two speeches.[20] James addressed Peter "Simeon." "The Greek form of Hebrew *Simeon*, introduced mimetically, along with the heavy biblical phrasing of the two speeches, recreates the sacred atmosphere of the conference."[21] He continues, "God first visited the Gentiles, to take out of them a people for his name." The divine initiative and its relationship to the present are the restatement of the speech made by Peter (Acts 15:7). But the expression, "God visited" belongs to the OT vocabulary of divine saving actions and so it introduces an important enlargement of our perspective on the Cornelius event and its effects. James asserts the full participation of Gentile converts in the people of God.[22] James quotes from prophet Amos 9:11-12.[23] It confirms God's rule of pagan nations. It clarifies the relation of the newly elect people to Israel. David's "fallen dwelling" is to be rebuilt so that all nations may "seek the Lord." It signifies the "ingathering of all nations into Israel," which has been begun with the apostolic teaching and now expanding to embrace the Gentiles.

---

19 Signs and wonders are seen as prophetic certification (cf. Acts 2:19, 22).

20 J. Dupont, "Un peuple d'entre les nations," *NTS* 31 (1985) 321-325, 323. But P. Debergé, *Saint Pierre*, Paris, Les Editions de l'Atelier, 2003, 97, argues that James did not share the position of Peter. He states "the nuance in 15:14 is important, for the Gentile nation became "a people" without being as much "the people," which is confirmed in the following quotation from Amos."

21 R.J. Dillon, "Acts of the Apostles," in R.E. Brown, *et al.*, (eds.), *New Jerome Biblical Commentary*, Bangalore, TPI, 1992, 722-767, 752.

22 "People," has its pregnant sense of God's elect. It is consistent with Luke's writing because Luke refers the same word again for Gentile converts (cf. Acts 18:10).

23 Doubts have been raised against the historicity of James' quotation of Amos 9:11-12. This is basically on the ground that James is quoting the LXX version of Amos, but he would have been familiar with the Masoretic text. There are no conclusive evidences to prove that James would have been familiar with LXX or Masoretic text. Moreover, it was common to all historical narratives that the author chose to embellish his accounts of historical speeches with elements of his own style and language. For a detailed discussion of this topic see, R. Bauckham, "James and the Gentiles (Acts 15:13-21)," in B. Witherington (ed.), *History, Literature and Society in the Book of Acts*, Cambridge, Cambridge University Press, 1996, 185-217.

James, therefore, recommends[24] "not to trouble those Gentiles who are returning to God" and proposes a solution which would make it possible for the Jews and Gentiles to live in fellowship, without a clash: "But should write to them to abstain from the pollutions of idols and from unchastity and from what is strangled and from blood" (Acts 15:20). The "decree" sounds to be a concession rather than an imposition, making common life and common table possible without laying any burden on the newcomers. The four clauses stated in Acts 15:20 correspond to the four things prescribed by the Book of Leviticus (chapters 17-18) for aliens residing in Israel: meat offered to idols, the eating of blood and of strangled animals (not ritually slaughtered) and sexual intercourse with close kin (Lev 17:8-9, 10-12; 18:6-18). The mention of "unchastity" disturbs the sequence of the other three items, which concern diet. If it is to be understood in the light of Lev 18, it corresponds to "fornication," which is often applied specifically to incestuous unions.[25] Moreover, eating food offered to idols and committing fornication were notorious Gentile practices and would cause major problems in the Christian fellowship if they were not prohibited.

Suggesting to abide by the decrees prescribed for the aliens in the OT, James invites the Gentiles to have access to the terrain of the chosen people, kept sacred by the "holiness code." Observance of decrees allows coexistence between the Christians of Jewish origin, those who remained attached to the

24 Peter was the acknowledged leader of the Christian community in Jerusalem. However, James' confirmation and amendments of Peter's speech suggests that at some point between early Christian movement and the apostolic council Peter has been displaced by James, the Lord's brother. D.C. Sim, *The Gospel of Matthew and Christian Judaism*, 80-81, suggests that the displacement of Peter from leadership would have happened between 36 CE and 48 CE. According to Sim the apostolic council took place around the year 48 CE. When did this shift of power precisely take place? According to Acts 12:1-5 during the reign of Herod Agrippa I (37-44 CE) a persecution of the Jerusalem church took place. As a result James, the brother of John was killed and Peter was imprisoned. After his liberation from the prison Peter left Jerusalem to an unknown place (Acts 12:17). On the basis of this account we could deduce that James was made to fill the vacuum left by the departure of Peter. As a member of Jesus' family and a recipient of a revelation of the risen Jesus (1 Cor 15:7), James assumed the leadership of the Christian community in Jerusalem. He might have retained the leadership even when Peter returned to Jerusalem. See M. Hengel, *Acts and History of Earliest Christianity*, Philadelphia, Fortress Press, 1980, 95; R.E. Brown, *et al.*, (eds.), *Peter in the New Testament*, London, Geoffrey Chapman, 1973, 48-49; R.R. Hann, "Judaism and Jewish Christianity in Antioch: Charisma and Conflict in the First Century," *JRH* 14 (1987) 341-360, 344. But R. Bauckham, "James and the Jerusalem church," in R. Bauckham, (ed.), *The Book of Acts in its First Century Setting. Vol 4. The Book of Acts in its Palestinian Setting*, Grand Rapids, W.E. Eerdmans Publishing Company, 1995, 415-480, 439-441, argues that during the persecution of Agrippa the leadership of the Jerusalem church transferred from the twelve disciples to a group of elders headed by James.

25 J.A. Fitzmyer, *To Advance the Gospel: New Testament Studies*, Grand Rapids, W.B. Eerdmans Publishing Company, 1981, 91-97.

Law and the requirements for ritual purity, and the Christians of Gentile origin. The two Christian groups could thus live together, and, more importantly share the Eucharistic meal. It is a compromise formula, which made the Christians of Gentile origin a kind of associated people, with a unique status to that of "God-fearers" or the proselytes in Judaism.[26]

4. Decision of the Council (Acts 15:22-29)

In verses 22-29 Luke records the consequence of the Council. The Council drafted a letter[27] addressed to Christians of Gentile origin. Paul and Barnabas were entrusted to carry the letter to Antioch, while Judas and Silas were entrusted with the responsibility of carrying the letter to Syria and Cilicia. The decision was taken with the consent of "the apostles and the elders" (Acts 15:22-23). Thus we understand that the resolution was passed by the authorship of plenary mother church. In fact, Paul and Barnabas are sent by the church at Antioch and there is no difficulty in comprehending the fact that they went back to Antioch with the letter. We don't hear about Judas anywhere else. Silas will be a companion of Paul in his second missionary journey (Acts 15:40-18:5; cf. "Silvanus," 1Thess 1:1; 2 Cor 1:19). For Luke, Silas is one more link binding Paul's mission to the mother church. The letter is destined beyond the inquiring church of Antioch (Acts 15:23), to its expanding mission territories, Syria and Cilicia.

The decision to send letters to different churches of Gentile origin is not only in confirmation with all gathered but also with the inspiration of the Holy Spirit (Acts 15:28). This suitably tallies up the deliberations, which have so emphasized the divine initiative. Church authority does not act on power or an agenda of its own; it is legitimate only in carrying out the saving will of God. The four clauses of proposal of James in the form of a decree, expressed in verse 20, puts in order corresponding to Lev 17-18 in verse 29, thus accentuating the addition of Golden Rule.[28]

5. Aftermath (Acts 15:30-35)

The closing paragraph of the council presents an ideal picture of Antioch's joyous reception of the resolution. This would have been the response expected by the mother church in Jerusalem. "They delivered the letter. And when they read it, they rejoiced at the exhortation" (Acts 15:30-31). The unity between the Christian communities of Jewish origin and Gentile origin has now been safeguarded. The conflict, which prevented the growth of a Christian

26 P. Debergé, *Saint Pierre*, 98.

27 The apostolic letter is a "document" of Luke's confection, quite keeping with Hellenistic historian's convention. H. Cadbury, *The Making of Luke-Acts*, London, SPCK, ^{2}1958, 191, suggests that the prescript is standard in all Hellenistic letters.

28 Cf. P. Debergé, *Saint Pierre*, 99.

community in Gentile regions, has been resolved by an acceptable and wise resolution. Moreover, the community at Antioch can now live peacefully by spreading the Word of God: "Paul and Barnabas remained in Antioch, teaching and preaching the word of the Lord, with many others also" (Acts 15:35).

D. Paul's departure from Antioch: Acts 15:36-41

Paul and Barnabas remained in Antioch. Paul later decides to depart. According to Luke, the immediate reason for Paul to depart from Antioch was due to a sharp disagreement with Barnabas. Paul suggested to Barnabas that they both go on a mission "in every city" where they proclaimed the word of the Lord, and see how they are (Acts 15:36). But the suggestion of Barnabas to take "John called Mark" along with them was not welcomed by Paul. Thus Luke recounts that Paul departed from Antioch with Silas. The break between them, we understand, was due to a sharp disagreement over whether John Mark should accompany them. Luke leaves us wondering about its deeper causes.

Paul left Antioch with Silas to conduct a mission to Syria and Cilicia, in Asia Minor and Greece. Paul's experience at Antioch probably marked a new stage in his missionary journey. His mission among the Gentiles made him consider himself to be the apostle to the Gentiles. D.C. Sim observes, "With no permanent base, he (Paul) travelled extensively between Asia Minor and Greece and kept well away from Antioch and the surrounding regions."[29] But Acts does state that he visited Antioch on one further occasion (Acts 18:22-23), probably either "to form closer relations between Antioch and the churches he had founded in Greece"[30] or "to renew relations with the Antiochene church."[31]

II. Texts from Galatians

Important passages in Galatians chapter 2 also shed more light on the nature of Christian community in Antioch.

A. Another Version of Council at Jerusalem: Gal 2:1-10

In order to understand the events which took place in Jerusalem, we are dependent also upon Paul's version of the council. We discuss the following essential elements in the light of Paul's version concerning Jerusalem Council:

1. Agreements and differences in comparison to Luke's version

Though many problems remain about the nature of the narrative, Gal 2:1-10 refers back to some event as that in Acts 15:1-21. A rapid comparison between the two accounts clarifies common points as well as notable differences. Both

---

29 D.C. Sim, *The Gospel of Matthew and Christian Judaism*, 101.

30 E. Haenchen, *Acts of the Apostles*, 548.

31 H. Conzelmann, *History of Primitive Christianity*, London, Longman & Todd, 1973, 90.

the accounts imply a council in Jerusalem, which was attended by Peter, James, Paul and Barnabas (Gal 2:1, 9; Acts 15:2, 6, 13). Paul's mission among the Gentiles is also assumed in both accounts, though not in the same manner (Gal 2:7; Acts 15:2). We note two fundamental differences in the accounts. First of all, according to Paul's version, he went to Jerusalem with Barnabas and Titus in response to a revelation (Gal 2:1-2). But according to Luke, Paul, Barnabas and some others were appointed by the church of Antioch to go to Jerusalem (Acts 15:2). Secondly, while the account in Acts eventually reaches in drafting a letter concerning four requirements in line with Lev 17-18 (Acts 15:20), the account in Galatians concerns the recognition of Gospel preached by Paul, division of mission field and a request to "remember the poor" (Gal 2:9-10).

2. Reasons Leading to the Council

Paul explains the origin of the apostolic council. After fourteen years, Paul and Barnabas, prophets or teachers of church at Antioch (Acts 13:1) together with Titus, a Gentile Christian (cf. Gal 2:3), who smoothes over Paul's relations with the Corinthian community,[32] come to Jerusalem (Gal 2:1). The correlation of this visit to Jerusalem with the data in Acts is one of the most difficult exegetical problems in the NT. However, one cannot escape the impression that Gal 2 refers to the same event as that in Acts 15. All other attempts to identify it otherwise is notwithstanding. Yet many problems remain. Paul came to Jerusalem in response to a revelation (Gal 2:2). Here Paul implies that he has not been summoned by the Jerusalem church. Paul refers to another reason for his coming to Jerusalem. [33] It is because some "false believers" destroyed the freedom, which the church of Antioch had in Christ (Gal 2:4). [34] In Acts 15:5 similar Jewish-Christian converts, said to be of Pharisaic background,

32 Cf. 2 Cor 2:13; 7:6, 13-14; 8:6, 16, 23; 12:18.

33 We have seen in Acts 15:2 that the reason for the visit is given as a decision of the Antiochene community.

34 There is some dispute over whether Paul's reference to these false believers and his defence of the Gospel applies to the apostolic council or is a note which actually describes earlier events in Antioch. For the latter view, see F. Watson, *Paul, Judaism and the Gentiles: A Sociological Approach*, SNTSMS 56, Cambridge, Cambridge University Press, 1986, 50-51; E. Haenchen, *The Acts of the Apostles*, 467; M. Hengel, *Acts and the History of Earliest Christianity*, 113; H.D. Betz, *Galatians: A Commentary on Paul's Letter to the Churches in Galatia*, Hermeneia, Philadelphia, Fortress Press, 1979, 89-90. According to D.C. Sim, *The Gospel of Matthew and Christian Judaism*, 83, such an interpretation runs against the natural sense of the text and it is more likely that the "false believers" did in fact have their say at the meeting in Jerusalem. This argument can be confirmed by Acts 15:5 where Luke describes a group of Christian Pharisees attempting to circumcise and impose the Torah on the Gentile delegates from Antioch. Certainly Paul's description of these events does cohere with Luke's description in Acts 15:1-2 of the men from Judea with whom Paul disputed prior to the council.

press for the circumcision of the Gentiles and their obligation to observe the Mosaic Law.

3. Submission of Gospel Preached to Gentiles

Paul submits before the acknowledged leaders of the Jerusalem church the Gospel that he preached to the Gentiles (Gal 2:2), thus acknowledging the prominence of "Jerusalem pillars" who were apostles before him. To confirm his Law-free mission to the Gentiles, Paul puts forth the case of Titus who is present with him: "But even Titus, who was with me, was not compelled to be circumcised, though he was a Greek" (Gal 2:3). Paul emphasizes on "the freedom we have in Christ." In Christ everyone is freed of the Law (cf. Gal 5:1, 13).

4. Uncompromising Tone of Paul

Paul presents before the meeting his contribution. He explains, "We did not yield to their submission even for a moment" (Gal 2:5). This gives the tone that Paul has influenced the assembly. The account in Acts gives importance to Peter (Acts 15:7-11) whose recommendations were later accepted by the assembly with minor changes. In Paul's view James, Peter and John contributed nothing to his mission. Paul seems not to have been intimidated by the prestige gained by the "pillars of Jerusalem church"[35] for having been eyewitnesses of Jesus' ministry. Such an experience and prestige, according to Paul, could not out-weigh the truth of the God-given Gospel (Gal 2:6). According to Paul, the council added nothing to the Gospel that he presented. In other words, he confirms that his Gospel was recognized by "pillars of Jerusalem church" as not deficient, despite the claims of the "false believers."

5. Recommendations of the Council

The mission field is divided between Peter and Paul: "When they saw that I had been entrusted with the Gospel to the uncircumcised, just as Peter had been entrusted with the Gospel to the circumcised…me and Barnabas…should go to the Gentiles and they to the circumcised" (Gal 2:7-9; cf. Rom 15:7-12; Acts 15:12).[36] Thus, "the acknowledged pillars" of Jerusalem church confirm Paul's

---

35 There are wide rages of view on the Jerusalem apostles as "pillars." Cf. D.M. Hay, "Paul's Indifference to Authority," *JBL* 88 (1969) 36-44; R.Y.K. Fung, "A Note on Galatians 2:3-8," *JETS* 25 (1982) 49-52.

36 Whether to consider the division geographically or ethically remains a question. Peter first preached to the Jews (Acts 2:14-42) and then initiated the mission among the Gentiles (Acts 10:1-11:18). Moreover, he supports the legitimacy of Gentile mission (Acts 15:7-13). Paul often begins his evangelization of an area with the Jews (1 Cor 9:23-24; Rom 2:10-11; Acts 13:46; 17:1-8; 18:4) and then undertook a wide ranging Gentile mission. After the Council probably both Peter and Paul returned to Antioch and concentrated their

"Gospel for the uncircumcised" (Gal 2:9), his apostleship (Gal 2:9), but for the Gentile.[37] In the last verse we are informed of an additional recommendation of the council, "remember the poor" (Gal 2:10). The poor are probably the "poor among the saints in Jerusalem" (Rom 15:26), those economically poor when compared with Gentile Christians of Hellenistic cities.[38] However, the account in Acts, as we have seen, evoked four requirements (Acts 15:20) to be followed by the Gentiles desiring to join the Church.

6. Outcome of the Council

The outcome of this Jerusalem conference was a confirmation of Paul's Gospel ministry and an official division of the mission field with respect to apostolic activity; Paul and Barnabas were commended to work with Gentiles, whereas James, Peter, and John continued in their commitment to the circumcised (Gal 2:7-10). In every way, Paul's Gospel ministry had been recognized and authenticated as being of divine origin and direction.

B. Conflict between Peter and Paul: Gal 2:11-14

Another valuable piece of information concerning the church at Antioch is given in Gal 2:11-14. It narrates the clash that took place between Peter and Paul at Antioch. It mentions about the stay of Peter in Antioch. Presumably, both Peter and Paul came to Antioch shortly after the decision on circumcision at the Jerusalem council.[39] The fact that the clash between Peter and Paul is reported after the account of meeting at Jerusalem (Gal 2:1-10) allows us to suppose that this incident took place sometime later.[40] Noteworthy points of this passage are the following:

---

mission among the Jews and Gentiles respectively. So in the particular context of Antioch the division of mission field would have been ethical in nature.

37 When Paul spoke in Gal 2:9 of the "grace" that had been given him, this was his favourite term for Christ's calling him and appointing him as the apostle to the Gentiles (Gal 1:15-16; Rom 1:5; 15:15-16; 1 Cor 3:10; 15:10-11; Eph 3:1-13; Phil 1:3-7). This term became a sort of theological abbreviation for the doctrine of the universal nature of the Gospel. Cf. H.D. Betz, *Galatians*, 27-28

38 J. Dupont, *Les Béatitudes*, 3 vols, Paris, 1958-1969, 2.15-51; J.A. Fitzmyer, "The Letter to the Galatians," in R.E. Brown, *et al.*, (eds.), *NJBC*, Bangalore, TPI, 1992, 780-790, 784.

39 J.A. Fitzmyer, "The Letter to the Galatians," 784.

40 A minority of scholars have attempted to place the incident at Antioch earlier than the council on the grounds that the former event could have happened subsequent to the agreement reached in Jerusalem. See J. Munck, *Paul and the Salvation of Mankind*, London, SCM Press, 1977, 100-103; G. Lüdemann, *Paul: Apostle to the Gentiles*, Philadelphia, Fortress Press, 1984, 75-77. But this view hardly does justice to the text and it misses the point Paul is making to his readers. See N. Taylor, *Paul, Antioch and Jerusalem: A Study in Relationships and Authority in Earliest Christianity*, JSNTSS 66, Sheffield, Sheffield Academic Press, 1992, 54.

1. Paul's Discontent Over Peter's Divergence

According to Paul, Peter came to Antioch after the apostolic council. He happily associated and ate with the Gentile Christians in Antioch. But when "certain men from James," from Jerusalem, came to Antioch, he disassociated himself from the table fellowship with the Gentiles. Paul was discontent over Peter's divergence. So Paul frankly asserted: "But when Cephas came to Antioch I opposed him to his face, because he stood condemned" (Gal 2:11). Paul always regarded Peter as a person of greater consequence than himself. This fact can be understood from the previous episodes for number of reasons. First of all, Peter served Paul as a source of tradition about Jesus (Gal 1:18). Secondly, Peter was the leader in Jerusalem at the time of Paul's visit after conversion (Gal 1:18). Thirdly, Peter had a role in the apostolate to the circumcised (Gal 2:8).[41] But Peter's inconsistency provoked Paul.

2. Reasons for Paul's Contention

According to Paul, Peter stood condemned by his own actions. His actions are explained in v 12. "For before certain men came from James, he ate with the Gentiles" (Gal 2:12a). The men who came from James may not be the "false brothers" of Gal 2:4 because the issue now concerns Jewish dietary laws, quite distinct from the issue of circumcision, which had been settled at Jerusalem (Gal 2:3-9; Acts 15:1-12). Until they arrived Peter led an exemplary life at Antioch. He shared meals with Christians of Gentile origin. He did not restrict himself to Jewish regulations, which prohibited meals with non-Jews. Thus Peter regarded the Gentile converts as Christians who are one with Christ and equal before God. This behaviour of Peter was appropriate and delighted Paul. "But when they came he drew back and separated himself, fearing the circumcision party" (Gal 2:12b). The behavioural change in Peter was due to the "fear of circumcision party." Why did Peter fear is not clear; but it is considered by Paul as a sign of his lack of conviction about the Gospel. According to Paul, Peter thus gave a feeling that only Jewish Christians, who observed such laws as Lev 17:8-9, 10-12, 15, were the real Christians.

3. Consequences of Peter's Action

Consequently, "with him the rest of the Jews acted insincerely" (Gal 2:13a).[42] The attitude of Peter could have influenced the Jewish Christians, thus, separating themselves, even from the common participation in table fellowship. Even Barnabas, the faithful companion of Paul, was influenced (Gal 2:13b). The attitude of Peter and others were not consistent with the "truth of the

41 R. E. Brown, *et al.* (eds.), *Peter in the New Testament*, 23-24.

42 The Greek word used here is ὑπόκρισις. Therefore, it is possible that Paul is describing Peter as a hypocrite and the rest of the Jews joining his hypocrisy.

Gospel" (Gal 2:14). For Paul, "truth of the Gospel" is the "freedom we have in Christ" (Gal 2:4-5), not only from the custom of circumcision, but also from Jewish dietary laws. Paul found fault with Peter because he was not walking straight according to this truth. So Paul reproached Peter: "If you, though a Jew, live like a Gentile and not like a Jew, how can you compel the Gentiles to live like Jews" (Gal 2:14). Since Peter's example had already misled Barnabas and others, Paul would have feared that it would affect other Gentile Christian communities outside Antioch.[43] Hence from Paul's view point Peter should be challenged when he failed to act in accordance with the truth of the Gospel.

Conclusion

The important passages in Acts of the Apostles and Galatians provide us with the early witness of Christian community in Antioch:

1. Hellenist Jewish Christians in Antioch: Hellenists were scattered because of the persecution that took place following the death of Stephen. Those who were scattered went from place to place, proclaiming the Word. We understand, therefore, the Hellenists did not forsake their belief in Jesus due to the persecution, instead, they continued their mission in new environments. Some of the Hellenists travelled as far as Antioch in Syria. These Greek speaking Jewish followers of Jesus then began to form Christian community devoting to missionary efforts. They were convinced that following Jesus no longer necessarily entailed acknowledging the validity of the temple cult in Jerusalem and adhering to the Law of Moses.
2. Gospel to Jews and Gentiles: At Antioch, the Hellenists preached the Word first to the Jews and then to the Gentiles (Acts 11:19-20). As it was for the first time that Word was preached to the Gentiles in Antioch, it would have been a Law-free mission. Thus the church at Antioch became a large and growing one. It developed into one of the most important Christian communities of the first century. The Antiochene church eventually became a unique community, comprising of both Jews and Gentiles. This would explain the presence of Jewish and Gentile elements in the Gospel according to Matthew.
3. Paul set out on a mission journey from Antioch: Paul's missionary activity apparently began under the influence of Hellenistic Jewish Christians, who were headquartered in Antioch. Paul emanated to an elaborate operation with many co-workers from Antioch. He ran well-organized campaigns in regions of Asia Minor, Greece and Rome starting from Syria Antioch. Thus the Antiochene church, in

43 J.A. Fitzmyer, "The Letter to the Galatians," 784.

a calculated manner, widened its missionary field. Jesus' acceptance of Gentiles like the Roman centurion and the Canaanite woman and his great commandment to preach the Good News to "all nations" in the Gospel point to the spread of the Gospel to the Gentile mission field.

4. Jerusalem Council: The community in Antioch is not concerned with the issue of circumcision for the Gentile converts. This could mean either that the church was still within a thoroughly Jewish context where circumcision was assumed, or that the church had become so thoroughly oriented to the Gentile mission that circumcision was no longer issue. The latter possibility remains valid since we assume that the community originated with the Jewish converts to Christianity and later a large number of Gentile converts joined the church. The Antiochene community, which comprised of Jews and Gentiles, progressed without strict adherence to Jewish laws, especially circumcision and dietary proscriptions.
5. Prominent role of Peter: Paul separated himself from Barnanbas and left Antioch. After his departure, Paul returns to Antioch only once for a brief visit (Acrs 18:22). In the meantime, Peter enjoyed an obvious authority in Antioch. He knew that certain prudence was recommended to him to accommodate both Jewish and Gentile elements in the Antiochene church. Therefore, wanting to avoid a conflict, which would necessarily have turned against the unity of the Christian community, Peter agreed to the compromise formula of observance of Jewish food law from the part of Gentile Christians in the common-table. This moderating leadership of Peter contributed to protect the tie between Jewish Christians and the Gentile Christians. This fundamental leadership of Peter in the Antiochene church, to keep united the Christians of Jewish and Gentile origin, reflects itself in the major place that Matthew reserves for him in his Gospel.

Thus early evidences on the identity of Matthean community reflected in Acts of the Apostles and Galatians show that Matthew's community first began in Syria Antioch with the Jews and then an increasing number of the Gentile converts joined the community, becoming a new people of God, where Peter was a prominent figure.

9

Quest for Identity Traits in Community Formation
Luke-Acts

Virginia Rajakumari Sandiyagu SAB

Introduction

Quest for identity is a perennial search as well as a struggle. In a time of hectic activities of individuals and communities, groups and races, there is always craving to know who and where I am. Jesus too had this interest. To the question of Jesus, 'who do people say that I am?' there were list of signifiers: John the Baptist, Elijah, one of the prophets… this litany of names is followed by a new question: 'and you, who do you say that I am?' to which the proposal is 'You are the Christ.' (Mk 8:27-33; cf. Mt 16:13-20; Lk 9:18-22). The busy-ness of modernism has not satiated the hunger for one's identity. The Christian community of today is no different in this search. The interest in the study of quest for identity of community in the Bible seems to indicate the urgent need to respond to the multiple and distorted issues such as: Who am I in this society? Who am I in the church? What is the nature of my community? Who are the members of my community and what is the identity of the other in comparison with my community? Etc. This quest for identity is although personal; it does become the concern of the whole society as the discussion progresses. The identity of a community is appropriate with its lifestyle, values and goals. It remains to be discovered how this quest progresses and climaxes especially in the writings of Luke-Acts. In this paper, we will ascertain that Luke describes an inclusive Christian community and his theologies fit into this context.

I. OT Background to the Formation of Community

Identity is the sum total of specific qualities that reflects an individual or a community. In the Old Testament understanding, *People of Israel*, *the Chosen People* were identified as the 'community.' They did not become a community or even a nation overnight. Rather, this band of nomads was slowly welded into God's people, for which they had to struggle through history facing various types of difficulties and hard situations. The formator of this community is Yahweh and his agents (Abraham, Moses, Judges, Kings and Prophets). The Israelites were chosen by Yahweh only because of his immeasurable love which is particularly expressed in redeeming them from slavery in Egypt. The great unifying force at this moment in their history could be the common desire to escape slavery. However, that would not be enough to sustain a true community in the days to follow. It was only when they came face to face with Yahweh in the desert on Mt. Sinai that they realized what it meant to be his people. Further, when they shared together the experiences of the desert, recalling the common experience of the Covenant forged at Mt. Sinai and remembered the common history, they were formed into a community. In all, the covenant with its stipulations namely, Laws and Commandments, Prayer and Worship, Doctrines and Beliefs was the basis and guiding principle of the Israelite community.[1] These principles will give a unique identity to the community as the קהל יהוה 'Community of God'. Hence the formation of a community, or a family, or a clan, or a tribe involves a goal and the means to reach it through requirements, which can be termed as the radical demands. If a community is in pain and confusion, then it has to examine its conscience for failure in keeping and fulfilling these requirements.

However, this election does not exclude others; rather the elected are asked to be the channels of God's love to others, thereby making the community more inclusive in nature. God said to Abraham "in you *all families* of the earth will be blessed" (Gen 12:1-4). Thus, we have the examples of Rahab the Canaanite prostitute becoming part of Israel along with her relatives, because she understood what God was doing at that point in history with Israel (Josh 2:6,22-27). The Gibeonites who resorted to a ruse too became part of God's people (Jos 9). Ruth, the Moabite became the member of the family of Israel, and in particular the grandmother of king David (Ruth 4:13-22). The people of Israel who came out of Egypt under the leadership of Moses were indeed a *diverse crowd* of people. They were crowd of mixed ancestry (Ex 12:38). Thus by incorporating the non-Israelites, the Israel community becomes inclusive in nature.

---

1 See Francis J. Maloney, *Disciples and Prophets: A Biblical Model for the Religious Life* (London: Darton, Longman and Todd, 1980), 50-51. See also Frederick Gast, "The Biblical Community," *Spiritual Life* 15 (1969), 19.

II. Formation of Community in Luke-Acts

In the Old Testament, the community was formed through covenant requirements that God made with certain individuals such as Abraham and Moses. This quest for the formation of community is carried out in the New Testament too through Jesus and his agents (Peter, Paul, Philip, Stephen, Barnabas and others). The Lukan gospel itself mentions about the Christian community in an indirect manner. Here Jesus does not herald his mission as founding a 'new' or a different covenant. Rather he proclaims continuity with the traditional covenant. He repeatedly points to the Old Testament texts as prophecies which he is fulfilling, thus maintaining his continuity with the history of God's covenant people (Lk 4:21; 24:27,44-47).[2]

We need to identify how the community of Jesus' time and of the apostolic time adapted itself to circumstances and what bound them as members of the community. In other words, what was the true identity of the 'Christian' community? What were the essential requisites for the formation of this community? What events shaped the community and what is its *Sitz-im Leben*? Although the precise *Sitz-im Leben* is difficult to pin down, the mood or the vision of the author is not. It appears that the writings of Luke, namely Luke-Acts has certain traits in presenting the community of Jesus and the early church.

III. Identity Traits of the Christian Community in Luke-Acts

While defining the community in Luke-Acts, we need to pay attention to the plot of Luke in shaping the community and to its characteristic traits. We will present these traits one by one.

A. The Founder/Formator/s

Every founder or formator has a goal to reach and a mission to accomplish. Jesus was the first formator of the New Testament community. God had long before planned the mission of Jesus as the messiah to save his people. He promised the Israelites that he would send the messiah. Hence the coming of Jesus into this world was to save and unite all people into the kingdom of God by giving his own life. He proclaimed the values of the Kingdom namely, love, forgiveness, compassion and forbearing. These values were opposed to that of the Pharisees, Sadducees and the high priests, who were bent on ritual observance of the laws. Jesus had to give up his life for his stance, but he made sure that his community members live and carry forward his mission.

Jesus seems to have founded a wholly unstructured community of disciples but it is this community which is the starting point of the movement

2 See Jerome H. Neyrey, *Christ Is Community: The Christologies of the New Testament*, Good News Studies 13 (Wilmington, Delaware: Michael Glazier, 1985), 123.

which later emerges and is identified as the church, more visibly as the *New Israel*[3]*, the Christian Community. In Acts, Luke focuses upon the Holy Spirit as the formator of the church community. He works through the missionary activities of some of the prominent disciples like Peter and Paul. Peter along with the other apostles is one of the major links between the time of Jesus and that of the early community. Peter's work of spreading of Good News and the establishment of new Christian communities are particularly evident in the three Pentecosts: Jewish (Acts 2:1-13), Samaritan (Acts 8:5-17), and Gentile (Acts 10:1-48). Special attention has been given to Peter and to his role in the early part of Acts. He is the spokesperson for the twelve whose speeches formulate the basic Christian Kerygma and whose activity is related to the beginnings of Christian life and mission. However, it is the figure of Paul according to the texts in Acts that has claimed the lion's share in establishing the communities. Luke demonstrates the continuity of establishment of Christian communities through Paul after Peter. Paul is a great witness, a preacher and a missionary who builds up a relation between Jewish and gentile missions. His mission is invariably related to the gospel and the activity of the Spirit.*[4] *Besides Peter and Paul, we have Stephen and Philip who were initially chosen to serve at the table but later having filled with the Spirit, served the word of God and added members to the believing community (Acts 6-8). At Corinth, we find also the functioning of Apollos an eloquent preacher from Alexandria taking up the task of forming the believing community (Acts 18:24-28; cf. 1Cor 1:10-17).*

Jesus in the gospels does not function as a sole founder. He shares his power with his apostles and disciples and sends them on mission to form communities (Lk 9:1ff and Lk 10:1ff). The same is found in the Acts of the Apostles, where the Holy Spirit delegates not only the apostles of the gospel but also others who later became believers like Barnabas, Stephen, Philip, Paul and Apollos. Thus there is inclusiveness in the functioning of the formation of the community.

---

3 The concept of *New Israel* is more evident in the gospel of Matthew where Jesus is presented as the New Moses and the community as the New Israel. However, Luke is no different. He refers to the OT texts right from the birth narratives to the Ascension and again in the life of the early community. Jesus prepares a foundation for authority within the people to replace the Jewish leaders who reject the prophet. He sends out the twelve with power and authority. That these twelve will take over the leadership of Israel is suggested in Lukan parables of pounds (Lk 19:11-27) and the Vineyard (Lk 20:9-18). At the last supper, Jesus explicitly bestows authority on the twelve to judge the twelve tribes of Israel (Lk 22:30). In the speeches of Peter, Stephen and Paul the proclamation of the resurrection of Jesus is on the basis of the history of the Israel. See Luke Timothy Johnson, *The Writings of the New Testament: An Interpretation* (Bangalore: TPI, 2009), 232.

4 See Earl Richard, "Luke-Writer, Theologian, Historian: Research and Orientation of the 1970's," *Biblical Theology Bulletin* 13(1983), 7.

B. The Call

There are two initial ways of forming a community as found in the writings of Luke. Firstly, through a direct call as is the case of the inner circle, namely, Peter, James and John (Lk 5:1-11), and others like Levi (Lk 5:27-28), the twelve (Lk 6:12-16) and some disciples (Lk 9:23,59; cf. 14:27; 18:22). This call to a relationship does not stem from any merit on their side, but is the result of Jesus' love and compassion. The locations where the call is given are: by the sea shore, wayside or at dining table etc. Secondly, the voluntary following of persons as seen in the case of number of male and female disciples (6:1; 6:12; 6:17; 8:1-3). It appears that these were moved by the charisma of the person of Jesus and found an inner urge to follow him freely without explicit call given by the master. However, not all who volunteered to follow Jesus were accepted by Jesus and vice-versa (cf. Lk 5:14-20; 9:57-62).This association happens in a number of ways throughout the story– mainly at meals, but also through healings performed and teachings he taught. Exclusion from the community is also a reality similarly taking place at meals, and through bitter arguments about the law and miracles (Lk 9:57-62; 14:15-33; 18:18-25; 20:9-19; 22:21-23,47-53).[5]

The Jesus' community later extends itself into forming a church community. The apostles and disciples who took the mission of Jesus to the corners of the ancient world, did not give an explicit call to "follow," but presented Jesus and his values and asked them to "repent and be baptized" (Acts 2:38; 3:19). This invitation was so convincing that many became the followers of the "Way" (Acts 2:41; 4:4; 6:7; 9:31; 12:24; 16:5; 19:20).

The call given to the followers is not an end in itself. They are to remain with him. Although Luke does not state explicitly like Mark that Jesus chose the twelve to be with him and to be sent (Mk 3:19), he uses the expression συν αυτω to emphasize the physical presence of his followers with Jesus (Lk 8:1-3). The time spent by Jesus with his followers helps in increasing the quality and quantity of members to his community. Although the initial community consisted of the twelve apostles, the number grew reaching up at least to 70/72 members (Lk 10:1ff) in the gospel. In the Acts, Luke uses almost thirteen verbs such as μενο and επιμενο to convey the importance of 'remaining' with the established community. This idea of remaining with the founding communities is evidently to consolidate the faith of those who had embraced Christianity. Peter stayed in Joppa for several days as resuscitation of Tabita had led to several conversions (Lk 9:43). Again Peter stays back with Cornelius and his

5 See Johann du Plessis, "The Christian Community in the Gospel of Luke: Looking for a Biblical Model for Church Renewal Today," 65. https://journals.co.za/docserver/fulltext/jortna/3/1/9.pdf?expires=1538942945 &id=id&accname=guest&checksum=CF1EEA7FF A08A7B6C66FC6A5FC754C1C access on 29.04.2018.

household after baptism to further instruct them in faith (Acts 10:48). Paul and Silas remained in the house of Lydia as there was need for a follow up of the faith of the Christians at Philippi (Acts 16:15). At Corinth, Paul remained with Priscilla and Aquila strengthening the new believers (Acts 18:1-4). Judas and Silas exhorted and strengthened the community in Antioch and Paul and Barnabas remained and proclaimed (Acts 15:32-35). At Thessalonica, when trouble arose Paul was sent away to Beroea and from there to Athens, but Silas and Timothy remained at Beroea (Acts 17:14) to instruct the community.[6]

If we observe the list of those who received the direct call and those who volunteered to follow, we see that there is no distinction made between the Jews and gentiles, between the haves and have-nots and between the righteous and sinners. Call is given to people of all strata of life and they are expected to commit themselves, and imitate Jesus and his activities and even share his fate.

C. Baptism

Baptism is an initiation procedure for an individual to be called a Christian. According to St. Paul, baptism is the concrete manifestation of one's faith in Jesus Christ. It is a unifying factor. By baptism all are united in Christ and we become the children of God through faith in Jesus. Then there is no distinction between Jew or Greek, slave or free, male or female. Because all are one in Christ (cf. Gal 3:26-29).[7] Luke refers to the baptism of John numerous times in his two volume work (Lk 3:7, 12, 16; 7:29-30; 20:4; Acts 1:5, 22; 10:37; 13:24; 11:16; 18:25; 19:3-4). He presents Jesus receiving baptism, but he does not mention that he was baptized by John the Baptist (Lk 3:21-22). Jesus himself does not baptize anyone. However, it appears that to be a member of the Christian community, Luke implies that besides repentance and belief in Jesus, there be a baptism in the name of Jesus. Although, the Lukan gospel does not state anywhere that baptism is absolutely necessary for salvation, and no mention is made that any of the original disciples were baptized, in the book of the Acts, he makes number references to baptism indicating its necessity. For example, Peter says "Repent and be baptized....." (Acts 2:38) and 3000 Pentecost day converts were baptized (Acts 2:41). Besides this, those who believed the preaching of Philip were baptized in Samaria (Acts 8:12); also in the stories about the conversion of the Ethiopian eunuch (Acts 8:37-38) and Cornelius (Acts 10:48) baptism is mentioned. Luke does not state that Apollos ever received Christian baptism but he mentions that he only knew the baptism of John (Acts 18:25). Luke speaks also of baptism of the Spirit

6 See Jose Varickasseril, "Remaining with the Community: A Lukan Strategy for Deepening the Faith of Christians," *Mission Today* 6 (2004), 48-63.

7 Jose Valliara, *Christian Discipleship: A Challenging Vocation* (Bangalore: Franciscan Missionary Brothers, 1983), 141.

and speaking in tongues. An important insight is that Luke gives priority to the reception of the Holy Spirit over water baptism. He suggests that it is possible to receive the Holy Spirit apart from water baptism (cf. Acts 8:12,15-17; 9:17-18; 10:44-48).[8] It may be understood that once, the baptism of John in water was a mark of repentance and forgiveness of sins (Lk 3:3), now the baptism of the Spirit is the mark of repentance and forgiveness of sins (Acts 1:5). Repentance and baptism in the name of Jesus could be for the purpose of sins being forgiven and as well as a preparation for the reception of the Spirit. Along with repentance and water baptism, the Spirit's coming is one of the components involved in the initiation of a person into a follower of Jesus (Acts 2:38,41). Luke did not think that speaking in tongues was the initial evidence of the coming of the Spirit, but the ability to speak in tongues could be the result and, by implication, evidence of being filled with the Spirit (2:4). For Luke, baptism is necessary by water or Spirit, and is fundamental to those who want to be admitted to the Christian community and its way of life.[9]

The above examples show that there is a shift of emphasis from water baptism which was meant for the Jews, to the baptism with the Holy Spirit. All, irrespective of gender, class, and age become the recipients of the Holy Spirit (cf. Acts 2:17-21). Thus, the community becomes inclusive in every respect.

D. Location of Community Formation

At the time of Jesus, Jerusalem continued to be the centre of Jewish religion and learning. Yet the first Christian community is not formed in Jerusalem. The members of this wandering community are from Galilee. In fact, Galilee was looked down upon by the religious authorities and perfectionists of the temple city, namely Jerusalem (cf. Jn 1:46; Acts 4:13). Galileans were on the fringe of the literal observance of the ordinances of the law. They even spoke a dialect which placed them somewhat in a class and accent of their own (cf. Mt 26:73). Majority of the Galileans were uneducated, ordinary farmers and fishermen (cf. Acts 4:13).[10] Jesus gives these insignificant persons a unique identity by accepting them to be the members of his community. The major part of Jesus' community formation is spent in Galilean region. Jesus makes these wandering community members witnesses of the "Christ-Event" in Jerusalem.

Although the first Church or the Christian community was founded in Jerusalem, they are not to be rooted there. They are asked to leave the centre

---

8 See Dennis M. Sweetland, "Following Jesus: Discipleship in Luke-Acts," in *New Views on Luke and Acts*, ed. Earl Richard (Collegeville, Mn: A Michael Glazier Book, 2018), 119.

9 See Graham H. Twelftree, *People of the Spirit: Exploring Luke's View of the Church* (Grand Rapids, MI: SPCK, 2009), 97-99.

10 See Maloney, *Disciples and Prophets,* 63-64.

and move to the peripheries. So in the Acts, we see the establishment of the communities taking place away from Jerusalem. The communities are spread, from Jerusalem to Judea, Samaria and to the ends of the earth (cf. Acts 1:8), namely to Cyprus, Antioch of Pisidia, Iconium, Lystra, Derbe, Philippi, Thessalonica, Beroea, Athens, Corinth, Ephesus, Rome and elsewhere. Thus the communities are not only located within Palestine but in the gentile world too.

E. The Ethoses of the Community in Luke-Acts

Ruth Benedict in her book *Patterns of Culture* writes: "No man ever looks at the world with immaculate eyes. He sees it edited by a definite set of customs and institutions and ways of thinking."[11] What were such customs and institutions that Jesus demanded of his community members? In seeking an answer to this question, we find that the demands which the Lukan Jesus presents to his members are to be realized in the radical following that is accentuated by certain ethoses. We enumerate a few of these important ethoses:

1. Prayer

Prayer is one of the most important aspects in the life of the community in Luke-Acts. In the gospel, the example that Jesus set and his teaching on prayer receive more attention.[12] The gospel of Luke begins (Lk 1:9-10) and ends with prayer (Lk 24:53). Before Jesus teaches his disciples to pray, he himself prays. He often withdrew himself from daily tasks to pray in lonely places (Lk 5:16; 9:18; 11:1). He especially prayed before significant events in his ministry. He prays at his baptism (Lk 3:21); before choosing the twelve (Lk 6:12); before speaking to his disciples about his death (Lk 9:18); before his transfiguration (Lk 9:28-29),[13] he prays for Simon so that his faith would not fail and that he would be able to strengthen his brothers (Lk 22:31-32).

He prays about his impending death and just before his arrest (Lk 22:41-46). He also prays as he hangs on the cross; in a loud cry he commits his spirit into the hands of his Father (Lk 23:46). Most of these examples are recorded by Luke alone and they reveal Jesus facing every crisis of life by prayer. In the gospel of Matthew, Jesus gave his disciples a model prayer, commonly known as the "Lord's Prayer" (Mt 6:9-15). But in the gospel of Luke, the Lord's Prayer is taught in response to the request of the disciples to teach them to pray (Lk 11:1-4). The disciples found Jesus often spending time in prayer and so they made a spontaneous request asking him 'please teach us to pray.' Beginners

11 Ruth Benedict, *Patterns of Culture* (New York: Mentor Books, 1934), 2.

12 The terms 'prayer' and 'pray' are found 13 times in Mark and 17 times in Matthew, they are found 21 times in Luke and 25 times in Acts.

13 See Du Plessis, "The Christian Community," 77-78.

must be initiated to prayer. Jesus became the model of a praying person for his disciples. Thereafter we find him admonishing the disciples to persist in prayer (Lk 18:1-8) especially in the face of temptation (Lk 22:40-46).

Thus, following the teachings of Jesus, the first thing the eleven along with the women and Jesus' mother and brothers do after the ascension is, with one accord, devote themselves to prayer (Acts 1:14). Before the election of Matthias they pray for the ability to speak the Lord's word boldly in the face of opposition (Acts 1:15ff). After being arrested for the first time and then being released the followers of Jesus pray (Acts 4:23-32). When the seven were chosen the apostles pray and lay their hands upon them (Acts 6:6). Stephen is portrayed praying as Jesus was in his suffering and death (Acts 7:59-60). When Peter was arrested and kept in prison, prayer was made to God by the Church (Acts 12:5,12). While Paul was in prison, he was praying and singing (Acts 16:25). Throughout Acts, Peter and Paul are depicted as praying often before key events (Acts 8:15; 9:40; 10:9;11:5 and 9:11; 14:23; 16:13,16,25; 20:36; 21:5; 22:17; 28:8).[14]

In short, Luke draws his reader's attention to the importance of prayer for the Christian community. Proper response to suffering and persecution is not to escape or to take revenge on the oppressors but like Jesus, they are to remain faithful to the Lord, praying for strength to face painful opposition with the help of the Holy Spirit. The real strength of the Christian community comes from praying.[15] Clearly for Luke, prayer is seen as vital and necessary part of the Christian life both individually and corporately.[16]

2. Breaking of the Bread

Along with the baptism and prayers, the celebration of the Breaking of the Bread forms the inner life of the new community. Luke envisions Christian life as organized and indicates that the Breaking of the Bread, rooted in the ministry of Jesus is an important celebration in the early Christian community. Breaking of the Bread is the miniature of the whole life of the community, as it strengthens and supports its growth.[17] The meal that Jesus shared with his disciples the evening before he was arrested (Lk 22:7-23) created a sense of mystery and awakened hope that were forever burned into the hearts of Jesus' followers. This motif appears in the multiplication of the loaves (Lk 9:10-17) and in the Emmaus story (Lk 24:30ff). The same formula – take, bless,

14 See Twelftree, *People of the Spirit*, 33-34.

15 *Ibid*, 106-107.

16 Robert H. Stein, *Luke*, The New American Commentary: An Exegetical and Theological Exposition of Holy Scripture, Vol. 24 (Nashville, Tennesse: Broadman Press, 1992), 53.

17 See Justin Taylor, "Acts of the Apostles," *The International Bible Commentary*, Ed., William R. Farmer (Bangalore: TPI, 2004), 1587.

break and give – appears in all three pericopes (Lk 9:16; 22:19; 24:30). It was when Jesus blessed and broke and gave it the disciples that they recognized the Risen Lord.[18]

The Christian community as Luke presents it, is very much concerned with the celebration of the Breaking of the Bread. In Acts, the life of the community is seen centered on the Breaking of the Bread. Within the Jewish community, the simple act of breaking bread with another person frequently signified an important event. Friendships, covenants, contracts, alliances and marriage might all be sealed by shared bread. In addition, Israelites' religious life was marked by feasts that celebrated God's blessings. The most important was the Passover meal. Thus, after the ascension, it is not at all surprising that the mystery of Jesus' life and death was celebrated by his disciples through a commemorative meal. When the disciples looked back in later years, the events of that Last Supper evening, the words that Jesus spoke became laden with inexplicable power. It was the single moment of Jesus' life that they would re-enact again and again. The disciples believed that by performing a ritual Last supper, they expressed and somehow touched the heart and power of his life and death.[19] Thus the believers met regularly to break the bread (Acts 2:42, 46; 20:7,11), which served as a sign of encouragement for the believers. It was a continuation of the meals described in the appearances of Jesus after the resurrection.[20] Breaking of the Bread is indeed a sign of unity among the members of the community.

3. Laws and Teachings

A community that comes into existence has to follow certain guidelines. Luke maintains that the Laws and Teachings are of continuing relevance for Christians. Jesus was not simply a great expositor of the Law. He, living in the overlap between the old covenant and the new is generally obedient to the Mosaic Law, but at the same time he makes clear that he has sovereign rights both to interpret and to set aside that Law (Lk 16:16 // Mt 11:12-13). On this basis he criticizes people who develop the oral law to prove their point that denied the very heart and purpose of the Law. He categorically states that some things cannot coexist (Lk 5:33-39 – the pair of parables dealing with new and old cloth, and new and old wineskins).[21] The Law itself is never ridiculed, but

18 See Dennis M. Sweetland, "The Lord's Supper and the Lukan Community," *Biblical Theology Bulletin* 13(1983), 27.

19 See Alma E. Guinness (ed.), *Mysteries of the Bible: The Enduring Questions of the Scriptures*, Reader's Digest (Plesantville, NY: Reader's Digest Association, Inc, 1988), 324.

20 See Sweetland, "Following Jesus: Discipleship in Luke-Acts," 120-121.

21 See D.J. Moo, "Law," in *Dictionary of Jesus and the Gospels*, eds. J.B. Green, S. McKnight and I.H. Marshall (England: InterVarsity Press, 1992), 450.

is in a sense broadened or supplemented by Jesus' preaching of the kingdom characterized by love and compassion. The mission of Jesus represents the culmination of the law, not its abrogation. In fact Jesus explains how he is the fulfilment of the law and the prophets (Lk 24: 26-27, 44).

The community of Jesus in the gospel of Luke is obliged to obey the Law as interpreted by Jesus, vis-à-vis the prevailing interpretation of that time represented by the Jewish leaders. **Firstly**, he demands that his community must follow the law of love (Lk 10:25-28) thereby emphasizing the importance of following the Ten Commandments (Lk 18:19-20). It is in the dual command to 'love God' and 'neighbour' that Jesus found the heart of the Law, and he used these basic demands to interpret and apply the Law. He specially criticizes those who are judgmental of sinners, outsiders and marginal Jews. Those with a highly restricted sense of who belongs in God's covenant (e.g. only those learned the law, the observant etc.) are corrected by Jesus and told to practice a more inclusive acceptance into the covenant community. So 'love' takes on a special meaning; inclusiveness and respect for less honourable and less perfect members of God's covenant. This is made evident in Jesus' instructions on who should be invited to share one's table. The elite tend to accept only other elite as companions at table. But Jesus commanded a more open table and so a more open covenant: "when you give feast invite the poor, the maimed, the lame, the blind" (Lk 14:13). Jesus himself dramatized this openness by repeatedly eating with sinners and offering them covenant fellowship (Lk 5:29; 15:1-2; 19:5-7; 24:29-30).[22]

Secondly, the teaching, not the Law, is the focus of the Gospels, and the Law remains authoritative for the disciple of Jesus only insofar as it is taken up into Jesus' own teaching.[23] The most beneficial teaching of Jesus is found in his teaching on the plain, which is called the 'Beatitudes.' Unlike Matthew who gives Jesus' sermon on the mount to the disciples in general before the election of the twelve, Luke gives his sermon on the plain after the election of the twelve, keeping them as the target group. He does not use obscure language; his commands are clearly stated. It contains the core of his moral teaching. His statements are clearly applicable to Christian communal life. These statements became a way of reaching into the hearts of those hearers, challenging their basic values and setting them on a lifelong quest for God's kingdom. His teaching revealed a morality beyond the letter of the Law. He spoke about the lifestyle of those who intend to live in the kingdom. He challenges them to make a complete change of heart and life. Practising

22 See Neyrey, *Christ Is Community*, 119-120.

23 See Moo, "Law," 460.

religion certainly involves behaviour but it also goes beyond an outward show of spirituality.[24]

To make sure that his teachings touched the heart of his hearers, Jesus put great emphasis on stories which are called parables. They were full of subjects easily recognizable in the everyday life of ancient Palestine –fishing nets, seeds, wheat, vineyard, coin, sheep, servants, widows, farmers and kings. The kernel of the parable is a message of comparison; hence there is always more than one level of meaning in a parable. The story may be entertaining in itself, but it always points beyond itself to something deeper that Jesus wanted his audience to perceive more clearly. He wanted a simple story to become a door that allowed access to the mystery of the kingdom. Parables avail the possibility of self-discovery and restored love relationship. Through parables, Jesus directed the attention of his disciples to shift their routine life to a transformed life.[25] In the Acts, the need of the time was Hope. Therefore, the preaching and teaching center on the resurrection of Jesus.

4. Renunciation

There is widely recognized concern about the relationship between the Christian community and wealth in the writings of Luke. We assume that his addressees consisted of members of relatively good socio-economic standing. As concerns the formation of the community and renunciation, we see two demands in the Lukan writings: **firstly**, Jesus demands that any member who wishes to be part of his community must leave "everything" and follow him (Lk 18:22). The most common view among Jews even into the NT times was that wealth was a sign of God's special favour and that poverty was likely a sign of God's disapproval (Prov 10:15). The Pharisees, for example, believed this and opposed Jesus (Lk 16:14) because of his contrasting view of money and wealth (Lk 6:20; 16:13; 18:24-25). It is almost clear that rather than being content merely to rehearse earlier Christian traditions (Markan and Q periscopes) devoted to wealth, Luke had his own particular views to express.

A number of redactional changes point to this concern. Luke adds to Mark's description of the call of the first disciples the detail that they *left everything* (ἀφέντες πάντα) to follow Jesus (Mk 1:18-20// Lk 5:11). In the call of Levi too (Mk 2:14// Lk 5:28), Luke adds the detail that he too *left everything* (καταλιπων παντα). Similarly, the rich young man (Mk 10:21//Lk 18:22) is told to *sell all* he has (πάντα ὅσα ἔχεις πώλησον). Besides this, he includes many other relevant passages not found elsewhere in the NT.[26] He cautions the

24 See Guinness (ed.), *Mysteries of the Bible,* 301.

25 *Ibid*, 304-305.

26 The more important of these are the Magnificat (1:47-55); the preaching of the John the Baptist (3:10-14); the woes of the rich (6:24-26); the exhortation to lend without hoping for

rich by pronouncing woes (Lk 6:24) for they live in a false sense of security (Lk 12:15ff) that leads them into all kinds of troubles, temptations and harmful desires. For this reason, no Christian should be driven by a desire to get rich. Through these redactions and additions, Luke presents the radical attitude expected of a member who wishes to be a member of Jesus' community.[27]

Secondly, Jesus demands that mere renunciation is no good, rather it must lead to love others by sharing one's wealth. This is the meaning of right use of wealth. There are three major sections of teaching about possessions in the Jerusalem travel narrative (12:13-34; 16:1-31; 18:18-30). Repeated points in these three sections bring out the central emphases in Jesus' teaching on this subject. The rich estate owner who experienced a bumper crop was severely reproached by God for he laid up treasure for himself but was not rich with God (Lk 12:16-21). The command to the disciples in 12:33 "sell your possessions and give charity" is basically equivalent to Jesus' command to the rich man in 18:22 "sell all that you have and give to the poor." By sharing riches with others, we honour the less fortunate or the non-elite who possess full status as covenant members. Comparably, the wicked steward was told to face a severe audit by his landlord (16:1-2). He was later praised (Lk 16:8).

One may infer that he spent his riches and surplus on members in need. This principle is dramatized most clearly in the subsequent parable of Lazarus and the rich man; God regarded Lazarus as a full member of the covenant, although the rich man did not; for this failure of love, God did not regard the rich man as a member.[28] These parables do not concentrate on money and its use; rather on relationship between a disciple and his love for the poor. One must show openness, respect and love to the poor, the sinners, the tax collectors the unclean and other folk who are considered marginal to the covenant membership. Through all these commands Jesus enjoins on his followers an inclusive openness to other covenant members.[29]

---

repayment (6:34-35); the friend at midnight (11:5-8), the parable of the rich fool (12:13-21), the instruction on whom to invite to banquets (14:12-14), the connection between discipleship and total renunciation of possessions (14:33), the parable of the unjust steward (16:1-9), the accusation against the money-loving Pharisees (16:14), the story of the rich man and Lazarus (16:19-31) and the conversion of Zacchaeus (19:1-10). In Acts, there are descriptions of the donations of property by richer members of the community for the use of all (2:44-45; 4:32-37 and the difficulties which arose in connection with this 5:1-11; 6:1-4).

27 Luke does not portray possessions as evil in themselves, nor do they necessarily prevent a positive response to the word of God (cf. Lk 18:28). But one must be convinced and choose between serving God and serving mammon (Lk 16:13). Wealth can be used for good, but in many cases it creates priorities which prohibit the rich from doing the will of God. See, Sweetland, "Following Jesus: Discipleship in Luke-Acts,"122-123.

28 See Neyrey, *Christ Is Community,* 120-121.

29 *Ibid*, 122.

The command to sell and give is not obsolete after the ascension of Jesus. In Acts, Luke presents several positive examples of almsgiving and describes the early Jerusalem community sharing wealth and possessions. The statement that the Jerusalem community was "having all things in common" does not mean that a new legal system was established involving collective ownership, which would end the right of individuals to sell property. Rather, it is a regularized system of charity in which those with saleable assets would liquidate their property in order to care for the needs of the poor (Acts 2:45; 4:34-37). The expressions for 'sell' and 'distribute' in Acts 2:45 (πιπρασκω and διαμεριζω) and in Acts 4:34-35 (πωλεω and διαδιδωμι) correspond to the commands of Jesus in Lk 12:33 (πωλεω and διδωμι) and 18:22 (πωλεω and διαδιδωμι). Even though the situation of Jesus' followers has changed with the existence of a settled community, the early Jerusalem church found a way to obey Jesus' teaching about possessions in its new context.[30] It appears that this conception of actual renunciation of one's property as a requirement for discipleship during the time of Jesus' earthly wayfaring (Lk 6:20;18:22) is now replaced during the time of the church by a *Willingness* to part with one's property for the good of the community. It was the concrete manifestation of their profound union in faith.[31]

5. Fellowship

The community of Jesus is marked by some special traits of fellowship. **Firstly**, *the community is pluralistic and inclusive*. At the very beginning of the gospel, we see that traditional observant Jews like Elizabeth (Lk 1:40-44), Simeon and Anna accept Jesus (Lk 2:25,38). There are also other Jews who are perhaps not so observant, but who likewise join the community of Jesus, namely, Peter, James, John and others (Lk 5:1-11; 6:12-16), as did certain women (Lk 8:1-3). The community extends itself to include the marginal Jews, whom the orthodox and observant would place on the fringes of the covenant. They are the Jews, who were "unclean," by virtue of defiling illness. They are ministered to by Jesus; lepers (Lk 5:12-16), cripples (Lk 5:17-26), and the blind (Lk 7:21). In Luke's gospel, we also find, Jesus giving specific instructions to invite the marginal people of Jewish society to one's feasts, thus indicating their full acceptance and complete status as the authentic members of the covenant (Lk 14:13). Jesus conducts a special mission to tax collectors. He associates freely with them (Lk 5:29-30; 7:29,34; 15:1; cf. 18:9-14; 19:1-10). While association with sinners was something to be avoided according

30 See Robert C. Tannehill, *The Narrative Unity of Luke-Acts: A Literary Interpretation*, Vol. I: The Gospel According to Luke (Philadelphia: Fortress Press, 1986), 247-248.

31 See Paul J. Bernadicou, "Christian Community According to Luke," *Worship* 44 (1970), 214-215.

to the Pharisees, Luke presents Jesus as operating on a different principle, associating with them (Lk 7:36-50; cf. 6:32-34). Besides favourably using a Samaritan's act of kindness in a teaching story which expands the concept of neighbour far beyond the members of the covenant community (Lk 10:29-37), Jesus healed also a Samaritan leper (Lk 17:14-18).

This inclusive vision of Jesus is carried into the Christian community. Jesus commands a mission which would include Jews, Samaritans and the rest (Acts 1:8). The prophecy of Joel is fulfilled in the first Pentecost community. It is an inclusive community as there are sons and daughters, men servants and maid servants, young and old, all who receive the Spirit (Acts 2:16-21). The apostolic preaching leads thousands of Jews to accept Jesus (Acts 2:41, 47; 4:4). The Ethiopian eunuch is baptized and given Christian membership (Acts 8:26-38). Paul, son of a Pharisee, a strict religious becomes a follower of Jesus (Acts 9, 22, 26). The rejected lame are healed in Jesus' name (Acts 3:1-10; 9:32-35; 14:8-11).[32] Peter and others initially protested against the inclusion of the gentiles as that was against the way they formerly understood covenant membership. It took a heavenly vision to convince Peter that God's covenant included both Jews and gentiles (Acts 10-11). Whether the new converts were to be circumcised and made to keep the traditional law of the Mosaic covenant was discussed in the Council of Jerusalem. The assembly decided against those distinguishing Jewish customs (Acts 15). The mission of Paul was completely towards making gentiles believers in Christ (Acts 13-28). So there is consciousness of a major change towards community of inclusiveness.[33]

Secondly, *equality is the hallmark of a Christian community*. Jesus once spoke about his disciples' conduct toward one another in such an authoritative way that this instruction was to be forever the rule for their community. The occasion was the disciples' argument about which of them was the greatest, as everyone's place in the community depended upon his greatness. Jesus took a child and illustrated the aim to which they were to turn. Thereby Jesus demanded from the disciples the renunciation of any exhibition of their strength or assertion of their significance, not only in their dealings with God but also in their dealings with one another (Lk 9:46-48/Mk 9:33-37/ Mt 18:1-5). Greatness belonged to the one who possesses the heart of a child. This rule had greater significance for the disciple's common life.[34]

In the economy of salvation, Lukan Jesus makes salvation universal (Lk 2:10; 2:29-32; 24:47). He traces the genealogy of Jesus to Adam (Lk 3:23-28); he calls attention to gentiles (parable of Good Samaritan; story of the Ten

32 See Neyrey, *Christ Is Community*, 108-110.

33 *Ibid*, 105-106.

34 See Adolf Schlatter, *The History of the Christ: The Foundation of New Testament Theology*, Trans. Andreas J. Koestenberger (Grand Rapids, MI: Baker Books, 1997), 298-299.

Lepers etc.). The inferior status of women in the Jewish society of Jesus' day is well known. It is widely recognized that in Luke's two-volume work, stories about a man are frequently paralleled by stories about a woman. In suggesting that equality exists between men and women, Luke is more progressive than his Jewish or Greco-Roman contemporaries. Women are in association with Jesus, just as the men are (Lk 8:1-3). Luke shows that women received the good news and helped to promote it in the church. [35] This aspect of equality of the members is continued in the early church. The infant community of men and women prayed together (Acts 1:14); received the Spirit together (Acts 2:16-21); Jews and gentiles are equally the members of the new covenant community.

Thirdly, *Table-Fellowship or the banquet is a most common biblical motif* that describes the community. It towers among others as a very significant characteristic of a community. It is both a source and a communion among persons, and between persons and God (Ex 24:3-11; Deut 27:7; Ps 50:5). Eating together establishes a covenant communion on a purely human level (Gen 26:26-31; 31:45-55; Josh 9:3-19). The shared meal commits one to a bond of loyalty so that one who betrays the community with whom he feasts is especially culpable (Gen 43:32; Ps 41:10).[36] In Luke's gospel the banquet motif is employed to communicate the multifaceted significance of the people of God, in a type of primitive ecclesiology: i. there exists a ranking at tables which symbolizes status (Lk 14:7-11; 22:24); ii. Table-talk also becomes a mode of teaching (Lk 5:29-32; 7:36-50; 10:38-42; 11:37-41; 14:7, 12; 22:14-38); iii. eating and drinking also indicates a symbol of luxury, positive and negative (Lk 6:24-25; 12:19, 45-46; 13:27-30; 14:15; 15:1-2; 16:19-31; 17:26-29; 21:34); iv. table service connotes community service (Lk 4:38-39; 7:36-50; 10:38-42; 12:42-46; 17:7-10; 22:24-27; Acts 2:46; 6:1-6) v. and table fellowship is a symbol for community fellowship (Lk 14:16-24). Among these, the primary function of the table meal is to maintain, grow and deepen social relationships. It promotes group identity and solidarity. The parable of the banquet Lk 14:16-24 exhibits this theme very prominently.[37]

As is the case with Jesus[38], the disciples are also instructed to welcome the needy at their table. Socially marginalized and the lower classes in particular

---

35 See Dennis M. Sweetland, "Luke the Christian," in *New Views on Luke and Acts*, ed. Earl Richard (Collegeville, MN: A Michael Glazier Book, 2018), 60-61.

36 See John Navonne, "The Lucan Banquet Community" *Bible Today* (1970 Dec), 155-161.

37 See Jacob Mullor, *Demolishing the Divide: A Lukan Reading of Fraternity* (Kochi, Kerala: Karunikan Books, 2011), 128. See also Dennis E. Smith, "Table Fellowship as a Literary Motif in the Gospel of Luke" *Journal of Biblical Literature* 106 (1987), 617-637.

38 It is in the table fellowship with Levi the tax collector that we hear the statement from Jesus: I have not come to call the righteous, but sinners to the repentance (Lk 5:29-32). Again we see Jesus at the dinner table of a Pharisee, where he offered forgiveness to the sinner

should be invited to share in this fellowship (Lk 14:21-24), but it should also be extended to and enjoyed with all people (Lk 9:2-5; 10:4-12). Meals in the community are therefore also seen as type scenes where people can be included in a relationship with Jesus, or excluded from the fellowship because of their rejection of him.[39] There are several features in Luke-Acts which alert us to the fact that Jewish-gentile table fellowship had been a matter of intense controversy in the early church. The most prominent indication comes in the account of the conversion of Cornelius in Acts 10-11. The central issue in this narrative is not only that the gospel has been preached to the gentiles but also the far more particular fact of great ethnic and social significance that Peter had lived and eaten with them (Act 11:3). This problem was resolved in the Council of Jerusalem.[40]

Fourthly, *the Community of Jesus and the Church is characterized by Joy*. Throughout Luke-Acts different expressions for joy are found. The note of joy is sounded no less than ten times in the very first chapter of Luke about the birth of Jesus and John the Baptist. To Zachariah it was told, 'your heart will thrill with joy and many will be glad that he is born' (Lk 1:14). As Elizabeth meets Mary, the unborn John the Baptist leaps for joy (Lk 1:44). Mary responds by saying that her spirit rejoices in the Saviour (Lk 1:47). Elizabeth's neighbours and relatives were as delighted as she was over the birth of John the Baptist (Lk 1:58). The angels announce to the shepherds the good news of great joy (Lk 2:10). The new joy brought into the world by Jesus finds expression in his teaching. Beatitudes is one such example. True happiness does not lie in the amount of possessions (Lk 12:15). Festive joy occurs within the parable of the rich fool (Lk 12:19; 13:17; 14:14f). The seventy (two) return from their mission with joy and are taught that they should be happier to have their names written in heaven (Lk 10:17,20). Repentance and acceptance of the invitation to salvation are the basis of joy according to the three parables of the lost sheep, the lost son, the lost coin (Lk 15:1-32) and also in the story of Zaccaheus (Lk 19:1-10). The crowd of disciples also rejoices over the triumphant entry of Jesus to Jerusalem (Lk 19:37). After the return of two disciples of Emmaus event, Jesus appears to the disciples and they disbelieved for joy (Lk 24:41).[41] Thus Luke's gospel ends on a joyous note (Lk 24:49-53).

---

woman (Lk 7:36-50). Jesus is further seen at the dinner table of the Pharisee challenging the Pharasaic purity laws (Lk 11:37-54).

39 See Du Plessis, "The Christian Community," 74-75.

40 See Philip Francis Esler, *Community and Gospel in Luke-Acts: The Social and Political Motivations of Lucan Theology*, SNTSMS 57 (New York, NY: Cambridge University Press, 1987), 93.

41 See William G. Morrice, *Joy in the New Testament* (Exeter, Devon: Paternoster Press, 1984), 91-92.

There is a long list of events and occasions related to joy in the Acts. On the day of Pentecost Peter spoke of the resurrection and the resultant gladness and joy (Acts 2:24-28); the first Christians are said to dine together in gladness (Acts 2:46). Peter and John rejoiced on leaving the Jewish council that they had been counted worthy to suffer dishonour for the sake of Jesus (Acts 5:41). Philip's ministry in preaching, healing and exorcism in Samaria was received with much joy (Acts 8:8) and the converted eunuch went on his way rejoicing after being baptized (Acts 8:39). Rhoda was joyful on hearing Peter outside the door (Acts 12:14). The gentiles rejoiced to hear Paul's message and they were filled with the Holy Spirit and joy (Acts 13: 48, 52). The reports of Paul and Barnabas gave joy to the brethren (Acts 15:3). The Jailer at Philippi rejoiced with his household as he became a believer in God (Acts 16:34), Paul and Barnabas describe God satisfying their hearers' hearts with food and gladness (Acts 14:17). [42]

6. Crises

Externally, the community of Jesus appears to be a triumphant and trouble-free community. Thus a call to emulate this community is fulfilling. However, the community that is formed with the ethoses prescribed by Jesus is not free from crisis. Even from a superficial reading of Luke-Acts, we need to admit that the narratives report a plethora of problems in the community. This crisis could be explained on the basis of enemies, persecutions and failures.

Enemies: the crisis in the community was caused both by internal and external forces. Jesus himself had opponents outside the community who can be identified as Pharisees, Sadducees, Scribes, leaders of the synagogues, High Priests and priests – in short, the leaders of the Jewish society. The resentment felt towards Jesus is developed in several episodes throughout the Lukan story, especially regarding the Law (Lk 5:33-6:11), and his authority (Lk 20:1-47). This hostility against Jesus constantly grows in intensity, until it reaches its climax with the trial of Jesus and his eventual crucifixion.[43] Besides the external enemies, the enemies from within could be pointed out as Judas Iscariot and even Peter. Immediately after the words of institution, Jesus announces that the one who will betray him is present at the table. Judas remained and participated in the Breaking of the Bread only to be singled out later.[44] Peter though he denies about wanting to betray Jesus, he does betray his master. Luke occasionally mentions conflicts between the disciples (Lk 9:46-48; 22:24-30); between the disciples and other followers (Lk 9:49-50); and between the disciples and the Samaritans (Lk 9:51-56). Jesus teaches how

42 See Twelftree, *People of the Spirit*, 108-109.

43 See Du Plessis, "The Christian Community," 61-62.

44 See Sweetland, "The Lord's Supper and the Lukan Community," 25.

his disciples are to solve conflicts (Lk 17:1-6).[45] The early church was not free from crises. Ananias and Sapphira's greed and deception cause Peter to pronounce punishment (Acts 5:1-12). There is dissatisfaction concerning the table service to the Jewish and Hellenist widows in Jerusalem (Acts 6:1-6). Similarly the issue of circumcision of the gentiles caused unrest among the members of the community until it was settled in the council of Jerusalem (Acts 15). Paul was the leader of the opposition and even found it necessary "to oppose Peter to his face" (Gal 2:11) on the issue.

Failure in Mission: Every community involves mission. But this mission is not always fully successful. There is a hint of failure of mission in Luke-Acts. One of the hints of failure is the mission in the synagogue in Nazareth. Those present in the synagogue were filled with rage, wanted to drive Jesus out of the town and hurl him off the cliff (Lk 4:16-30). The disciples, especially the twelve really did not grasp the message and purpose of Jesus despite being in his company all the time. In Acts 1:6 it appears that Jesus' mission was a failure because the disciples question Jesus, 'when will you restore the kingdom?[46] Despite the success of mission, Paul's missionary activities are met with severe opposition. In Damascus, Antioch of Pisidia, Iconium, Lystra, Philippi, Thessalonica, Beroea, Athens, Corinth, Ephesus and Jerusalem, in all these places, to some extent mission was failure due to instigation and accusations.

Persecution: It is reasonable to assume that persecution was important in what Luke wanted to say about the life of the Church. At the beginning of the gospel the topic of persecution is introduced in Simeon's otherwise joyous song that the child is destined to be a sign that will be opposed (Lk 2:34). That the opposition will be from his own people is presaged in Jesus being said to be the reason for the falling and rising of many in Israel (cf. 12:51-53; Isa 8:14-15). Also echoing the OT passages, Simeon says to Mary, 'a sword will pierce through your own soul also', telling not only of the anguish that Mary will suffer over her son's rejection but also of his death (Lk 2:35). Then throughout his gospel, Luke portrays Jesus predicting his fate, suffering rejection and eventual death (4:28-29; 9:22;44;52-53; 18:31-34; 23:44-48).[47] Luke also develops the theme of suffering of the followers of Jesus. In Lk 21:12-19, we find that before the 'end,' there will be persecution. "They will lay their hands on you and persecute you, delivering you up to the synagogues

45 See Du Plessis, "The Christian Community," 60.

46 See, Twelftree, *People of the Spirit*, 180-181. In addition to the above, Twelftree adds the story of the call of first disciples (Lk 5:1-11), in which the response of Simon "master we toiled all night and took nothing" is considered as a failure of Jesus' mission. Again in the story of the mission of the seventy the statement "harvest is plentiful, but the labourers are few' (Lk 10:2) is also marked as failure of the mission of Jesus. We see eisegesis here.

47 See Twelftree, *People of the Spirit*, 101-102.

and prisons, and you will be brought up before kings and governors for my sake" (Lk 21:12). Family and friends will hand over the followers of Jesus to be put to death (Lk 21:16) by both Jews and gentiles (Lk 12:4-12).

In Acts, we find a litany of stories of whipping, trumped-up trial, suffering, persecution and death. Peter and John are arrested and taken before the Jewish Sanhedrin (Acts 4:1-22); the apostles are imprisoned (Acts 5:18); Stephen is stoned to death (Acts 7:54-60). Persecution in Jerusalem scatters all disciples but the apostles; Saul ravages the church (Acts 8:1-3); Herod lays violent hands on some who belong to the Church and then kills James by the sword (Acts 12:1-2). There are also stories of the persecution and imprisonment of Paul, Silas, Barnabas and Stephen, the archetypal suffering – followers of Jesus.[48]

Ironically, the effect of persecution is the spread of the Christian witnesses and communities. Often, the Christian presence in a new territory was on account of forceful expulsion from the old territory (centripetalism to centrigugalism). In addition, there is a show of strength and joy at the face of the suffering. Expressions of joy resulted from seeing persecution as an opportunity to show and bring honour to the name of Christ. At times it leads to prayer of the heart (4:23-31). Luke does not present persecution as the main point to focus but concentrates on believers' fidelity in living the life of witness.[49]

7. Mission-Witness

The Synoptic gospels climax not with resurrection appearances but with a mission command. Jesus was himself a missionary. His mission was to proclaim the Good News of the Kingdom of God (Lk 4:43). A call given to be the members of the community of Jesus includes a missionary responsibility. Luke deviates from his source (Mk 6:6-13), and informs the reader that Jesus sent out the twelve specifically "to preach the kingdom of God" (Lk 9:2) in addition to other apostolic activities. Besides the mission of the twelve (Lk 9:1-6), Luke is the only gospel writer to mention the mission of the seventy (Lk 10:1-16). These 70/72 missionaries like the twelve, are closely associated with the mission of Jesus. They use the given power and authority to exorcise, heal, and preach the kingdom of God (Lk 10:9,11).[50] Jesus also refers to the future missionary activity when he says to Peter, "henceforth you will be catching men" (Lk 5:10). However, the more prominent and ultimate mission responsibility of his followers is to be a "Witness." Giving witness to the risen

48 *Ibid*, 102.

49 See John J. Kilgallen, "Persecution in the Acts of the Apostles," in *Luke and Acts*, eds. Gerald O'Collins and Gilberto Marconi (Mahwah, N.J: Paulist Press, 1993), 155ff.

50 See Sweetland, "Following Jesus: Discipleship in Luke-Acts," 114.

Christ is an important constituent of the community in Luke-Acts (Lk 24:48; Acts 1:8).[51]

Very often we think that the mission of Jesus was to perform miracles. But these miracles in most cases have a temporary value. The real mission of Jesus was to be a witness to God's love. He became a witness of the love and compassion of God. The miracles he performed are not meant to prove his strength and power over others but rather to tell us how God has been gracious to people through him. Prior to commanding his community members to be witnesses, he himself lived a life of witness. He himself received baptism (Lk 3:21-22), he prayed before asking others to pray (5:16; 6:12–13; 9:18, 29; 10:21–22; 11:1) he showed compassion (Lk 7:13; cf. 10:33; 15:20) and he forgave his enemies (Lk 23:34 cf. 5:24; 17:3-4; 24:47). Having shown the path of being a witness to the Kingdom values, he commands his disciples to do the same.

What does it mean to bear witness? Bearing witness involves "a total re-enactment of the journey of Jesus, including his suffering in Jerusalem. The followers of Jesus are not witnesses because they suffer and die but they suffer and die because they are witnesses."[52] In his final mission command, Jesus assigns his followers to be witnesses to the proclamation of repentance and forgiveness (Lk 24:47). Yet again in the command given in the Acts, there is a re-emphasis on being a witness once they are clothed with power from on high (Lk 24:49; Acts 1:8). Those that are called to be witnesses receive God's power which will enable them to fulfil their task (Lk 12:11-12; 21:15; 24:49). This promise is important, because hostility and severe persecution will meet their testimony (Lk 21:12-19). Thus the disciples are called to endure sufferings because of their convictions and their loyalty to Jesus (Lk 6:22; cf. 6:26; 9:1-6; 9:57-62; 10:1-16; 12:11-12; 21:12-19). Jesus says, when the followers will be persecuted and brought before kings and governors for his sake, that will be the time to witness (Lk 21:13).

Initially, the role of a witness is exclusive to the apostles; it eventually includes Paul, Stephen and others (Acts 7:55-56; 22:15-20; 26:16). In Acts 10:43 Peter speaks of all prophets as witnesses. This extends the way to the whole church to be witnesses. In their commitment to Jesus, the Christian community should follow their leader's example and be steadfast in the face of suffering. Persecution is in fact an opportunity to witness (Lk 12:11; 21:13-15). Those who stood by Jesus in his trials will be richly rewarded (Lk 22:28-30).[53] Hence, we find the Christian missionaries Peter (2:32; 3;15; 10:39-41;

51 *Ibid*, 111.

52 Twelftree, *People of the Spirit*, 197-198.

53 See Du Plessis, "The Christian Community," 77.

cf. 5:29-32) and Paul (13:30-31; 22:14-15,20; cf. 20;21,24; 23;11) frequently claiming that they are witnesses.

Conclusion

The meaning and the formation of a community can be better understood if we analyze its characteristics. It is these characteristics that decide whether a group is a community or not. First of all, there must be a founder with a vision to form a community. He or she will then invite some to be the members or some volunteer themselves to be the members. They are accepted into the community through an initiation of baptism. A group of people forms community only when they reside in a definite territory; but this territory need not be fixed forever. A group of people like nomadic persons may change their habituations. However, what binds the community together is the ethoses of the community because of which the community experiences unity and solidarity.

Analyzing the community formation in the Luke-Acts, we find that besides the external elements of a community formation, we have seen that Jesus as well as his disciples in the early church were not mere founders of a community, but they were witnesses and their very life also attracted many to become the members of their community. The presence of the founder in a founding community yields rich dividends. The Lukan community is built on the ethoses set by Jesus, namely, Prayer, Breaking of the Bread, Laws and Teachings, Renunciation, Fellowship and a Mission to be a Witness. All these cannot be achieved without crises and struggles. Through the hardships, members are refined to be witnesses.

From our study, we understand that there is an inclusive believing community in Luke-Acts. Unimportant places and persons are recognized and given dignity in Luke-Acts. Imposing the ideas and attitudes of one community or an individual can be one of the greatest obstacles to Christian credibility and Christian proclamation. Hence, one must be ready for mental, structural and theological changes. The concept of inclusive community in Luke-Acts may not be purely a Lukan creation. Luke could have been influenced by the Hebrew texts which enumerates clearly that God of the OT was indeed an inclusive God and his community was from a diverse crowd. Hence there is a succession of thought from OT to Luke-Acts. We have seen a number of traits inherent to the formation of a believing community which gives it a unique identity. All these traits culminate in the believers becoming witnesses. Knowledge of the traits has no bearing, if it does not show itself in action. Crises and persecutions are means to leave the comfort zone and explore other areas in search of likely believers. Salvation is made universal and it is the gift and task of the disciples to become channels of this salvation.

10

Quest for Identity in Community Formation in the Gospel of John and its Relevance to the Indian Context

C. Gregory Thomas Basker

The question of identity, or rather, the 'quest' of it, seems to pervade the Gospel of John. Questions, like "*who* is Jesus", "*who* are the disciples in relation to Jesus", "how is the believing community defined", form a large part of the narrative of the Gospel. The Johannine community has been variously defined and described by a host of scholars including, Brown, Cullmann, Culpepper, Ringe, and Carter.[1] However, the question is still open and there has not been any final consensus among scholars on the nature of the Johannine community. This paper is an attempt to understand the 'community' in the Gospel of John from an anthropological, trans-ethnic, -lingual, -racial and -religious perspective. It is my contention that the message of the Fourth Gospel in terms of the quest for identity or community formation, is nothing but a call to *transcend* the idea of "identity" or "community formation".

---

1 Raymond Brown, *The Community of the Beloved Disciple: The Life, Loves and Hates of an Individual Church in New Testament Times,* New York/Ramsey/Toronto: Paulist Press, 1979; Oscar Cullmann, The Johannine Circle: Its Place in Judaism, among the disciples of Jesus and in early Christianity (London: SCM Press Ltd., 1976); R.A. Culpepper, *John, the Son of Zebedee: The Life of a Legend*, Edinburgh: T & T Clark, 2000; Sharon H. Ringe, *Wisdom's Friends: Community and Christology in the Fourth Gospel*, (Louisville, Kentucky: Westminster John Knox Press, 1999); Warren Carter, *John and Empire: Initial Explorations*, (New York/London: T & T Clark, 2008)

The essay is divided into three parts. In the first section, the paper seeks to understand the 'Johannine community' from an anthropological perspective in order to derive meaning outside the ethnic, racial and political realms. Here, only the community of the disciples along with Jesus is considered. Second, there is an attempt to redefine 'identity' in the Fourth Gospel. And finally, the paper represents a few Indian readings of the Gospel of John with a view to presenting an anthropological understanding of identity in John's Gospel.

1. Anthropological Understanding of the Johannine Community

John's Gospel explains the history of Jesus differently from the Synoptics, both chronologically and geographically. The Synoptics represent only about one year of Jesus' ministry/life, which takes place to a large extent in Galilee. Jesus travels only once to the Passover feast in Jerusalem, and he is captured and arrested, tried and executed there. In John, one sees the activity of Jesus stretched to more than two years. There is a frequent change of place between East Jordan, Galilee and Judea and central Jerusalem. Undoubtedly, Jerusalem is emphasized. To the question as to which of the accounts is more historical, Synoptics or John, Wengst opines that John could be more historically valid, since it is consistent with the then customs of religious Galilean Jews in the background of the pilgrimage to Jerusalem.[2]

1.1. Community of the Disciples vis-à-vis Jesus

The fundamental question has always been, "Does the term 'disciple' (μαθητής) always refer to one of the twelve or does it have a broader connotation?" It is now widely accepted that in John's Gospel, μαθητής does not always refer to the Twelve.[3] Garvie believes that the "Twelve," who were constant companions of Jesus did not accompany him everywhere because there was a circle of disciples in Judea who, due to the hostility of Jewish rulers preferred to remain in secrecy.[4] Hence, when disciples are mentioned in John's Gospel, we cannot assume at once that the twelve are meant. In support of Garvie, Brown raises a question: "We have not heard of Jesus' disciples being with him since ch. vi in Galilee. If these disciples are the twelve, this is the first

2 Klaus Wengst, *Das Johannesevangelium*, Vol.I, (Stuttgart: Kohlhammer, 2000), 33, footnote 19

3 Contra Bultmann who states that except in certain places (e.g.2:1-12 NRSV) when the combination of narratives are taken seriously (for only five are called in 1:35-51), "there can be no doubt that in the Gospel, μαθηταὶ refers to the traditional twelve". (Rudolf Bultmann, *The Gospel of John: A Commentary*. Tr. by G.R Beasley-Murray, R.W.N.Hoare, & J.K. Riches, (Philadelphia: The Westminster Press, 1971) 115, footnote 5

4 Alfred E. Garvie, *The Beloved Disciple: Studies of the Fourth Gospel*, (London: Hodder and Stoughton Ltd., 1922), 130.

indication that they came up to Jerusalem with Jesus. Or are they the obscure Judean disciples of vii 3?"[5]

Following this, other instances can also be cited: the 'disciples' in 7:3 (NRSV) cannot be proved to refer to the twelve. Again in 9:2 we are not sure that John refers to the twelve. Consequently, the "Twelve" did not possess any ethnic or racial significance, in order to be chosen. The choice was freely made. This aspect could be confirmed by how John portrays them.[6]

a) The Twelve did not choose Jesus but Jesus chose them (15:16);
b) They cannot come to Jesus except drawn by the Father (6:44);
c) In spite of their long companionship with Jesus, they fail to understand the true subject of his revelation (14:9);
d) When they think their faith has been perfected, they receive the devastating reply: Do you now believe?" Jesus replied. [32] "A time is coming and in fact has come when you will be scattered, each to your own home. You will leave me all alone. Yet I am not alone, for my Father is with me. (16:31 – 32)

The Fourth Gospel, therefore features the community of disciples as a significant group which accompanies Jesus after its 'call' (2:2, 11, 17; cf.1:37 – 43) and is involved in a deep relationship with him. Hence, the concept of 'call' bears a lot of significance here.

1.2. Jesus and the Beloved Disciple

The Beloved Disciple (BD) plays a distinct role in John's Gospel (13:23-25; 19:26-27, 35; 20:2-10; 21:7, 20-24) It is an agreed opinion that the BD was both a real historical person as well as one who had "representative, paradigmatic, or symbolic significance in John."[7] He is the ideal disciple, who has no misunderstandings, loved by Jesus and reclining on his chest, indicating not only favoured position and intimacy, but also recalls Jesus' relationship to the Father in 1:18. It is observed that, even as Jesus was "in the bosom" of the Father and revealed him, so the BD is able to make Jesus known.[8]

The theory that the BD is a model disciple is further proved because it is to him that Jesus offers the responsibility of his earthly mother at his crucifixion. The BD's relationship with Jesus can be likened to sibling kinship or something that involved consanguinity. He is first introduced not as the

5 Raymond Brown. *The Gospel According to John*. AB, Vol. 1, (Garden City, New York: Doubleday & Company, Inc., 1966) 371.

6 C.K. Barrett, *The Gospel According to St. John: An Introduction with Commentary and Notes on the Greek Text*, (London: SPCK, 1955) 80.

7 R. A. Culpepper, *Anatomy of the Fourth Gospel: A Study in Literary Design* (Philadelphia: Fortress Press, 1983) 121.

8 Against Barrett *John,* 373.

one whom Jesus loved but the one "reclining close to the breast of Jesus" (ἐν τῷ κόλπῳ τοῦ Ἰησοῦ, 13:23). The intimacy is further enhanced by the characteristically Eastern way of sitting (especially of the BD) – instead of being seated about a Table (*a` la Leonardo da Vinci*!), the company was reclining on cushions.

1.3. Jesus and Judas Iscariot

Judas' status as one of the Twelve is always emphasized in John, as also in Mk.14:10, 18, 20, and with it Jesus' foreknowledge of what he is about to do. In all Synoptic Gospels, Judas is mentioned as the one who turned traitor (10:4; Mk.3:19; Lk.6:16), and John does the same.[9] Judas' betrayal is portrayed as an act being induced by Satan himself (13:2; cf.Lk.22:3). John introduces Judas as the betrayer (6:64; cf.21:20). It is true that John does not attribute any psychological or political motivations for Judas' actions. Judas does not betray Jesus for money – the silver is not mentioned in John – though he was guilty of pilfering from the common purse (12:6). It is important to note that John's characterization of Judas attains greater depth by his assertion that Judas, along with the other disciples, was given by the Father to Jesus (17:12; cf.6:65).[10] Hence, Brown writes: "Judas' betrayal has an air of inevitability; this is not a denial of free will but reflects the inevitability of the plan of salvation."[11]

Consequently, it may be surmised that both the BD and Judas Iscariot, in addition to having their historical and specific identities, also appear to fulfil a representative role in the Fourth Gospel. Whereas the former is a classic example of how a disciple is a witness, the latter has been understood as the "humanization of the cosmic forces of evil."[12]

1.4. True Discipleship as 'Johannine Community'

In the Jesus-disciple relationship, there was a code that the disciples had to fulfil in order to be true disciples. It meant that those who have believed in Jesus had to remain in him and know the truth, and be freed by the truth. (8:31). In Judaism the truth was the Law; and the study of the Law made a person free. Barrett sees the expressions, "truth" and "freedom," as primarily referring to the Christian liberation from sin.[13] The disciples are instructed that hatred and persecution of the world are part of discipleship (16:33; 15:18-20; 16:2). There are two worlds, one heavenly and one earthly and the disciples belonged to the former (6:27; 17:14; 18:36). They do not attach much importance to the

9 See C.H. Dodd, *Historical Tradition in the Fourth Gospel*. (Cambridge Univ., 1963) 72 f.

10 See Culpepper, *Anatomy of the Fourth Gospel,* 124 f.

11 Brown, *John* Vol. I, 299.

12 Culpepper, *Anatomy of the Fourth Gospel*, 125.

13 Barrett, *John,* 285.

present world but regard it as a preparatory ground for the next, heavenly life.[14] They are ready to die, given the predicament of this world. A supportive view is seen in Bultmann's explanation, where he contends that the 'Johannine misunderstandings' did not arise from words having more than one meaning but from "concepts and statements, which at first sight refer to earthly matters, but properly refer to divine matters. The misunderstanding comes when someone sees the right meaning of the word but mistakenly imagines that its meaning is exhausted by the reference to earthly matters…."[15]

2. Construction of a New (no?) Johannine Identity

Generally, identity is perceived on the basis of one's sense of belonging to a group or community. It is also the significance and meaning that individuals attribute to membership in an ethnic group. There is a subtle difference between racial identity and ethnic identity. Racial identity is how individuals construct their identities in response to an oppressive and highly racialized society and ethnic identity is how individuals see themselves relative to their cultural beliefs, values, and behaviours.

In the Gospel of John, identity is created by how the author defines it - particularly in the introduction of characters, what they say, what they do, and how other characters react to them. According to M. Davies, the author of John has inside out information about his characters' beliefs, understanding and emotions. Of the disciples, the author knows when and what they believe (2:11; 2:22; 20:8); he is aware of their suppositions (13:29); he knows when and what they remember, so that they come to a new understanding in retrospect (2:22; 12:16; 20:9); and he also recognizes when they are startled (4:27; 6:21; 20:20).[16] In other words, the author ascribes identity to each one of his characters, in order to make them perform his objective.

John had primarily Jewish addressees in mind when he wrote the Gospel, those who found themselves as a threatened community among their own (majority) Jewish people and were searching for a new identity. According to Klaus Wengst, the issue in John's Gospel is one of an inner-Jewish conflict (*innerjuedische Konflikt*), wherein the minority, threatened Jewish community with its faith in Jesus, suffering, religious discrimination, social isolation and economic boycott, climaxed in the excommunication (9:22; 12:42; 16:2) from

14 Most, if not all, Western interpreters find this idea hard to accept, and keep emphasizing the idea of "realized eschatology" in John. Asian readers, particularly those living in India can easily understand this concept, probably because of the socio-economic condition of their country.

15 R. Bultmann, *The Gospel of John: A Commentary*. Tr. by G.R Beasley-Murray, R.W.N.Hoare, & J.K. Riches, (Philadelphia: The Westminster Press, 1971) 135, n.1.

16 See Margaret Davies, *Rhetoric and Reference in the Fourth Gospel*, JSOT, (Sheffield: Sheffield Academic Press, 1992), 32 – 33.

the Synagogue.[17] There was not a perceptible ethnic conflict. There were "Jewishnesses" and "Judaisms" that had to be dealt with – diaspora Judaism with its inferior status as against the religiously powerful Palestinian Judaism, aspects of interpretations of ethnic purity and the use of excommunication as a controlling strategy.

Consequently, identity construction in John necessitated "bordering" and "othering", "us/them", "you-we" representations, etc., in order to establish a common identity, even though such differences were fluid. What one sees in John is a 'mixed-identity', an 'imagined community' perpetuated through symbols and rituals of a common past. Some examples could be:

> "*we* speak of what *we* know, yet *you* do not receive our testimony" (3,11)
>
> "*You* worship what *you* do not know, *we* worship what *we* know" (4, 22)
>
> "*You* were born entirely in your sins, and are *you* trying to teach *us*?" (9, 34)

However, what is striking here is that there is constant effort to remove this schism. There are efforts to resocialize, build bridges and to establish newer, transnational, trans-ethnic patterns of community construction (e.gs. Samaritan woman, Nicodemus, the man who was healed of his blindness). This is done by presenting Jesus as a matrix for change. As Culpepper puts it, "Jesus is the protagonist and most of the other characters [in the Gospel of John] are ficelles."[18] In the narrative, individual personalities derive importance only by their encounter with Jesus. Jesus is the bread to be eaten; a relationship which is wholly other-worldly. Hence, an identity formation is completely other-worldly! The calling of disciples as "friends" is yet another example of how identity is formed – irrespective of hierarchy or protocol! Hence, belonging to Jesus meant adopting a new identity or *no identity*.

Therefore, it may not be incorrect to state that the idea of identity present in the Gospel of John is designed to negate the construction of identity. The phrases, "I in them, you in me…." (17:23), "I am the vine, you are the branches," (15:5), etc., reinstate the necessity of abandoning identity. James and John are presented as desirous of constructing a hierarchical community with Jesus as the leader. But the categorical rejection of them by Jesus is again a statement against identity construction. Another significant model of identity

17 Klaus Wengst, *Jesus zwischen Juden und Christen: Revisionen im Verhaeltnis der Kirche zu Israel*, 2nd Rev. edn. (W. Kohlhammer GmbH Stuttgart. 2004), 78 f.

18 Culpepper, *Anatomy of the Fourth Gospel*, 104.

construction (read destruction) is represented in the I-AM motif of the Gospel of John, particularly 14:1-14.

After speaking about his betrayal, Jesus addresses the confused and threatened situation of the disciples and exhorts them to place their trust in God. He states that he is going to his father, so that he may prepare a place for them. The main objective of this "going" is, "where I am, there you may be also" (14:3). According to Wengst, Jesus' going to the father does not mean that God is not present in the current situation, nor is it pointing to a God in the beyond or afterlife. Rather, the following verses (v.4 – 14) point to the idea that God is ever-present among the disciples in Jesus.[19]

Notably, one seldom finds a direct allusion to divinity, as in the case of the Gospel of John. After referring to God as his father several times (Jn.2:16; 5:19 ff. 26f., 45; 8:42), Jesus equates himself with the father by phrases such as, "whoever has seen me has seen the father" (14:9), "I am in the Father and the Father is in me" (14:10,11), and "I am the way, the truth and the life" (14:6), all, pointing to the divine nature of Christ. So, the question is, "what type of a community was Jesus trying to construct here?" "Where do the disciples situate their identity?"

The self-acclamation in 14:1-14, particularly in v. 6 has been understood and interpreted from early times. The Church fathers interpreted 'the way' as that which led to a goal. Along this line 'the way' was sometimes interpreted as itself 'the truth' which led to eternal life. Augustine believed that 'the way' led to a goal, and along with Clement of Alexandria and Origen, possibly under the influence of Platonist thought, related 'the truth and life' as this goal to the Logos. According to Maldonatus, 'the truth' had to be taken adjectivally; the rendering should be 'I am the true way to life'. Aquinas, interpreting according to medieval thought forms, maintained that Christ was 'the way' according to his humanity, but 'the truth and the life' according to his divinity.[20]

As such, the text has been interpreted against a variety of backgrounds: gnostic, Mandaean and Hermetic. Some have seen the origin of 'the way' in the Old Testament concept of walking in God's way, referring to the Torah, while others have seen the origin in Mandaean literature, for e.g. in such statements as 'you show us the way of life, and let us walk upon the paths of truth and faith.[21] Interestingly, Bultmann identifies four distinctive forms in the 'I am" formula.[22]

---

19 Wengst, *Das Johannesvangelium*, 115 f.

20 Elizabeth Harris, *Prologue and Gospel: The Theology of the Fourth Evangelist*, (London/New York: T & T Clark International, 1994), 149.

21 Quoted in Harris, *Prologue and Gospel*, 150f.

22 Bultmann, John, 225 f.

a) Presentation formula: Here the 'I' is the subject, and the speaker introduces himself in reply to the question 'Who are you?'
b) Qualificatory formula: Here the subject is "I", and the question 'what are you?' receives a reply in terms of 'I am that and that' or 'I am the one who…'.
c) Identification formula: which proliferates in religious syncretism, for here the speaker identifies himself with another person or object, as when the Egyptian god Re says, 'I am he who arose as Chopre': or Isis says, 'I am everything that was and is and will be'.
d) Recognition formula: This is distinguished from the other three in that the 'I' is not the subject but the predicate. It answers the question 'Who is the one who is expected, spoken to, asked for?' with the reply 'It is I who am'.

So, according to Bultmann, this line of usage in the text would represent the "identification formula", wherein 'identity' is constructed on the basis of the identity of Jesus, who, in turn identifies himself with the "Father", who is the "I am". Subsequently, the idea in John is to rather lose one's identity, than to seek to form or establish it. One has to refrain from going after an identity, but rest content with the fact that the Johannine group was "not of this world" (but), "from above" (3:3-8). In other words, one's "identity" derived existence only from the "I am", which does not ascertain ones identity, but ascertains the reality of the "I am".[23]

A pertinent study of John 14:1-14, by Tod Swanson emphasizes a trans-ethnic, trans-race construction of community in the Gospel of John. According to Swanson, the 'preparation' of a place for the disciples (14:2) was a direct

23 Unlike the above interpretation, Warren Carter, calling it the "sacred identity", gives a sociological explanation of identity in the Gospel of John. He presents five aspects of this identity: the sacred household or temple of God, faithfulness (fides), loving service, greater works, and living as a community of friends. Alluding to Mary Coloe, who points out that, the "transfer or better, extension of the temple imagery from Jesus to the community of Jesus-believers takes place…in chapter 14", Carter states that in ch. 14, one could discover a community with a sacred identity on the basis of the temple, which "interacts with and provides an alternative community to the imperially constituted and Artemis-blessed civic identity of Ephesus." Warren Carter, *John and Empire: Initial Explorations*, (New York/London: T & T Clark, 2008), 257 ff. See also Biju Chacko, who, in his article "Can anything good come out of (John's Gospel)? Christological Articulations of John's Subaltern-intercultural community: Search for an Alternative Space to Carry out the Task of Hermeneutics" states that the community of John was a "subaltern-intercultural community" (in Bangalore Theological Forum Vol. L, No.1, June 2018, 128-151). Asish Thomas Koshy, in his monograph, "Identity, Mission and Community: A study of the Johannine Resurrection Narrative", portrays the Johannine Community, in familial terms, extending the image of family to include socio-political and soteriological aspects. (See Asish Thomas Koshy, Identity, Mission and Community: A Study of the Johannine Resurrection Narrative, Christian World Imprints: New Delhi, 2018)

reaction to definitions of identity based on "this-worldly construals of ethnic territory." This meant that "sacred topographies of this world" had to end and that "true worship would no longer take place 'on this mountain' [Mt Gerizim, the center of Samaritan identity], nor in Jerusalem [the center of Jewish identity]', but 'spirit' (4:21-23)." For Swanson, such a stance was provocative, since it posited that "the place-bound character of ethnic identity [w]as something to be overcome in the newly opened placeless place of Johannine worship."[24]

Interestingly, for Swanson, the signs of Jesus in John actually re-enact the foundational deeds of local patriarchs, in that they intend to "reconnect the fathers of specific places with the one Father, and the geographies they founded with the one true country."[25] So, any preference of physical territory of a patriarch, over the unity that the Gospel pointed to, was to be a schismatic. Accordingly, schismatics were the cause of conflict and turmoil, and the killing of Jesus too finalized "the judgment of the *Ioudaioi* because it pushes their rejection of unity to its murderous conclusion."[26] In this regard, Swanson states:

> On the eve of his death Jesus tells his followers that he must exit this world in order to 'prepare a place' for them in the 'Father's House'. By performing the *semeia*, Jesus had already transferred ethnic allegiance from the territorial shrines to his own body. But his body was still one space in the world alongside other competing spaces. As long as his body is there incarnating the *logoi* of the patriarchal territories, no 'true country', or unembodied 'space' for unity could really emerge. In order to open the spaceless rooms of the Father's House, the body space of the one who had incarnated the symbols of the patriarchal homelands also had to be erased. And in fact it is the dissolution of Jesus' body that finally clears a space for the coming of the unifying spirit.[27]

Therefore, for Swanson, the early Johannine Christians aspired to abandon the boundaried world of ethnic territories. They hoped for a spaceless world, but they were accused of being exclusive, and a danger to Jewish society and were branded as heretics and also as non-Jews, by the leaders of the majority Jews

24 Tod D. Swanson, "To Prepare a Place: Johannine Christianity and the Collapse of Ethnic Territory" in Musa W. Dube and Jeffrey L. Staley (Eds.), *John and Postcolonialism: Travel, Space and Power*, London/New York: Sheffield Academic Press, 2002), 14 (11-31)

25 Swanson, "To Prepare a Place", 18

26 Swanson, "To Prepare a Place", 24

27 Swanson, "To Prepare a Place", 26

of rabbinical Judaism.[28] To be conformed to an 'identity' was restrictive to the Johannine Christians, who wanted to surpass the tag of 'identity'. Their main objective seems to have been to overcome the 'identity' that was attributed to them. The 'identity' that they wanted was beyond political, religio-cultural and social horizon. It was an 'identity' derived from the Father.

A so-called "high Christology" in John, has been understood as idolatrous from a Jewish perspective. Jesus Christ, who is the word, is the cause of "being" (1:12ff). Beneath this personification or representation is the formation of a community. The community is understood as the new creation of the end-time. The community in John is conceived as the discipleship to Jesus and Jesus calls his disciples as "friends" (15:14-15). This new creation as the community is reflected in the creation in the beginning (1:12-13; 3:3.5), for it is part of the whole creation.

3. Reflections for the Indian Context on the Quest for Identity in Community Formation in the Gospel of John

The Johannine vision of a new community can provide fresh impetus to community formation in India. The Gospel of John has been considered to be relevant to Indian spirituality. An Indian understanding of community in John, needs to consider two important trajectories in the reception of the Fourth Gospel in India, one by the so-called 'elites' who were said to have formed the dominant tradition of interpreting the Gospel of John along the Hindu, (neo-advaitic) religious background, and the other, newer approach, which emphasized the social and political perspective of India. The following argument, however, seeks to remove this distinction in Indian Johannine hermeneutics.

In Interpretations that proceed in comparing Johannine thought with Indian (Read Hindu) religious thought, the first concept to be identified is the 'unknowability of God' (John 1: 18). This aspect has been time and again deliberated by western thinkers like Plotinus and Aquinas. This unknowability of God is portrayed in the Bible, as "God in the heavens", whereas in Indian spirituality, it is spoken of as the 'indwelling God'.[29] In the Gospel of John, the coming together of transcendence and immanence envisions the divine element of community. This community distinguishes itself from Marxist or socialist images, in that, it categorically rejects the polarisation of the world as spiritual and material. Hence, Johannine emphasis on history needs to be perceived from the Indian transcendent view of existence. The idea of atman in Advaita Vedanta, can be connected to the Johannine logos. According to

28 See Wengst, Das Johannesevangelium, 25. Cf. Swanson, "To Prepare a Place", 28.

29 Abhishiktananda, Saccidananda: A Christian Approach to Advaitic Experience, (New Delhi: ISPCK, 1984), 11

Abhishiktananda, one of the proponents of intercultural reading of the Bible, Advaita does not distinguish between matter and soul, since atman both transcends as well as indwells everything and does not have any dichotomies and transcends reason. Therefore, an anthropological understanding of community, takes history seriously, and the logos concept of John (full of grace and truth, 1:14) explicates this idea.[30]

As has been demonstrated, identity in John is constructed on the basis of one's allegiance to Jesus, upon one's belief/disbelief in him. Focussing on the verse, "I am the way, the truth and the life" (14:6), we see the concept of "I am" running across the Gospel of John. In Indian spirituality, the Self or *Paramatman* has divine status. Similarly, even in the Old Testament, God is defined as "I am that I am" (Gen.3:14). This is one of the best definitions of God. Even the Sanskrit *aham brahmasmi* (I am God) is not as direct as the OT declaration. God is none other than the Self or the *Paramatman*.

Contrary to conservative interpretations that have viewed the Johannine words, "I am the way, the truth and the life" (14:6) as exclusively referring to Jesus' physical self/person, and have, as a result, claimed exclusivity of the historical Jesus in matters concerning faith and salvation, to the Indian mind, there need not be any distinction between Jesus' physical self and spiritual self. It is all but one unified entity. Jesus, himself did not see any distinction within himself and understood himself, as the one true Self. Since in John, Jesus is described as the beginning and end of creation and all realities (John 1:1-3), wherever, "I" occurs, with reference to Christ, the attribution is to Christ's essence, one being in constant communion with God. An Indian commentator commenting on John 14: 6 states: "When Jesus says, 'I am the way, the truth, and the life', the actual meaning is *I am* is the way, the truth and the life".[31] Hence, the phrase here is actually a call to recognize God/Reality in the Self, because the Self is divine.

The concept of viewing the self as divine has been time and again accentuated by Hindu religious belief systems. The realization of the Self's limitless nature led the Indian sages to speak of it as the inner reality or the subtle essence of all things. This view is set forth in the following famous dialogue between a teacher and a student illustrated in one of the Upanishads:

"Bring me a fruit from a banyan tree"
"Here it is, sir."
"Open it"
"It is open, sir."
"What do you see there?"

30 Abhishiktananda, Saccidananda, 52ff.

31 Sri Parananda, An Eastern Exposition of the Gospel of Jesus according to St. John being an interpretation thereof. Ed. By R.L. Harrison, (London: William Hitchinson and Co.1902)

"Some very small seeds, Sir."
"Open one of those small seeds."
"It is open, sir".
"What do you see there?"
"Nothing at all, sir."

The teacher then replied, "My son, that 'nothing' is the subtle essence of all things, which appears as nothing, because you cannot perceive it. But from this nothing this great and ancient tree has grown. That infinite source of the whole universe, the Self of all that is, the ocean of pure consciousness – that is truth, the way and the life. That is the unmanifest Self. Of that you are created. That thou art (*tat tvam aci*)".[32]

Further, Indian interpreters have presented Jesus as the 'guru' or sanctified teacher who would enlighten the soul (14:4ff). The guru dwells in the soul and bestows it with the power to discern the way of the knowledge of the indwelling God and of eternal life. For an Indian, it is not difficult to accept Jesus as a guru, who shows the way to God. In Indian spirituality, the guru is God and grants grace. It is the Self that takes the form of a guru and guides the soul towards realization.[33]

On the contrary, the Gospel of John, despite its special significance to Indian religiosity, has also been critiqued due to its 'other-worldly' emphasis. Particularly in India, where poverty and inequality form the social reality, this Gospel is considered to be irrelevant. What significance can a 'spiritual' interpretation have for the deprived and discriminated masses? Such 'elite' interpretations can only serve the 'intellectuals'! These are some of the accusations that prevail among those in the margins.

A counter argument, however, would be that the portrayal of Self as God promotes the idea of a 'divine community' in the Gospel of John, with a 'divine identity'. Such an identification enhances one's solidarity with the oppressed. The unity of the Self presupposes the unity of the whole created order. If this unity is taken seriously, there is no question of any distinction or discrimination. The upanishadic tradition advocates a continual connection between God and humans, and between human beings, each with one another. This connection could be compared with the Johannine reconciliatory idea of oneness of all human beings, where both, masters and the oppressed come together, where there is no more hierarchy and all things done, whether to one's own self or to the other are done on the basis of love. A 'community' feeling is perceived here, that echoes a unity among the believers. As a result, the words of Jesus have both transcendent as well as social implications. Therefore, identity in

32 Chandogya VI. 12. 1 – 3

33 See G.T. Basker, *Interpreting biblical texts: John and his Tamil readers.* (New Delhi: ISPCK, 2016), 7 f., 23 f.

John is based on anthropological reality, devoid of ethnic, caste, nationality, gender tags, but defined by the existential oneness of all who believe.

Interestingly, a Dalit writer of the 19th Century has discovered this trans-ethnic concept of identity in the Gospel of John. Iyothee Thass (1845-1914), an author and activist, wrote on Dalit emancipation as early as in the latter half of the 19th Century. His literary work predominantly reflects on the thought of the Gospel of John. According to him, the Tamil word *Kiṟistavaṉ* (Christian) is an analogue to *kiṟisthu avaṉ- avaṉ kiṟisthu-* Christ is he – he is Christ). Alluding to John 15:4, he uses the term *amarntavaṉ* to depict the idea of *remaining*. According to him, one could only be a Christian when he/she abides in Christ (*Kiṟistu avaṉukkuḷḷum avaṉ kiṟistuvukkuḷḷum amarntavaṉē kiṟistavaṉāvāṉ* - the one in whom Christ abides and he who abides in Christ, he is Christian).[34] For Thass, to "abide in Christ" (*amarntiruttal*), means to follow the works and way of Jesus (*naṉmārkka oḻukkattuḷ*) which defines one's identity as a Christian. In this way, he prefers a pragmatic understanding of identity and community formation. Thass limits himself mainly to the human situation and does not concern himself with an other-worldly, mystical level or divine intervention. He uses the term *nuḻaital* in order to stress the possibility of abiding in Jesus.[35] Interestingly, he describes the Tamil Saiva religion by the words, *taṉṉai aṟiyum camayamē caivam* (knowing one's self is Saiva religion), and thereby defines religion as one that advocated self-realization

It is now clear that, though a persistent search for identity underlies Johannine thought, the objective was to actually transcend identity. Throughout its narrative, the Fourth Gospel, envisages a community, which is devoid of identity construction, but strives to be identified as a community not defined by ethnic, racial, religio-cultural and political labels/terms. Rather, the 'Johannine community' imagined a boundary-less, inclusive society, fundamentally anthropocentric, defined by its belief in Christ. Despite the diversity of the context of India, Indian interpretations of John have advocated such a community. This unified construction of identity and community formation are the needs of the day, to effectively recount segmentation and sectarianism.

---

34 Ayothee Thasan, Ayothee Thasar Cinthanaikal, II, G. Aloysius (ed.), (Palayamkottai: Camayam, Ilakkiyam Folklore Resources and Research Centre, St. Xavier's College, 1999) 99

35 Ayothee Thasan, Ayothee Thasar Cinthanaikal, 100.

11

Identity Formation of the Christian Community in 1 Peter Dialectic of Continuity and Discontinuity

Prema Vakayil CSST

Introduction

Pauline and Gospel centered readings have too long provided the normative understanding of Christian identity. Recent studies[1] on the General Epistles, commonly known as Catholic Epistles taken collectively or individually, explore a common thread namely identity formation of Christian community, and they broaden the perspectives of Early Christian identity. They answer questions like what do the Catholic Epistles uniquely contribute to Christian identity? How do the authors of the epistles shape the identity of their respective community whom they address? What are the potential results of the identities constructed in these epistles for early Christian communities? And, could these epistles have influenced and shaped Christian identity years later? It is in this context we make an attempt in this paper to understand the meaning of titles and identity associated with the Old Testament People of God in 1 Peter with a focus on 2: 9-10. The paper is divided into 3 parts:

I. Christian identity in continuity with the Jewish identity in 1 Pet 2: 9-10

1 A mention to be made of the recent studies in K. M Hockey, M. N Pierce, F. Watson (eds), *The Muted Voices of the New Testament: Readings in the Catholic Epistles and Hebrews,* Library of the New Testament Studies 565 (New York: Bloomsbury Publishing: 2017).

II. Christian identity in discontinuity with the Jewish identity in 1 Pet 2: 9-10
III The newness of the Christian identity in 1 Pet 2: 9-10

I. Christian Identity in Continuity with the Jewish Identity in 1 Pet 2:9-10

The most central and relevant text with regard to the identity of the Christians in 1 Peter is Chapter 2. In vv. 9-10 the author declares: "But you are a chosen race, a royal priesthood, a holy nation, God's own people ... Once you were not a people, but now you are the people of God; once you had not received mercy, but now you have received mercy". The importance of this text is in his declaration in a cluster of titles in v.9: *hymeis genos eklekton* (You are a chosen race), *Basileion hierateuma* (Royal Priesthood), *ethnos hagion*, (Holy nation), *laos eis peripoiēsin* (People of His possession). Here the identity of the readers as Kingdom of priests or royal priesthood, holy nation and a people of God's possession derive from their special status as God's elect. That is, these titles of honour are the elements of election. Peter in this text draws upon some very distinctively Jewish titles of honour that are specifically attributed to the people of Israel using Ex 19: 5-6 and perhaps Is 9: 2; 43: 21; 61:6; Deut 7:6; 14:2; Hosea 1: 9-10; 2:23 to give an identity and status to the Christian community whom he is addressing.

1. Chosen Race (1 Pet 2:9)

The writer of the letter describes his addressees as the "chosen sojourners of the dispersion" (v.1), thus underlining a central theme that controls the message of the epistle. The title applies both to the author and recipients in 1 Peter. It is addressed to the "chosen" at the beginning (1:1-2) and sends greetings from the "likewise chosen" at the end (5:13), "thus bracketing the whole letter by an inclusio"[2] It also appears in other forms "Chosen and precious" (2:4, 6) thus appearing five times in one form or another in the entire epistle, more than in any other books of the NT. While its occurrences may not necessarily justify any claim to importance or centrality, the elect motif is known to underlie the message of the epistle, thus stressing further its importance right from the outset[3].

2 D. L. Balch, *Let Wives Be Submissive. The Domestic Code in 1 Peter*, SBL MS, 26 (Atlanta, GA: Scholars Press, 1981), 123.

3 J. H. Elliott, *1 Peter. A New Translation with Introduction and Commentary,* Anc B, 37B, (Garden City, NY: Doubleday, 2000), 446. S.A. Fagbemi, "The Identity of the Elect in 1 Peter: Its Present Significance and Implications for the Believers", ed. J. Schlosser, *The Catholic Epistles and the Tradition*, Bibliotheca Ephemeridum Theologicarum Lovaniensium CLXXVI (Leuven: University Press, 2004), 367-380, 368.

a. The elect identity of Israel

It is important to acknowledge that these titles of honour derive from the Hebrew Scriptures where they originally applied to Israel. Peter's references to the election motif manifest dependence on OT texts such as Ex 19: 6, Deut 7: 6-8 and Isa 43: 20-21. In examining these texts, there is a consistent nuance that cannot be over emphasized namely the purpose and challenges of the election.

b. Purpose of the election of Israel

The author of the letter enumerates three components of 'election' which again are taken from Israel's self-identity. Yahweh chose Israel in order that she might be "a light" among the nations. Although it was based on divine love, the relationship required an ethical response - holiness of life - to distinguish her from other nations. Israel was called to be "holy to Yahweh," i.e., set apart, different, belonging exclusively to him[4]. Israel was like the s^{e}gulla "the private treasure of a king who owned everything else as well, but valued his personal possessions particularly (cf. 1 Chron 29:3; Eccl 2:8)."[5]This explains then why Gods' people are "chosen" (*genos eklekton),* to be *ethnos hagion'*. By being holy and obedient to Yahweh, they mediate God to the nations and thus fulfill their priestly role 'royal priesthood'.[6]

The author's quotation *Basileion hierateuma* from Exodus 19:6 comes, typically, from the Septuagint. The word has a functional and corporate meaning; a group or community engaged in the act of priestly service namely the worship of the God of Israel and regards the designation as a badge of its

---

4 C.J.H. Wright, *Deuteronomy* NIBC, (Peabody , M.A, Hendrickson: Paternoster, 1996), 111.

5 Ibid.

6 The two references to priesthood within the epistle are found in 2:5 and 2:9. The first of these refers to the churches receiving the letter as a 'holy priesthood', and the latter, as a 'royal priesthood'. The relationship between these two verses is a matter of some debate. The primary question surrounding the word *basileion* is whether it is to be understood as a noun or as an adjective. In other words, is the phrase as a whole to be read as two separate designations for those addressed (with *basileion* meaning 'palace' or 'kingdom'), or as a single, two-word phrase (*basileion* translated 'royal')? If the former of these two options is followed, and given the rhetorical flow of descriptive phrases, it seems on balance perhaps the more convincing, then whichever reading is right in the case of the Septuagint, in the case of 1 Peter 2:9, *basileion* means 'royal'; either the priests themselves are royal, or (perhaps more likely) it reflects their·service of God as King. *Hierateuma*, which is first found in the Septuagint, appears in extant literature only a small number of times up to and including the period of its inclusion in 1 Peter, and only in Jewish or Christian writings.(LXX Ex. 19:6; 23:22; one fragment of Test Levi 11:6 (Fragment 67) ; 2 Macc. 2:17) cf. J. R Michaels, *1 Peter* (WBC 49; Waco: Word Books, 1988) 108-9; E. G. Selwyn, *The First Epistle of Saint Peter* (London: Macmillan, 1955) 165-167; J.H. Elliott, *The Elect and the Holy : An Exegetical Examination of 1 Peter 2:4-10 and the Phrase basileion hierateuma* (Leiden: Brill, 1966), 149- 153.

identity. The concept of *hierateuma* is associated with the idea of *diaspora* Jews as a *politeuma*, meaning a community of one nationality living abroad. [7]

c. *Holy nation and royal priesthood: Challenges of early Jewish life in Diaspora*

The consciousness of Israel's self identity as the holy nation and royal priesthood developed more in the Diaspora. For the Jews, Diaspora was in a sense the logical conclusion of the 'exile' in that people of God was not only removed from its homeland but in a sense dismantled and dismembered as a nation. It was to be understood as the effect of God's punishment, a state to be lamented and there would have been in theory and perhaps in practice a longing to return to the Holy land.[8] Does this then imply that the Diaspora Jew, living as part of a *politeuma*, had no loyalty or commitment to the local city? It might be supposed that their choosing to continue living there, rather than relocating to Jerusalem or Judea would suggest that this is not the case as Diaspora communities retain a sense of belonging. In this sense Diaspora is a much more complex phenomenon than migration, since Diaspora community is neither a wandering body of people, nor simply a community of immigrants absorbed into new home." [9]

The Diaspora Jews at least in some of its manifestations- held a distinctive identity, not only as holy people in an unholy nation, but precisely as a community which is holy on behalf of the *unholy* just as the separated priesthood of the Temple maintained purity and offered worship on behalf of Israel and the dispersed Jews. The dispersed Jews saw themselves, as maintaining purity and offering synagogue worship on behalf of the nations. The Jews of the dispersion became "a priestly community charged with the worship of the true God "with a divinely endowed religious mission to fulfill.[10] Though this may appear to be speculative it seems broadly convincing. It does, at least provide some explanation as to why *hierateuma* which appears on few occasions, most of them originate in one Diaspora community (2 Macc 2:17; Philo, Abr. 56; Sobr. 66**).** Perhaps Diaspora Judaism, largely constituted of lay Jews, had a particular need to be corporately priestly, given its higher degree

7 J. H. Elliott, *The Elect and the Holy,* 69-70.

8 W. C van Unnik, *Das Selbstverstandnis der Judischen Diaspora in der hellenistisch Zeit* (Leiden: Brill 1993), 148-165. Cf. also J. M Scott, "Exile and Self-understanding of Diaspora Jews" in *Exile: Old Testament, Jewish and Christian Conception,* ed. J. M. Scott (Leiden: Brill, 1997), 206-208; A.T Kraabel, "Unity and Diversity among Diaspora Synagogues", in *The Synagogue in Late Antiquity* ed. L. I Levine (Philadelphia: American Schools of Oriental Research, 1987).

9 J. M. J. Barclay, *Negotiating Diaspora: Jewish Strategies in the Roman Empire*, eds. L. L. Grabbe and J. H. Charlesworth, (London: T&T Clark, 2004), 2.

10 J. H. Elliott, *The Elect and the Holy*, 69

of holiness than the local population as a whole and the probable shortage of designated priests in its midst.

The role of worship and the atonement which the priests perform on their behalf, they fulfill for the profane nations; this remains true for all Israel imbued with a priestly quality, but Diaspora is perhaps uniquely placed to appreciate such a status (Cf. Philo, *Spec* 2.162) and to this the fact that the Jewish communities in the dispersion generally lived with the status of outsiders, lacking the privileges of citizenship of either Rome or their own polis, and isolated from the centre of Jewish religious life, and we have a picture of a people potentially seeking an identity with status and value. By being exclusively committed to God and none other, which is the wish of the "jealous Yahweh", they fulfill their election as '*laos eis peripoiēsin*' (People of His possession).[11]

The interaction among these titles is interesting. They exemplify Yahweh's interest in electing Israel, delivering them from Egypt, and his covenant at Sinai. By worshiping Yahweh and living in the light of his revelation, Israel was fulfilling its mission to the nations. The corporate nature of the election of Israel is in one sense an indication that the priestly nature of the calling transcends cultic worship. Although this might not be a conscious missionary agenda, as scholars have pointed out12 the ethical and moral lifestyles of Jews constituted a significant missiological strategy, especially in the Diaspora. Subsequently, it resulted in proselytisation and conversion of Gentiles.13 Good Deeds have been identified to be about the most effective means of reaching Gentiles.14 It seems then that the election of Israel had ethical implications and such commitments further served missiological purpose in representing Yahweh and in bringing other nations to him.15 This probably indicates where we should look for the significance of the elect identity.

---

11 S.A. Fagbemi, "The Identity of the Elect in 1 Peter", 370-371

12 Cf. S. McKnight, *A Light Among the Gentiles. Jewish Missionary Activity in the Second Temple Judaism* (Minneapolis, MN.: Fortress, 1991).

13 S. Baron, *A Social and Religious History of the Jews to the Beginning of the Christian Era*, Vol1, (New York: Columbia University Press), 1952, 174- 175

14 S. McKnight, *A Light Among the Gentiles,* 67 n 27

15 S. A. Fagbemi, "The Identity of the Elect in 1 Peter", 372

2. The Elect Identity of the Believers in 1 Pet 2:9

In 1 Peter we find a deliberate combination of these texts[16] to appeal to the identity of the recipients as elect and a kingdom of priests. They betray a midrashic nature[17] that reformulates and reflects upon the original texts[18].

a. The chosen 'sojourners of dispersion" in 1 Peter

The letter is addressed to the Chosen Sojourners in the Dispersion. The meaning of the word 'Dispersion' needs be clarified since it is strictly a Jewish term.[19] The options vary in current scholarship: (1) Diaspora may refer exclusively to the Jewish Diaspora, so that the letter would be addressed to Christians in (the area of) the Jewish Diaspora of Asia Minor.[20] "In each of its three New Testament occurrences (John 7:35; Jas. 1:1; 1 Pet. 1:1) the term Diaspora circumscribes geographically and socially, as it did in its technical LXX usage, a body of people living beyond the limits of Eretz Israel (Palestine) in Jas.1:1 and 1 Pet. 1:1, contrary to conventional Jewish usage, Diaspora is used for the first time as a designation for *Christians* (most probably an admixture of both Jewish and Gentile converts) who, like their former Jewish counterparts, now also live beyond the borders of Palestine."[21] (2) Alternatively, Diaspora in 1 Peter may refer to a Christian Diaspora analogous to the Jewish Diaspora by virtue of its situation, in which the Christian addressees live like the Jews, but for other reasons— in a concrete dispersion ((3) Finally, some scholars think of Diaspora as an explicitly metaphoric statement, either (a) in the sense that Christians "must live in this world, but separate from this world," or (b) with the nuance that they are anyway strangers since they are remote from their heavenly home.[22]

As to the last nuance, it needs to be said that it is not explicitly present in 1 Peter (and not in James either). What is "kept in heaven" for the addressees

16 J .H. Elliott, *The Elect and the Holy*, 140.

17 E. G. Selwyn, *First Epistle of Peter,* 269 (n. 12). While 2, 4-5 reflect the LXX in formulation, the latter sections are midrashic in nature, as they are a reformulation and reflections upon the former.

18 J. H. Elliott, *The Elect and the Holy*, 17-22.

19 cf. W. C. van Unnik, "Diaspora' and 'Church' in the First Centuries of Christian History [1959]," in *Sparsa Collecta: The Collected Essays of W. C. van Unnik,* Part 3, *Patristica - Gnostica -Liturgica* (NovTSup 31; Leiden: Brill, 1983), 95-105.

20 Cf. J. H. Elliott, *Home for the Homeless : A Sociological Exegesis of 1 Peter , its Ssituation and Strategy,* (Philadelphia: Fortress Press 1981), 38.

21 Cf. J.H. Elliott, *1 Peter,* 314.

22 L. Doering, "First Peter as Early Christian Diaspora Letter" in K. W. Niebubr, R.W Wall (eds.), *The Catholic Epistles and Apostolic Tradition,* (Waco: Baylor University Press), 2009, 230.

(1 Pet 1:4) is not citizenship or a home but an imperishable future inheritance that is "vouchsafed by God."[23]

Over against James, in which the recipients are addressed as the twelve tribes (of Israel) in the Diaspora (Jas 1:1), the specific relation between Diaspora, election, and life as strangers in 1 Peter is different. The addressees are "the elect strangers of the Diaspora" in Pontus, Galatia, Cappodocia, Asia and Bithynia (1 Pet 1:1); they are urged "as exiles and strangers" (2:11) to abstain from fleshly desires, and exhorted to live in (reverent) fear in the time of their exile (1:17). 1 Peter draws here particularly on Jewish tradition that value life as strangers as counterpart to divine election. But the implication of election in wider Jewish discourse on Diaspora existence needs to be borne in mind as well. However predominately though not exclusively Gentile addresses of 1 Peter are members of the elect people (cf. 2: 9-10) by virtue not of their birth but of their rebirth (1: 3, 23; 2:1-3). Thus, a purely geographic understanding of the concept of Diaspora in 1 Peter misses part of the intention of Diaspora within its semantic field. Similarly, Diaspora in 1 Peter does not refer to a people who have been physically and historically dispersed from their homeland, but rather to addressees who have entered into a Diaspora existence by their rebirth. Even if we therefore prefer to call this a metaphoric use of Diaspora,[24] we shall not overlook that this concept is closely modeled on the analogy with Jewish Diaspora experience.

In this respect, two basic notions of Jewish identity in the Diaspora are the complementary concepts of election and otherness. In the vertical dimension, the story of election serves to create identity as the people of God, and in the horizontal dimension, the maintenance of boundaries and the perception of difference vis-a-vis the non-Jewish population.

First Peter takes these notions on board, but sharpens them by making election the intrinsic reason for Diaspora and re-conceiving otherness in terms of an existence as strangers, which figures positively only in a small string of Jewish tradition. The author has thus creatively reinterpreted the Diaspora metaphor to reflect the stance of the community chosen by rebirth and called to a life as strangers. Jewish Diaspora then to be seen as a symbol of the Christian community of 1 Peter which comprises both Gentiles and Jews. [25]

As in the case of the elect in the OT the purpose of the Christians as a chosen race has a purpose: "In order that you may proclaim the mighty acts of him who called you out of darkness into his marvellous light" (NRSV 1 Pet 2: 9b). The "electedness" and "holiness" of believers is for a present purpose, namely to declare God's might acts. It seems best to look at 2:11-12

23 Ibid.

24 Ibid 231.

25 Ibid

to understand how to "proclaim" or "declare" God's mighty deeds [26]. There, Peter is unequivocal that the way to declare or fulfill this task consists largely in "good conduct" and "good works" among the Gentiles. It must be seen entirely in the light of the duty consistent with the status and identity of God's people. It is to be done by acts and word. [27]

The context of Isaiah here relates to God's promise to deliver his people from Babylon and by inference in the Exodus Formula, it follows God's act of deliverance from Egypt. In either case, their deliverance was to result in the praises of God as well as living according to His will. In 1 Peter, it refers to God's gracious act of election and spiritual deliverance of God's people (including Gentiles) from the kingdom of darkness and spiritual oppression to God's marvelous light. The expression "out of darkness into light" is a typical NT description of the changes that the Gospel brings into the lives of converts from heathenism (Acts 26: 18; Eph 5: 8; Col 1:13).[28] Interestingly, the acts or duties associated with the transition from darkness to light[29] are to be shown in the believer's life for people to see; they are a practical demonstration and outward manifestation to the outside world. It does involve individual and corporate dimensions. The emphasis of this text points towards open acts of declaration of God's deeds as the basic intent for the salvation or election of the people. This is neither about the past nor the future, but about the present purpose for which the believer has been elected and sprinkled with the blood of Christ- holiness and good conduct.

Like Israel, this has a missiological end that is vital for Peter. Through a consistent and enduring holy living, the believers can be asked by nonbelievers to give an *apologia f*or their faith. Peter enjoins that it be done with reverence and gentleness (1 Pet 3: 15) [30]. This presents an interesting opportunity for evangelism, but it is in response to the inquirer. It is "reactive" rather than "proactive". Its motivation lies in the character and conduct of the believer. It is unavoidable then that the declaration of God's mighty acts will have to be done by word, having been preceded by "good conduct".

---

26 F. B .Craddock, *First and Second Peter and Jude* , (Louisville . KY , Westminster: John Knox Press, 1995), 40-41.

27 P.J. Achtemeier, *1 Peter: A Commentary on First Peter* (Minneapolis: Fortress Press, 1996), 166, n 15

28 A. M. Stibbs, A. F. Walls, *1Peter , A Commentary*, (London: Tyndale Press), 1971, 104.

29 C. Bigg, *A Critical and Exegetical Commentary on the Epistles of St. Peter and St. Jude* , (California: C. Scribner's Sons Pub: 1909), 134-135, n.34

30 M. Volf , "Soft Difference, Theological Reflections on the Relation Between Church and Culture in 1 Peter" in *Journal of the Northpark Symposium on the Theological Interpretation of Scripture* , 10.

II. Christian Identity in Discontinuity with the Jewish Identity in 1 Pet 2:10

If 1 Pet 2: 9 employs the terminologies commonly used in reference to Israel to give an identity to the Christian community, in v.10 however there is a shift.

Hosea is Reinterpreted to Reveal Discontinuity from Jewish Identity

The two phrases that are used in 1Pet 2: 10 refer to the calling of the Gentiles by using Hosea 1: 9-10 and 2: 23.

a. Once you were no people but now you are God's people

There is an allusion here to the passage in Hosea 2:23, "And I will have mercy upon her that had not obtained mercy; and I will say to them which were not my people, Thou art my people; and they shall say, Thou art my God." Peter takes the experience of Israel as an analogy to express his idea centered on two paired verbs *pote* and *nun*. They are used not to underscore the parallel between biblical times and the present experience as in 1 Pet 3: 20-21 but to underscore the contrast between past and present status of the Gentile Christians before God. In Hosea, the passage refers evidently to the reception of one portion of the Israelites into favour of God after their rejection; in Peter, it refers mainly to those who had been Gentiles, and who had never been recognized as the people of God. The reference here is to Christians of Greco-Roman background who became God's people not by election but by their conversion. Their conversion guarantees them incorporation into the people of God. Hence Christian community in Asia Minor addressed by 1 Peter is a mixture of Jews and Gentiles.[31] Among the biblical designation for the church are those which more naturally apply to those converted from outside the chosen race who prior to their conversion are not a people (1 Pet 2:10). They become God's people or children of Sarah (3:6) by conversion rather than by birth. Those references more applicable to Jews on other hand refer to those dispersed from a homeland identifiable not as Judea but as God's heavenly kingdom (cf. 1: 4; cf 1: 12; 3: 21f ; 5:10).

Meanwhile references to their life before becoming Christian suggest a Greco-Roman background (cf. 1:14, 18; 2: 10-12; 3:5f; 4:3f), while the fact that many of the churches in the area are of Pauline foundation might tentatively add to the conclusion that they are predominantly Gentile. Given Christianity's Jewish root the *Tanakh* was authoritative from the beginning so it is not surprising that it should be used to such an extent, even in addressing Gentiles.

31 P. J Achtemeier, *1 Peter: A Commentary on First Peter*, 50-51; J.H Elliott, *I Peter*, Anchor Bible (Garden City, NY: Doubleday, 2000), 89-90; R. Feldmeier, *The First Letter of Peter: A Commentary on Greek Text*, trans. P. H. Davids (Waco: Baylor, University Press, 2008), 42.

These are then Gentiles who have become part of what is still essentially a Jewish sect; it would seem probable that this would raise questions of identity for such Christians. They are not obviously an unambiguously included sect within the unique relationship which the people Israel have with their God; They are not for instance, permitted within the inner courts of the Temple in which the most holy rituals were performed. This is confirmed by the next half of the verse.

b. Once you had not received mercy but now you have received mercy

The language of mercy also comes from Hosea 1:6-8 LXX. But the structure of the clause like that of the previous one peter's own, built around the implied contrast of *pote* and *nun*. Peter uses the terminology to remind his Gentile readers that they are Gentiles and they have become people of God by God's mercy now revealed in Jesus Christ. In their transformation from not a people to God's people these Gentile Christians are reenacting a chapter of Israel's own history - the very language that identifies them as Gentile at the same time identifies their identity as Israel. The experience of being no people or destitute of mercy was Israel's experience by virtue of her disobedience, Long before it was the experience of these Gentiles.

Not much more can be known about those who first received and preserved the book, but we must speculate that 1 Peter's recipients were generally lacking in political or domestic power, perhaps on account of a lower social status.[32] The church clearly contained slaves (2: 18-20) and women (3: 1-6) and the instruction is directed to these two groups with no equivalent for masters, and relatively little for husbands (3:7).

3. The Wider Context of the Letter

Another point of discontinuity with the Jewish identity is the wider context of the letter. It appears to have been written for those who suffer. The form of suffering is unclear it could plausibly be persecution by the state authorities[33] or the determined, possibly violent, opposition of neighbours or families (Peter 2:10). 1 Pet 3: 13-17 speaks of a general opposition, although the 'defence' (*apologian*) and the 'abusers' (*eperezontes*) might refer to a court room trial (3: 15f). The comparison in the following passage (v. 18ff), with the sufferings of Christ may also imply that Christians also risked death at the hands of the law or violent mobs, or simply were called to take as their model Christ who suffered unjustly. The preceding passage (2:11-3:12) is concerned with their daily conduct, advocating submission to authority, humility, piety and mutual

32 J.H Elliott, *A Home for the Homeless: A sociological exegesis of 1 Peter, its situation and Strategy* (Philadelphia: Fortress Press, 1981) 70-72.

33 F.W Beare, *The First Epistle of Peter*, 3rd ed. (Oxford: Blackwell, 1970) , 32-33, 188

love, so that their godly life will leave their accusers without an accusation or, if not preventing persecution, will at least ensure that their suffering is for the sake of Christ, which brings blessing (3:13f; cf. 4:14).[34]

III. I Pet 2: 9-10: The New Identity of the Christian

The implications of the titles and identities drawn from the Jewish nation are associated with the newness that has attended the believers' lives namely that of conversion and new birth. (1: 3-4; 1:23). The verb participle aorist active nominative *anagenesis* used in v.3 derives from *anagennao*, and it implies "to give new life or new birth to." They have been born anew into a living hope and through the imperishable and living word of God. Being born anew, they are converted from their previous state to another, such as is found in 1 Pet 2:9 where the elect are called "out of darkness into the marvellous light". It is remarkable that the author of the letter subsequently shows this experience as the basis for new ethics and lifestyle (1:23-2:3). The newness that characterizes the present identity of the recipients of the letter is clearly underlined in 2:10 where our author, using Hosean texts (2:10; 2:23: Cf. Rom 9: 25f) contrasts the past with the present status of the believers.

The use of *pote* and *nun* brings out the distinct and sharp contrast between their "present" life and their "former life" to underline the importance of the "present" status and life of the believers and its subsequent demands. Unambiguously, he charges believers to live a distinct and new life as a necessary corollary of this status, saying "...For you have spent enough time in the past doing what pagans used to do..." (4: 2-4). Hence as rightly remarked by Stribbs, the recipients of 1Peter, like the old Israel, constitute a community characterized by election, royalty, priesthood, holiness and privileged relation to God as His special people.[35]

The distinct Christian identity is fashioned by their willingness to face a fiery ordeal (4:12), in daring to be a *Christianos* (4:16) and by entrusting their souls to a faithful creator (4:19). The term *Chrstianos* appears in 1Peter only in 4:16[36] in the context of the "fiery ordeal" (4:12). The fiery ordeal the Christians must bear precisely because they bear the name *Christianos*.

The context in which the word *Christianos* appears in 1 Peter is highly significant for understanding the origin and importance of the term in the history of early Christianity. The setting is one of hostility and suffering where the believers are ridiculed for their allegiance to Christ. The statement

34 A. Saldanha, "From Fearing the emperor to Fearing God: A Kenotic Response of the Exiles in 1 Peter", P. Vakayil and L. Culas (eds.), *Call to Self Emptying Biblical Perspectives* CBAI Seminar papers (Bangalore: TPI, 2017), 171-211 also *1Peter* in *ITS* 49 (2012): 113-146. A. Saldanha has written extensively on this point.

35 A. M. Stibbs, A. F. Walls, *1Peter , A Commentary,* 105, n 51

36 The word *Christianos* appears only thrice in the NT, Acts 11: 26; 26: 28 and 1Pet 4:16

of David G. Horrell could be recalled here: "The label *Christianos* is a stigmatizing label associated not with facet of personal identity- such as disability or disfigurement- but a feature of social identity deriving from group membership. In relation to the term *Christianos*, one thing that is interesting is that it is outsiders who heighten the salience of the label, not only by coining it in the first place but also by making it in judicial settings, the crucial identifier that determines whether a person is or is not a social deviant whether they can be permitted to remain in society or not."[37] *Christianos* is a label applied from outsiders in the context of accusation. It is meant to bring shame, degradation and humiliation to the Christians.[38]

In a hostile situation, an unbeliever may legally accuse a Christian and bring him to trial before the governor. The popular slander against the Christian included incest, murder, cannibalism etc.[39] It is against such charges that 1 Peter is insistent that they take care that none of them may be found guilty (1 Pet 4: 15). It is precisely because of this that one of the themes of the letter has been the need for Christians to do good, to conduct themselves honourably in the sight of the world (eg. 2: 11-12, 20; 3: 8-17). They are urged to ensure that none of them suffers as a consequence of wicked conduct which must result in a person's being labeled a murder, a thief or any kind of evil doer. Such occasion and their consequent suffering are not occasion for rejoicing but are rightly seen as a cause for shame in contrast to suffering as Christians for the glory of God which is no cause of shame (4:16). Given this background the new converts are exhorted to holy conduct in the same way Israel of old was. It is highly possible that the titles are meant to aid the alien sojourners in understanding their place in society. For those tempted to blend into their environment in hopes of suppressing shame and hostility 1Peter offers a message of election holiness and separateness.[40] By resisting Roman imperial cult and emperor worship the converts live a life worthy of their call. That sense of being formed into a new community one with its ethnic roots elsewhere but living out that identity in this world as exiles and aliens is valuable for them.

Conclusion

In the quest for forming a Christian identity the author of 1Peter draws upon two identities; the elect identity of Israel, the chosen people of God and the

37 D.G. Horrell, "The Label *Christianos*: 1 Peter 4: 16 and the Formation of Christian Identity" *Journal of Biblical Literature*, 126 (2007): 361-381, 377

38 Ibid 379-380.

39 Ibid 375-376.

40 N.K Gupta "Spiritual Home of Royal Priests Chosen and Honoured: The Presence and Function of Cultic Imagery in 1Peter", *Perspectives in Religious Studies* 36 (2009): 61-76, 65.

identity of the Gentiles who were incorporated into the chosen race by the reception of the Word. For this he develops Jewish titles and identities and adapts them to suit a new readership. It is not about replacing Israel, rather it is a newness that is determined by the encounter with Christ. It is an adaptation by the Christian author for the Christian reader. In this context the identity formation of the Christian community in 1 Peter is the dialectic of continuity with the Jewish tradition as well as a discontinuity with it as far as it is in dialogue with the Greco-Roman culture and tradition.

The new identity introduces a dynamic quality into their status; they hold a status and identity which is epitomized by the idea that they once were not a people but now are God's holy people, but that is an identity which is not merely fixed and eternal but is also being lived in reference to the worlds around them, presumably being shaped by the reality of that life. It is an identity which is found in the tension between the homeland and the host city, and that tension should lend to it a creative edge, which allows it to grow, develop and eventually come to full fruition. The sense that theirs is not a completed status, but one which is being refined is also seen in the idea that they are being (or should be built 2: 5) into a spiritual house.

There is perhaps in the Catholic Epistles the clear emergence of the place of suffering death as integral part of the Christian identity – something that is being understood and therefore more willingly borne. The concern of the communities such as identity, unity, behavior and spiritual warfare that the epistle reveals may also be found to constitute relevant pressing issues for today's faith communities.

Dr. Prema Vakayil CSST
St. Peter's Pontifical Institute
Bangalore

12

Redefining *Mammon* Implicit and Ignored Teachings of Jesus on Wealth from Socio-Economic Approach

H. Joseph Lalfakmawia
NIIPGTS (NT)

Introduction

The term '*mammon*' is generally translated into 'wealth'. Current sociological study of the first century Mediterranean world is quite hostile towards wealth and riches or the rich. Therefore, a casual reader can be misled either to simplify the term *mammon* or to miss the original intent of the term itself due to the unfavourable sociological implication of the first century.

A saying in the ancient Mediterranean stated that 'every rich man is either unjust or the heir of an unjust person' or 'every rich person is a thief or the heir of a thief'.[1] This saying is warmly welcomed by various social scientists today. This mindset influences negatively that wealth/rich and God are considered antagonistic. In the midst of this, our paper attempts to objectively see if *mammon* indicates negative connotation or how far, the term bears negative remark. We also try to find out why did Jesus add ἀδικίας to μαμωνᾶ to mean 'unrighteous *mammon*'. The interpretation of 'μαμωνᾶ τῆς

1 Jerome, In *Hieremiam*, II, V, 2, CCL LXXIV 61; and similarly in *Tract*, de Ps LXXXIII, lines 29-30, CCLLXXVIII 96; Epistle 120: To Hedebia, PL XXII, 984, quoted in Malina, "Wealth and Poverty in the New Testament and Its World," 363.

ἀδικίας' determines a lot for what Jesus would really mean to tell this parable. Our current discussion is centred around two issues: 1) what does '*mammon'* basically mean and, 2) is 'wealth' itself really 'dishonest/unrighteous'?

1. The Term *Mammon*

As seen in many English Bible versions and elsewhere, *mammon* is commonly translated as 'wealth'.[2] The deciding point, here, is how do we interpret 'wealth' or its technical term '*mammon*'.

2. Etymological Studies on *Mammon*

The term '*mammon*' (μαμωνᾶς), though popularly used in Greek, is most probably of Chaldaic origin, but not Greek. Grundmann's finding states,

> Originally the Aramaic noun served to describe anything of cash value, the 'property' and the 'fortune' without any depraved ethical or religious connotations. Only when the emphasis shifted toward 'profit,' especially 'unjust profit' (see Lk 16:9 *mammonas täs adikias)* and 'bribe,' the term '*mammon*' received its negative accent, for 'profit' is aiming at something beyond the honorable ordinary business, it is something for the sole benefit of one party only. This made the term take on its pejorative character in which we encounter it in the rabbinic sources and the said four New Testament verses. '*Mammon*' has thus become a term denoting the personal attitude 'trust in material goods,'...[3]

The term μαμωνᾶς appears only four times in two passages throughout the New Testament, Mt. 6:24; Lk. 16:9, 11, 13.[4] It is not only a pregnant term, but also ambiguous. It has socio-economic root and implication. According to Friedrich Hauck, the Greek term has a rendering of the *status emphaticus* of the Aramaic noun מָמוֹן.[5] Eb Nestle made extensive list of its probable etymology out of which, the most suitable one is Nm) as he said that this (trust or what is entrusted or that which supports and nourishes human beings) is supported even by Syriac lexicographers.[6] Following this, Hauck assumed that

2 For instance, ESV, NRSV etc.

3 Christoffer H. Grundmann, "*Mammon* - Its Biblical Perception," *Mission Studies* 12, no. 2 (1995): 158.

4 Grundmann, "*Mammon* - Its Biblical Perception," 157.

5 Friedrich Hauck, "μαμωνᾶς," *Theological Dictionary of the New Testament*, ed. Gerhard Kittel, vol. 4 (Grand Rapids: William B. Eerdmans Publishing Company, [1967] 2006), 388.

6 Eb Nestle, "*Mammon*," in *Encyclopedia Biblica: A Dictionary of the Bible,* ed. T. K. Cheyne and J. Sutherland Black, vol. 3 (London: The MacMillan Company, 1902), 2914.

it is derived from the verbal root אמן (אמן that in which one trusts).[7] On the other hand, ממון does not occur in the Old Testament except in Targum and rabbinic literature. In Mishnah,[8] it is used to denote resources, not merely in money, but also in property and anything of value (for instance, slaves). Rabbinic usages interestingly depicted that there is a *mammon* which is free from ethical objection. It was neutrally used in Targum as a property and goods. Not only that, there was a command to honour God with one's substance that shows that there is no ethical incompatibility between ממון and God.[9] Black interpreted Palestinian Pentateuch Targum to Gen. 34:23 as a rendering of Hebrew *miqneh*, 'cattle', the 'wealth' of the Hebrew farmer. Babylonian Talmud (*Berach.* 61b), according to Black, has the sense of 'profit', 'money' and no negative remark is attached with.[10]

However, Targum simultaneously used ממון with negative sense. Targum Gen. 37:26 used ממון for 'profit' while בצע is used in MT (BHS) to mean 'gain made by violence, unjust gain.'[11] LXX used χρήσιμον[12] rather than μαμωνᾶς in which, no negative aspect is explicitly implied.[13] The exact word μαμωνᾶς is not used in LXX. According to Hauck, Targum tends ממון to mean 'gain' especially 'dishonest gain', 'damage', 'spoiling one's neighbour's property' to denote the dishonest profit which a man makes in a matter or transaction by selfishly exploiting the situation of another.[14] It is also used to mean 'bribe' which is silently brought to the judge.[15] Generally speaking, in Judaism, μαμωνᾶς is used with the idea of impure, dishonest and worldly.[16]

---

7 Hauck, "μαμωνᾶς," *TDNT*, vol. 4, 388.

8 For instance, Ab., 2, 12; Sanh., 1, 1, etc. Cf. Hauck, "μαμωνᾶς," *TDNT*, vol. 4, 388.

9 Quoted in Hauck, "μαμωνᾶς," *TDNT*, vol. 4, 389.

10 Matthew Black, *An Aramaic Approach to the Gospels and Acts* (Oxford: Clarendon Press, 1946), 102.

11 Cf. Francis Brown, S. R. Driver and Charles A. Briggs, "בצע," in *The Brown-Driver-Briggs Hebrew and English Lexicon* (Peabody: Hendrickson Publishers, [1906] 2004), 130.

12 Useful, beneficial, advantageous, cf. Walter Bauer, "χρήσιμος," in *A Greek-English Lexicon of the New Testament and Other Early Christian Literature*, trans. William F. Arndt and F. Wilbur Gingrich, 2nd and rev. ed. (Chicago: The University of Chicago Press, [1957] 1979), 885.

13 The same word (χρήσιμος) appear in LXX Wisdom of Solomon 13:11 has '...a useful vessel that serves life's needs'. Here too, a positive connotation is seen. Other passages that have this word is Sirach 10:4; Epistle of Jeremiah 1:59; 2 Macc. 12:12 and Ezek. 15:4 and few more. Apart from Ezek. 15:4, other passages use the term positively.

14 Hauck quoted from Targum Onkelos on Gen. 37:26; Jud. 5:19. Cf. Hauck, "μαμωνᾶς," *TDNT*, 4, 389.

15 Hauck, "μαμωνᾶς," *TDNT*, 4, 389.

16 Hauck, "μαμωνᾶς," *TDNT*, 4, 389.

Strictly speaking, Targum used ממון 36 times in two different senses:[17] 1) **Negative Sense**: Ex. 18:21; (dishonest gain – NASB, NRSV), (bribe – RSV; covetousness – KJV, NKJV); 1 Sam. 8:3[18] Ex. 21:30; Num. 35:30, 31 (money, to mean ransom – LXX translate it as λύτρον). 2) **Non-negative Sense**: Judge 5:19 (spoil of a war, which, though the result of war, could be taken as a positive one because it is a reward of the victors of wars); Mal. 3:14; Ps. 30:10 etc.

What we observe here is that the counterpart of Aramaic ממון in Hebrew Bible is almost consistently בקע[19] הון דנא [20]. Not only in Targum, but also in the Hebrew Bible, that these words denote both neutral and negative aspects. Lexical translation occasionally generalizes the meanings. This leads interpreters to prejudice; because contextual usages must bear the actual sense. For instance בקע is not always used for bad sense such as Judg. 5:19 (as Tar. Judg. 5:19 mentioned above); Job 22:3 (gain); Ps. 30:10 and Mal. 3:14 (profit in general). In the same manner, הון have positive sense such as the blessing of God in various places too (Ps. 112:3; 119:14; Prov. 8:18; 24:4; Ezek. 27:12, 18, 'wealth' in general). These Hebrew words are again almost consistently translated as 'dishonest gain', according to Hauck, even by some English Versions. However, LXX is inconsistent in selecting the equivalent word;

---

17 Gen. 37:26; Ex. 18:21; 21:30; Num. 35:30f; Judg. 5:19; 1 Sam. 8:3; 9:7; 12:3; 2 Sam. 14:14; Is. 5:23; Jer. 6:13; 8:10; Ezek. 22:13, 27; 33:31; Hos. 5:11; Joel 2:8; Amos 5:12; Mic. 2:8; Hab. 2:9; Mal. 3:14; Ps. 30:10; Job 22:3; 27:8; 36:18; Cant. 8:7; Qoh. 2:26; 3:9; 5:9; Lam. 3:39; Ess. 4:7; Lay. 3:39; Law 3:39; Prov. 15:27. Cf. *Targum Onkelos*, vol. 1 & 2 (Berlin: Gorzelaczyk & Co., 1884).

18 One has to mark that Targum used ממון while Hebrew used a seemingly counterpart בקע to mean dishonest wealth, as translated by some noted English versions such as NASB, NKJV etc. while other such as ESV, RSV, NRSV simply translate it as 'gain'. Hauck seemed to take the Hebrew sense and assimilated the same to Aramaic ממון to mean 'dishonest gain' while ממון, strictly speaking, even in this context does not explicitly connote any 'dishonesty'. Hauck probably took it to match the continuing words such as bribe, perverted justice etc. in the same verse. Apart from this, the term itself does not explicitly connote negative aspect. A striking fact is that the Hebrew word בצע is consistently used to mean unlawful gain (as in Gen. 37:26; Ex. 18:21; Judg. 5:19; 1 Sam 8:3; Is. 33:15; 56:11; 57:17). For this usage, cf. L. Koehler, W. Baumgartner, M. Richardson, and J. J. Stamm, *The Hebrew and Aramaic Lexicon of the Old Testament,* "בקע," vols. 1-4 combined (Leiden; New York: E.J. Brill, 1999), 148. In the meantime, Gesenius (while pointing out negative meaning such as 'unjust gain') maintained a neutrality of the term by making a category 'any gain' that do not simply connote negative sense. To him, Is. 56:11; Ezek. 33:31; Gen. 37:26; Job 22:3; Ps. 30:10 are in this category. Cf. William Gesenius, "בקע," *Hebrew and Chaldee Lexicon to the Old Testament Scriptures*, trans. Samuel Prideaux Tregelles (London: Samuel Bagstes & Sons Limited, 1846), 134.

19 בקע is used19 times: Gen. 37:26; Ex. 18:21; Judg. 5:19; Job 22:3; Ps. 30:10; 119:36; Prov. 1:19; 15:27; 28:16; Jer. 6:13; 8:10; Lam. 2:17; Ezek. 22:27; Hab. 2:9; Mal. 3:14.

20 הון is used 18 times: Ps. 44:13; 112:3; 119:14; Prov. 1:13; 6:31; 8:18; 10:15; 11:4; 13:11; 18:11; 19:4; 24:4; 29:3; 30:15f; Cant. 8:7; Ezek. 27:12, 18.

sometimes ὠφέλεια (Ps. 30:10), πλεονεξία (Hab. 2:9), χρήσιμον (Gen. 37:26), δῶρον (Judg. 5:019) and so on; in fact, according to the context. We can also say that while negative usage dominates, non-negative or neutral aspect of the term מָמוֹן בֶּצַע and הון cannot be underestimated because it is definitely there. It is also worth noting that this Aramaic term is not used at all in the Hebrew Old Testament; rather, a negative counterpart is being used. We ask why did the OT writers not use the term ממון but בֶּצַע and הון. Did they purposefully avoid this term to truly suit their intent while ממון might not be literal enough to imply their intent? This must make some sense.

Let us repeat that while ממון does not appear in the Hebrew Old Testament; rather בֶּצַע and הון are common, but as we said, not always in a negative sense. Furthermore, Franz Delitzsch's New Testament in Hebrew[21] employed ממונא (בממונה) to translate μαμωνᾶς back into Hebrew. This makes us think that other Hebrew words used in the Old Testament are not as critical as הממונה in its sense. Similarly, Old Syriac of both Curetonian and Sinaitic Palimpsest too retained the same word *mmona* for μαμωνᾶς. We resolve that the term *mammon*, from the Hebrew and Aramaic words technically, is not purely pejorative.

We summarize that Hauck's investigation is comprehensive and intellectual but not without a slight prejudice against *mammon*/wealth.

3. Ancient Near Eastern Texts on Wealth

Ancient Near Eastern texts witness much on the positive connotation on wealth, particularly as a blessing from god(s). Tablet VII:26, 27 of the Akkadian creation myth inscribed that the god Enbilulu is "The irrigator of the plantations of the gods; Lord of abundance, opulence, *and* of ample crops, who provides wealth, enriches all dwellings, who furnishes millet, causes barley to appear…."[22] Akkadian proverb,[23] the Akkadian rite,[24] Sumero-Akkadian hymn

21 Delitzsch utilized Textus Receptus (because of the wish of the Bible Society) instead of Codex Sinaiticus. His translation of the New Testament was in order to promote Christianity among the Jews. Cf. Gustav Dalman, "The Hebrew New Testament of Franz Delitzsch," *The Old and New Testament Student* 15, no. 3/4 (Sept. – Oct., 1892): 145f.

22 E. A. Speiser, trans. "Akkadian Myths and Epics," in *Ancient Near Eastern Texts Relating to the Old Testament*, ed. James B. Pritchard, 3rd ed. (Princeton: Princeton University Press, 1969), 71.

23 "Like a man's wealth, let your lips be precious." Robert H. Pfeiffer, trans., "Akkadian Proverbs and Counsels," in *Ancient Near Eastern Texts Relating to the Old Testament*, ed. James B. Pritchard, 3rd ed. with supplement (Princeton: Princeton University Press, 1969), 426.

24 The Akkadian rite recited to the goddess Beltiya, by the *urigallu*-priest of the temple Eudul, after withdrawing from the presence of the god Bel, bears exaltation of the goddess that says, "…Who impoverishes the rich, who causes the poor to become wealthy…" According to Sachs, this prayer was recited in the temple program for the New Year's Festivals at Babylon. Two duplicate texts are involved, one in Paris and the other in

to Shamash (Sun-god),[25] the Babylonian Theodicy[26] etc. There are many other texts that talk about wealth or riches. These texts clearly indicate that wealth was seen as a providence from god(s) or goddess(es).

Meanwhile, negative aspect on wealth is also found in the Ancient Near Eastern literature. For instance, the Aramaic proverb taught not to covet other's wealth,[27] a sort of lamentation that god brought the reciter scarcity instead of wealth[28] etc. As a whole, positive view on wealth is seen more in the texts.

4. Qumran Writings on Wealth

From the Qumran texts, הון בצע and נכס are commonly used to mean wealth and riches.[29] בקעם in 4Q457a Frag. 6 is translated as 'unjust profit'.[30] 4QS^b 18:6,[31]

London, both tablets dating to the Seleucid period. The program described may go back to a much earlier time. A. Sachs, trans., "Akkadian Rituals," in *Ancient Near Eastern Texts Relating to the Old Testament*, ed. James B. Pritchard, 3rd ed. with supplement (Princeton: Princeton University Press, 1969), 332.

25 This hymn exalts that the doer of good deeds and who is not crafty in his account will expand (his) family and will acquire wealth. Ferris J. Stephens, trans., "Sumero-Akkadian Hymns and Prayers: Hymn to the Sun-God; iii," in *Ancient Near Eastern Texts Relating to the Old Testament*, ed. James B. Pritchard, 3rd ed. with supplement (Princeton: Princeton University Press, 1969), 389.

26 The Babylonian Theodicy contains, "The humble man who fears his goddess accumulates wealth." The Theodicy is an acrostic poem of twenty-seven stanzas of eleven lines each, not all of which are preserved, and takes the form of a dialogue. Robert D. Biggs, trans., "Akkadian Didactic and Wisdom Literature: The Babylonian Theodicy," in *Ancient Near Eastern Texts Relating to the Old Testament*, ed. James B. Pritchard, 3rd ed. with supplement (Princeton: Princeton University Press, 1969), 602.

27 The text is preserved as the more recent writing on eleven sheets of palimpsest papyrus of the late fifth century BCE recovered by German excavators from the debris of Elephantine, Upper Egypt in the years 1906-7. Cf. H. L. Ginsberg, trans., "Aramaic Proverbs and Precepts," in *Ancient Near Eastern Texts Relating to the Old Testament*, ed. James B. Pritchard, 3rd ed. with supplement (Princeton: Princeton University Press, 1969), 427, 429.

28 Robert H Pfeiffer, trans., "Akkadian Observations on Life and the World Order: A Dialogue About Human Misery," in *Ancient Near Eastern Texts Relating to the Old Testament*, ed. James B. Pritchard, 3rd ed. with supplement (Princeton: Princeton University Press, 1969), 438f. According to Pfeiffer, This poem is sometimes called "The Babylonian Ecclesiastes." The extant tablets on which the poem is written are not earlier than 7th century BCE, but the poem may have originated a few centuries before then.

29 For text and primary translation of the Qumran text, cf. Florentino García Martínez and Eibert J. C. Tigchelaar, eds., *The Dead Sea Scrolls Study Edition*, vol. 1 & 2 (Leiden: Brill, 1999).

30 Martínez and Tigchelaar, *The Dead Sea Scrolls Study Edition*, 935.

31 4QS^b 18:6 (ובצע) says 'To them he should leave goods and profit like a servant to] his [mas] ter and like one oppressed before] someone do[mineering him …' Martínez and Tigchelaar, *The Dead Sea Scrolls Study Edition*, 515.

4QSM 2:3,[32] 4Q412 4:1 used עשׁרי (עשׁר)[33] which does not mean negative.[34] 4Q424 3:10, 11 and 11QT[a] 57:19-21[35] used הון to mean wealth[36] in which הון does not do with something that is unjust or gain/profit by violence.

In the meantime, Wealth (הון) can corrupt others (*1QpHab.* 8:3). Wicked Priest is condemned for hoarding wealth as he deserted God and betrayed God's law for the sake of riches (*1QpHab.* 8:10-12). In contrast to that, wealth (נכסיא) is counted as a blessing from God (*1QapGen ar.* 21:3; *1Q22* or *1QWords of Moses* 2:3). Abram gave tithe of all the wealth (נכסיא) of the king of Elam and his allies (*1QapGen ar.* 22:17). To be precise, there are several passages in the Dead Sea Scrolls that bear negative and positive characteristic of wealth.[37]

The above Qumran textual studies indicate that בקע, הון, נכס and עשׁר are used to denote 'wealth/riches'. As found in *1QpHab.* 8:10-12 where it is used negatively, it indicates 'hoarding', 'sufficiency or enough' in exclaim'. Borrowing Marshal's word, "It can express wealth of all kinds, and may have a good or a bad sense."[38] When it connotes negative remark, it is understood from the contexts. This again says that the term itself is not basically depreciatory, but its context determines.

5. New Testament Usages and its Interpretation

Throughout the New Testament, it is found only in the words of Jesus. Friberg suggests that the personification *mammon*, is the Syrian god of riches.[39] However, Eb Nestle convincingly ruled out this proposition as due to later thought developed by Milton.[40] Hauck quoted Mt. 6:19ff., 6:24 par., Lk. 12:15ff.; and Lk. 16:9 and saw derogative senses in all these passages and commented that the nature of God rules out all ideas of using *mammon* in the

---

32 4QSM 2:3 used 'profit' but too short to identify whether negative or positive. But it is used together with wealth הון which means 'wealth/sufficiency/high value'. *BDB*, "הון," 223.

33 'Riches' Cf. *BDB*, "רֹשֶׁע, " 799.

34 4Q412 4:1 used עשׁרי (עשׁר) which says, "my wealth he will give as an inheritance," which is rather not negative. Cf. Martínez and Tigchelaar, *The Dead Sea Scrolls Study Edition*, 843.

35 And he shall not pervert justice, and he shall not accept a bribe to pervert righteous judgment. And he shall not crave a field, a vineyard, any wealth, a house or any valuable thing in Israel and seize... cf. Martínez and Tigchelaar, *The Dead Sea Scrolls Study Edition*, 1279.

36 4Q424 3:10, 11 used different word (הון) to say "he will be] concerned with all who lack wealth, the sons of justice [...] 11 [...] with all wealth [...]." Martínez and Tigchelaar, *The Dead Sea Scrolls Study Edition*, 891.

37 For instance, *1QS* 10:19; *1Q28b* 3:19 *1QH[a]* 6:20; *4QHistorical Work* Frag. 1, Col. 2:4 and many more.

38 Marshall, *NIGTC: Luke*, 621.

39 T. Friberg, B. Friberg and N. F. Miller, "μαμωνας," in *Analytical Lexicon of the Greek New Testament*, vol. 4 (Grand Rapids: Baker Books, 2000), 253.

40 Nestle, "*Mammon*," *Encyclopedia Biblica*, 2915.

world to serve cultural aims and concerns. To Hauck, the only unobjectionable and religious use of the earthly wealth is clever use of money.[41] Louw and Nida too stressed its negative aspect.[42] In addition to that, Colin Brown rightly said, "In itself the word may be neutral, but it acquired in negative contexts the connotation of possessions dishonestly gained and wealth dishonestly used, as in bribery."[43]

It is clear to a great extent that the *mammon* in the words of Jesus has negative aspect. From its face value, it appears that the comparison is between God and *mammon*, the poles that will never have meeting point. Apart from the exclusive usage of the technical word *mammon*, other words such as wealth, riches, properties etc. are viewed with much suspicion as if they are inclined towards ungodly or sin. It leads to an estrangement of economic security or well-being.

The background study reveals that *mammon* is not simply a currency itself but hoarding of it so that the owner puts trust in it. Thus, it is realized that *mammon* is the idol legitimating the storing up of treasures (Mt. 6:19ff.) which was introduced by the Persians on an imperial scale in order to rationalise the collecting of tribute.[44] As theologically interpreted by Duchrow, *mammon* is "money accumulation by tribute, temple, slave production and trade taking away the means of life from the poor, and particularly the rural poor, which marks the political economic context of Jesus' rejection of *Mammon*."[45] Duchrow likened this *mammon* with today's 'capitalistic economy' and considered it as one that has to be avoided.[46]

Martin Hengel saw a total repudiation of possessions indicated in the use of the Aramaic-Phoenician word *mammon*. He assumed that since the early church borrowed it from the contemporary Jewish terminology, it is left untranslated because it is almost regarded as the name of an idol: the service of *mammon* is idolatry. So, it is demonic.[47] Radical criticism of property during the early church is witnessed clearly.[48]

41 Hauck, "μαμωνας," *TDNT*, 4, 390.

42 Louw and Nida, "μαμωνας," *Greek-English Lexicon,* 561 (57.34).

43 Colin Brown, "Possessions: μαμωνας," in *New International Dictionary of the New Testament Theology*, vol. 2, ed. Colin Brown (Grand Rapids: Regency Reference Library, 1976), 837.

44 Ulrich Duchrow, "God or *Mammon*: Economies in Conflict," *Mission Studies* 13, no. 1-2 (1996): 44, 49.

45 Duchrow, "God or *Mammon*," 50.

46 Duchrow, "God or *Mammon*," 53.

47 Martin Hengel, *Earliest Christianity*, trans. John Bowden (London: SCM Press Ltd., 1974), 172.

48 Martin Hengel, *Property and Riches in the Early Church* (London: SCM Press Ltd., 1974), 46.

Oakman pointed out that money in Jesus' day was an elite political tool, not a universal economic medium. It benefited the powerful inordinately, but held captive values esteem by common folk. For instance, money was for tax, in safety deposits, or on load to the weak. Jesus called these security arrangements '*Mammon'*. Therefore, he conjectured that the Aramaic root word means 'trust'. Taxes, deposits, and loan receipts were items trusted by the powerful to provide future security.[49] So, *mammon* does not simply mean 'money' in itself but with all its abusive and despotic power grabbed by the powerful/rich over against the poor. The essence is oppressive. As Oakman said, it is called negatively, evil, from agrarian perspective because it was perceived as gained unjustly. It led to the control of villages' agricultural increase.[50] The reason why Jesus was hostile against *mammon* is that money was used and misused on deposit or to commercial and money transactions in order to entangle the weak/poor into indebtedness.[51]

Socio-economic Reading of Mammon

When we employ socio-economic approach to study *mammon*, we do not fail to see the evil nature of wealth and riches. However, our main intent is to acknowledge positive aspect of wealth in the service of God and human beings, particularly the poor in the real sense.

Unjust *Mammon* and Just/True *Mammon*

As per the evidence made by Grundmann, *mammon*, in its original setting, is at least neutral, if not positive.[52] Therefore, the neutral usage of the term *mammon* has nothing to do with something unjust or violent. However, the source or outcome/consequence or both is always prone to something unjust or violent. Therefore, Jesus clearly saw how precarious is one withholding wealth. As a result, the term *mammon* requires addition of 'unjust' (ἀδικία) to serve Jesus' purpose of critique on it; hence, μαμωνᾶ τῆς ἀδικίας (the unrighteous *mammon*). J. A. Metzger rightly said that if *mammon* itself has a negative valence, then Jesus' qualifier would be redundant because μαμωνᾶ would already be having negative valence.[53] Since Jesus intentionally added this, we can take this as evidence that the term μαμωνᾶ does not automatically bear negative remark unless its context does not determine. A stronger argument

49 Douglas E. Oakman, "Money in the Moral Universe of the New Testament," in *The Social Setting of Jesus and the Gospels*, ed. Wolfgang Stegemann, Bruce J. Malina, Gerd Theissen (Minneapolis: Fortress Press, 2002), 334.

50 Oakman first interpreted it as 'accumulated wealth', corresponding to its Aramaic meaning 'wealth'. Cf. Oakman, "The Countryside in Luke-Acts," 167f.

51 Oakman, "Money in the Moral Universe of the New Testament," 345.

52 Grundmann, "*Mammon* - Its Biblical Perception," 158.

53 Metzger, *Consumption and Wealth in Luke's Travel Narrative*, 127.

probably is Lk. 16:11 in which Jesus said two opposing terms 'ἀδίκῳ μαμωνᾷ and ἀληθινὸν μαμωνᾷ'. Strictly speaking, ἀληθινὸν μαμωνᾷ (true wealth/ true *mammon*) is not used, instead, ἀληθινὸν. However, this adjectival usage indicates the existence of the word it qualifies, that is, μαμωνᾷ which is already said before. In this case, we argue that Jesus used both unrighteous μαμωνᾷ and true/right μαμωνᾷ, that indicates the neutrality of the term μαμωνᾷ. If unrighteous *mammon* exists, righteous/true *mammon* also exists (as we also provide internal evidence). Hence, μαμωνᾷ alone, without τῆς ἀδικίας is not pejorative.

False Dichotomy of God and *Mammon*

Martin Hengel believed that *mammon*, as indicated as 'unrighteous *mammon*', signified an act of idolatry, which constitutes the very essence of idolatry.[54] E. P. Groenewald strengthens his argument that the root word of *mammon* is derived from Aramaic *amen*, that in which one places trust, which is steadfast; which is reliable and true. He puts forward the view of God and *mammon* as if they are contrasting objects of worship. In his idea, God is the true Amen while *mammon* is the pretending Amen. Thus, *mammon* is the counter-God.[55] François Bovon straightforwardly put *mammon* as a 'negative counterpart of God'.[56] This can sound like a dichotomy between God and *mammon* as object of worship which legitimizes Jesus' word, "You cannot serve God and *mammon*" (Mt. 6:24).

In contrast to this view, we share Groenewald's comment, "Jesus does not commend the steward for his dishonest action, but for his sensible foresight and for the fact that he was not dominated by *Mammon*, but rather employed this *Mammon* as his servant…the employment of *Mammon* in the service of God."[57] Instead of the dichotomy of God and *mammon*, we tend to say subjugation of the *mammon* in the service of God carried out on others particularly for the poor. Jesus did not tend to mean that *mammon* is an object of worship against which God has to be chosen. Rather, it is a moral and ethical teaching of Jesus not to be enslaved and entangled in the clutches of wealth and hoarding of wealth because it is harmful for individual and community. Money or wealth or properties is not sinful; but it easily tempts the possessors towards sin because they put trust in it. Therefore, Jesus criticizes against it. Instead of idolizing it, it has to be subjugated and used to make friends.

---

54 Martin Hengel, "Property and Riches in the Early Church," in *The Earliest Christianity* (London: SCM Press Ltd., 1979), 172.

55 E. P. Groenewald, "God and *Mammon*," *Neotestamentica* 1 (1967): 62.

56 François Bovon, *Luke the Theologian: Fifty-five Years of Research (1950–2005)*, 2nd revised ed. (Waco: Baylor University Press, 2005), 498.

57 Groenewald, "God and *Mammon*," 65.

G. R. Beasley-Murray, in his comment on Rev. 18:17-19, suggested that the sin of Babylon is not in the commodities of the merchants and sailors (their wealth) but on how it used its riches to seduce human to adopt the kind of gross materialism and *mammon*-worship.[58] The language of '*mammon*-worship' is only in a metaphorical sense, not literally as God as an object of worship. Robert H. Stein rightly sees the play of word,

> This expression does not refer to wealth gained through dishonesty, for in 16:11 we are told to be trustworthy in our handling of the "*mammon* of unrighteousness," and one cannot be trustworthy with respect to wealth obtained dishonestly. The expression is idiomatic and refers to "filthy lucre" or as the NIV translates it "worldly wealth."[59]

Mammon is not necessarily wealth or money in a negative sense, but generally wealth of any kind. When it is technically used to bear negative overtone, it is right to ascribe negative label. In that context, we define *mammon* (to bear negative sense) as, "Unjustly obtained, unjustly used and unjustly hoarded wealth in which one puts trust." It is not something that can be worshipped literally because it is not an object of worship. It only pollutes human mind.

Enslaving the *Mammon*

According to Wright, Is. 23 and Ezek. 27-28 (oracles against Tyre and Sidon) was a prophetic indictment that was primarily because of economic arrogance and self-deification. God condemned these kings because they used economic criteria as the ultimate measure of all things.[60] This is economic abuse. Tyre and Sidon were not condemned because of their economic wealth, but because of their economic abuse. OT thought provided a middle way between being rich and poor as we see,

> give me neither poverty nor riches;
> feed me with the food that that I need,
> or I shall be full, and deny you, and say, "Who is the LORD?"
> or I shall be poor, and steal, and profane the name of my God
> (Prov. 30:8b-9).

58 G. R. Beasley-Murray, *The Book of Revelation: The New Century Bible Commentary* (Grand Rapids: William B. Eerdmans Publishing Company, [1974] 1987), 268.

59 Robert H. Stein, *Luke: The New American Commentary* (Nashville: Broadman Press, 1992), 416.

60 Wright, "God or *Mammon*," 154.

Beatitudes are spoken to the poor, and yet possessions can be used for good (Lk. 8:1–3; 10:29–37; 12:32–34).[61] Crossan thought that the beatitudes uttered by Jesus is the heart of the original movement about a shared egalitarian society of spiritual and material resources[62] in which expendables (the weak and the oppressed who were abused by the rich) and acts of oppression and injustice no longer exists.[63]

As we have discussed above, wealth itself is not sinful. Jesus called it as *the unrighteous mammon* because injustice is always involved in the process of accumulation and use of earthly possessions. But Jesus nowhere teaches that material possessions as such are sinful and unclean. It is human's sinful attitude and conduct in connection with worldly goods (money in particular) that make wealth a curse.[64]

We have also pointed out that wealth/*mammon* and God are not two opposing objects of faith/worship. *Mammon*/wealth is to be subjected or enslaved, and made use of it wisely and justly. It is not to be hoarded beyond the reach of others, particularly by the poor. Goetzmann cautiously commented, "[W]hile wealth is not to be sought for its own sake, wise and diligent stewardship of it in the master's service is important."[65] When wealth/*mammon* enslaves one, that is sinful; but if wealth/*mammon* is subjugated/enslaved and used for good cause, then wealth is good. If one puts trust in wealth, then it is sinful; but if one utilizes it for good cause, then wealth is honourable. Such was expressed by Plutarch who said that wealth is noble when used for human needs.[66]

Richard H. Hiers rightly argued that Lucan Jesus' economic concern oscillated between the rich and the poor. The material possessions have to be

---

61 Fred B. Craddock, *Luke: Interpretation* (Louisville: John Knox Press, 1990), 189.

62 John Dominic Crossan, *The Historical Jesus: The Life of a Mediterranean Jewish Peasant* (New York: HarperSanFrancisco, 1991), 341.

63 Trudinger, "Exposing the Depth of Oppression (Luke 16:1b-8a)," 136.

64 Norval Geldenhuys, *Commentary on the Gospel of Luke: New International Commentary on the New Testament* (Grand Rapids: William B. Eerdmans Publishing Company, 1979), 416.

65 Jürgen Goetzmann, "House: oivkonomi,a," in *New International Dictionary of the New Testament Theology,* vol. 2, ed. Colin Brown (Grand Rapids: Regency Reference Library, 1976), 255.

66 Quoted by Malherbe, "The Christianization of a Topos (Luke 12:13-34)," 126.

used for the benefit of the poor[67] while hoarding and withholding the same led exclusion from the Kingdom of God.[68]

We do not say that this parable does not talk about the eschatological issue or the Kingdom of God, but as Silva states, 'the parable advises eschatological readiness, but within it provides the key to its concrete application, namely the use of material goods.'[69] Derrett believed that failure to deal righteously with *mammon* leads to hell.[70]

One way to enslave *mammon*/wealth, with the rise of the first urban Christians outside of Palestine, was "conversion" of the wicked wealthy so that they would share their wealth with their fellow Christians.[71] Without sharing means hoarding. Hoarding was one of the key issues addressed by Jesus. Therefore, "The injunction is not to befriend *mammon* but to use *mammon* for the benefit of others."[72] Brown rightly said, "*Mammon* itself does not endure, but it may be used to achieve something which is enduring. *Mammon* itself is material, but its use has personal dimensions."[73] *Mammon* has to be enslaved before it enslaves us.

Prudent Use of Wealth: Ultimate Goal of the Parable

James Kizhakkeyil proposed a synthetic interpretation to find out the true intent of Jesus in approving the praise of the steward by the master. To Kizhakkeyil the main intent of the parable is to inculcate prudence.[74] T. W. Manson's statement bears a socio-economic sense, though in an obscure way (which he might not really intend though) as he said,

> If a bad man will take infinite trouble to get friends for his own selfish interests, the good man will surely take some trouble to make friends in a better way and for better ends. The point of this

67 He quoted Lk. 14:13f.; 19:8; 10:34f. etc. for his argument. Cf. Richard H. Hiers, "Friends by Unrighteous *Mammon*: The Eschatological Proletariat (Luke 16:9)," *Journal of the American Academy of Religion* 38, no. 1 (Mar., 1970): 33.

68 For instance, Lk. 6:24 f.; 12:15 ff.; 16:19 ff.; 18:24 etc. Cf. Hiers, "Friends by Unrighteous *Mammon*: The Eschatological Proletariat (Luke 16:9)," 33f.

69 Silva, "The Parable of the Prudent Steward and its Lucan Context," 266.

70 Derrett, *Law in the New Testament*, 90.

71 Malina, "Wealth and Poverty in the New Testament and Its World,"366.

72 Brown, "Possessions," *NIDNTT*, vol. 2, 837.

73 Brown, "Possessions," *NIDNTT*, vol. 2, 837.

74 Kizhakkeyil, "Decoding Luke," 374; This interpretation (prudence use of wealth) is held by various scholars such as Ireland, "A History of Recent Interpretation of the Parable of the Unjust Steward (Luke 16:1-13)," 295; Craddock, *Luke*, 189; Pickar, "The Unjust Steward (Lk. 16:1-9)," 253 and many more. Ireland, from his extensive studies, says that out of about 140 interpreters he surveyed, at least 50 understood this parable to connote a positive lesson about prudence or wisdom in the use of material possessions.

> saying [v 9] is rather that by disposing of worldly wealth in the proper way, one will have treasure in heaven.[75]

Craig L. Blomberg boldly translated the phrase 'μαμωνᾶ τῆς ἀδικίας' as 'worldly wealth' and interpreted that it does not mean ill-gotten gain but simply money in general. He continued to say, "Jesus thus commands his followers to use the possessions of this life for kingdom purposes - to gain friends for themselves by making and nurturing disciples and putting God's kingdom principles into practice."[76] Thus, he has no problem in using the material wealth/money to make friends by means of unrighteous *mammon*.[77] Paul Borgman straightforwardly commended that the story is a challenge to use money well. Whatever the complication in it, it illustrates a more complicated truth about letting go of possessions.[78] Bovon too agreed to mean that the best use that one can make of money is to make friends for the future life.[79]

Whatever is the interpretation of the steward's action, either as a dishonest one or a vindicated one, scholars' common parlance is that his prudence is praised/commended. To be precise, his prudence to secure himself so that he would be welcomed by the debtors, especially when he would need it most (right usage of time) or to restore the honour of his master is praiseworthy, and it was praised too. Our finding here is that wealth/money itself is not estranged but its right usage in life plays more significant role and the same is highly suggested, even by Jesus.

Conclusion

Material wealth as well as economic profit it very often misunderstood as '*mammon'* mainly because of the implication of the first century socio-economic senario. Sometimes, it is emphatically polarized as if it is antithesis of God. We found that wealth/riches itself is not called '*mammon'* negatively but wealth that is acquired unjustly, avariciously hoarded especially when it enslaves the possessors to overshadow God and the poor. Thus, we define *mammon* as "Unjustly obtained, unjustly used and unjustly hoarded wealth in which one puts trust." It is not something that can be worshipped literally because it is not an object of worship. But it pollutes human mind. Our finding is that *mammon* is not an antithesis of God as if it is an object of worship. Rather,

---

75 T. W. Manson, *Sayings of Jesus* (London: SCM Press Ltd., 1949), 292-293.

76 Craig L. Blomberg, *Neither Poverty nor Riches: A Biblical Theology of Material Possessions* (Leicester: Apollos, Inter-Varsity Press, 1999), 122.

77 Blomberg, *Neither Poverty nor Riches*, 122.

78 Paul Borgman, *The Way according to Luke Hearing the Whole Story of Luke-Acts* (Grand Rapids: William B. Eerdmans Publishing Company, 2006), 160f.

79 Bovon, *Luke the Theologian*, 72.

mammon has to be subdued and enslaved. Wealth must not be hoarded; instead, should be used wisely to serve the poor in particular, and society in general.

Therefore, we say that it is narrow-mindedness to think μαμωνᾶ as a sinful thing. If *mammon* itself has a negative connotation, then Jesus' qualifier τῆς ἀδικίας would be redundant because μαμωνᾶ would already be having negative valence.[80] Since Jesus intentionally added this, we can take this as evidence that the term μαμωνᾶ does not evidently bear negative remark.

Generally speaking, ἀδικίας is added to qualify the depreciatory character of *mammon*. When it is technically used to denote negative statement, it is also used simply as *mammon* (without ἀδικίας) but not limited to all wealth in general; rather, unjust wealth of any kind. Therefore, we resolve that 'wealth' is not a conventional translation of the term μαμωνᾶ. The best way is to retain the technical term as μαμωνᾶ/*mammon* and be defined and described cautiously according to contexts because it is detrimental to polarize earthly economy (vital for human existence) and God.

The next step after this is that engagement in business or trade or being rich (if it is with a clean hand) does not readily mean that one is sinful. Economic stability does not automatically mean antithesis of God or worshipping *mammon*. Wealth itself is not hostile to God. So, we challenge dichotomy between God and *Mammon* as if they are two opposing objects of worship. Justly obtained and utilized wealth (in the service of human, particularly the poor, and of God) is noble. Such is not a *mammon* in a negative sense (technical usage), but a *mammon* in a positive sense.

80 Metzger, *Consumption and Wealth in Luke's Travel Narrative*, 127.

13

The Significance of Torah in the Book of Proverbs
(*Synopsis of the DTh Dissertation*)

Enolyne Lyngdoh

Torah is significant in the history of the Jewish community in the Post-exilic period. The significance of Torah in the Book of Proverbs is presented as didactic instruction to the younger generation. The instruction intent to nurture the youth concerning the path of wisdom comprises attitude, social behaviours and actions. Further, the concept of social justice towards the emancipation of the disadvantaged section is mentioned. In the pursuit of justice, parents, sages and scribes instruct children the value of wisdom. Wisdom embraced Torah in the instructional discourse, and Torah is central to the understanding of liberation in Proverbs. The vitality of wisdom instruction in the Book of Proverbs aim to educate individuals to liberate oneself from the way of life that can destroy the 'self' and affect 'others' as well. Hence, the sages in Proverbs present Torah as a guiding principle to wisdom and knowledge. In the study of Proverbs, one can perceive that the Book contains independent sayings. Further, its diversity is observed in its limitation of the overall structure. Thus, the study argues that wisdom instruction in the Book of Proverbs does not confine to the educational structure of equipping the elite class. Besides the scribes, parents, elders and sages of different social strata play a prominent role in educating children. Torah appears in wisdom discourse as judicial wisdom to discern between social good and social evil. Hence, Torah embraced wisdom and wisdom is the obedience of Torah in the Book of Proverbs.

1. Why Torah Significant?

The Book of Proverbs emerged in the context where the Jewish community is confronted with the uncertainty of their very existence. The institutional loss of the Davidic monarchy and the experience in the exile has greatly shattered the Jews. Such unexpected challenges have led the community to question about their faith and history. The Post-exilic period[1] mark as fundamental because during this period the Jewish scribes and the sages are encouraged to reconstruct one's history under the sponsorship of the Persian Empire. Such event took place when the Babylonian Empire fell in the hand of the Persians, and the Persian court embarked upon a new policy toward captive nations by allowing the Jews to return and to re-settle in their homelands. But, the exiles are not free from the Persian rule. It was during this period that the scribes and the sages were motivated to reflect the importance of Torah to the socio-economic and religious life of the Post-exilic Israel. Eventually, this period contributes an important defining moment in the development of Jewish's history and theology. Hence, proverbs stay close to actual-life conditions that discern the best choices in ambiguous situations when the basic order of things are not obvious and have to be searched out.[2] In Proverbs, the ethical values of Torah are associated with words, thoughts, and actions in which the sages interpreted as the 'way of wisdom.' In addition to this, Justice, righteousness, and the fear of the YHWH (1:3; 2:9; 4:18; 8:6-8, 16, 20; 11:2-6, 18, 30; 12:5; 13:5-6; 15-9; 16:8, 13; 17:15, 23;19:1; 20:7, 28 21:7, 29; 23:23-24; 24:1) are the central concern in the quest for wisdom. Justice concerning the emancipation of the disadvantaged (the דל, אביון, עני, רש, מחסור, אלמנה and the יתום) is rooted from the socio-religious ethos of Torah in Proverbs. Thus, the socio-liberative reading is employed to interpret the significance of Torah in the Book of Proverbs.

1.1. The Socio-Liberative Hermeneutical Approach of Torah in Wisdom Discourse

The socio-liberative serves as a hermeneutical lens to examine the economic, political and social struggles of the Jewish community in the Post-exilic period. This reading is employed to examine if such values and norms of Torah function to enhance liberation to the oppressed and how these norms bring justice and equality in society. In a narrow sense of the term, Torah is understood as binding norms than liberative principle. It is, therefore, essential to interpret the function of Torah from the liberating perspective. In Proverbs, the traditional understanding of Torah as norms of behaviour is further interpreted as having socio-religious concerns. Socio-liberative reading is a deliberate

1 The term 'Post-exilic' is a historical reference of the end of exile (539/500–323 BCE).

2 Norman K. Gottwald, *The Hebrew Bible: A Socio-Literary Introduction* (Philadelphia: Fortress Press, 1987), 573.

focus on the community's responsibility towards the implementation of justice to the poor which is understood as an act of liberation from exploitation and oppression.[3] The interpretation of wisdom as the execution of justice in Proverbs is concerned with the oppressive action in a hierarchical power structure, and call for positive endeavors towards the disadvantaged sections.[4] The aspect of liberation and justice is a vision of the Deuteronomic historian. And such interpretation can be observed in the depiction concerning the value of human life and human dignity, in which, inter-personal social relation is emphasized.[5] One of the requirements for a 'just order' is a commitment to the implementation of justice to the poor (Prov. 14:31; 21:13; 22:2, 9, 22; 28:3). The sages in Proverbs further convey the disadvantaged sections using the predicate adjective and noun as 'poor one,' 'weak one' or 'dejected one.'[6] The interpretation of justice as a collective response is a vision for gaining wisdom that the Book of Proverbs incorporated the principles of Torah. It is therefore necessary to study the meaning of Torah in the Post-exilic Period to further understand the uniqueness of Torah in Proverbs.

1.2. The Meaning of Torah

The term 'Torah' is understood as the Law of Moses and the five books from Genesis to Deuteronomy.[7] However, 'Torah' in the Post-exilic and Second Temple Period has a wider connotation that comprises an extensive variety of literature and traditions.[8] The term תורה is derived from ירה which explicitly refer to the teaching activity carried out by parents, sages, and priest and the same valence attaches to Torah.[9] The root ירה implies nothing about any particular method, but one can observe that there is an element of mutual personal relationship when ירה is used.[10] There are occurrences of the derived substantive מירה 'moreh' which can be translated as 'teacher.'[11] The term ירה in

3 Rolf P. Knierim, *The Task of Old Testament Theology: Substance, Method and Cases* (Grand Rapids, MI: William B. Eerdmans Publishing Company, 1995), 94.

4 Bruce V. Malchow, *Social Justice in the Hebrew Bible* (Minnesota: The Liturgy Press, 1996), 22.

5 Peter T. Vogt, "Social Justice and the Vision of Deuteronomy," *JETS* 51/1 (2008): 35.

6 David J. A. Clines ed., *The Dictionary of Classical Hebrew*, vol. 2 (Sheffield: Academic Press, 1995), 437.

7 James W. Watts, "Torah," in *NIDB* vol. 5, ed. Katharine Doob Sakenfeld (Nashville: Abingdon Press, 2009), 630.

8 Watts, "Torah," 630.

9 Douglas A. Knight, *Law, Power and Justice in Ancient Israel* (Westminster: John Knox Press, 2011), 29.

10 Wagner, *TDOT* 6: 339.

11 The word מוסר is 'instruction' and it can be translated as to 'teach' or to 'instruct' with a double object which conveys 'teach someone something.' The root word תורה comes from

Wisdom Literature appears as a parental instruction to children that encompasses social behavior and conduct which suggest that wisdom instruction includes explicit ethical elements.[12] The sages and scribes in Proverbs teaches the fundamentals of Mosiac Torah in ירה wisdom discourse. Wisdom instruction conveys Torah values concerning social justice and 'the fear of God.' Hence, Torah enjoyed a status not just as a foundational educational document but as a unique standard of law that forms a community in the Second Temple Period.[13] There is a possibility that the late (or post) Deuteronomistic author of Deuteronomy 4 merges the idea of hearing and observing of the Mosaic commands in Deuteronomy 6:6-9.[14] The aim and purpose of instruction in Proverbs is to gain חכמה (wisdom), בינה (understanding, discernment), and דעת (knowledge) so that a person may be able to deal wisely as well as uphold righteousness, justice and the fear of the Lord (Prov. 1:1-7).

The usage of Torah is associated with the word חק (חָקַק from חקו in Prov. 8:29) which denotes commandments.[15] Further, the terms מִצְוָה and דבר in the Book of Proverbs is conveyed beyond the literal understanding of the term, bearing a 'hokmatic' meaning.[16] In Proverbs, the function of the plural דבר (1:23) denotes the covenant commandment.[17] The oral character of the Torah as instruction is indicated by Proverb 31:26 as well as the call to hear (Prov. 1:8) to the commandments מִצְוָה. The terms מִצְוַת and מִצְוֹת (3:1; 4:4; 6:20; 7:2) denotes to observe and to understand which is further interpreted as walking in the path that leads to life (cf. Ps. 1).[18] The Torah as 'instruction' is developed in connection to the way of life, which is something to be taught and learned, and in that process, it is to be rationalized and urged.[19] Consequently, human behavior is something that needs exhortation and explanation, reasons for

---

ירה and it is found in several Semitic languages and the verb appears 45 times in the Old Testament and mostly in hiphil. S. Wagner, "ירה," *TDOT* 6: 339-347

12 Wagner, *TDOT* 6: 339.

13 David M. Carr, "The Rise of Torah," in *The Pentateuch as Torah: New Models for Understanding its Promulgation and Acceptance*, eds. Gary N. Knoppers and Bernard M. Levinson (Winona Lake, IN: Eisenbrauns, 2007), 39.

14 Bernd U. Schipper, "Afterword: Wisdom and Torah: Insights and Perspectives," in *Wisdom and Torah: The Reception of 'Torah' in the Wisdom Literature of the Second Temple Period*, JSJSup., vol. 163, eds. Bernd U. Schipper and D. Andrew Teeter (Leiden, Boston: Brill, 2013), 314.

15 The term "טקק" means 'to insribe' and in Proverbs 8:15 and 31:5 conveys to establish justice, govern as in Isaiah 10:1 "טקק." It also indicates 'a lord's sovereign legislation regarding his subordinates. G. Liedke, "טקק," *TLOT* 2: 468-472.

16 G. Liedke and C. Petersen, "תורה," *TLOT* 3: 1415.

17 W. H. Schmidt, "דבר," *TDOT* 3: 94-125.

18 Liedke and Petersen, *TLOT* 3: 1415-1416.

19 Patrick D. Miller, *The Way of the Lord: Essays in Old Testament Theology* (Grand Rapids, MI: William B. Eerdmans Publishing Company, 2004),137.

obedience and motivations to indicate the attractiveness of the way described therein.[20] The possibility of Torah as a derivation from ירה might have emerged in the sense of showing the direction to extend the hand or finger to indicate the way.[21] The concept of Torah in Proverbs presents the social requirements and directs people to walk in the path of justice, righteousness, and the fear of the Lord. The liberative approach of Torah in Proverbs is addressed as a way of living that affirms life and encourages the child to avoid destructive behavior that can create a danger to oneself and society at large. Thus, Torah functions as a hermeneutical approach of gaining wisdom and knowledge in Proverbs.

2. The Function of Torah in Proverbs

The interpretation of Torah in Proverbs is assumed to have addressed the socio-economic and political struggles of the Post-exilic period. Despite the fact that the social context of the individual Saying in Proverbs is obscure, and the quest for the context of the text in its oral stages is unresolved, but the function of wisdom and law seems to have had a greater influence during this period. In Proverbs, the teaching about wisdom is assumed to have instructed by parents and sages to younger generation. It is presumed that in the pre-literary stage, the sage might have appeared among the simple ordinary people without having any specific function or office and lived in small villages, town, and capital. The wise men comprise of farmers, artisans, housewives, elders of the clan, scribes, priest, prophets, and royal court officials. Perhaps the prominent location for instruction in Israel is the family. The parental instruction is portrayed as important, and the home is an institution where values are acquired, and character is being shaped.[22] Wisdom instruction in Proverbs is seen as education concerning moral formation, particularly to the younger generation.[23] There is a possibility as the scribal circles flourished on the cultivation of 'wisdom,' the stress on the attitude to life through the observation of nature, human society, and the relations between human beings with God, and with the world is reflected.[24] Wisdom is a sensible approach that informs one's whole attitude to life.[25] The Book of Proverbs presents 'wisdom' as a compelling argument, and in doing so the concept of justice,

20 Miller, *The Way of the Lord*, 137.

21 Liedke and C. Petersen, 3: 1415.

22 James L. Crenshaw, *Old Testament Wisdom: An Introduction* (Louisville: Westminster John Knox Press, 1998), 13.

23 Katharine J. Dell, *The Book of Proverbs in Social and Theological Context* (Cambridge: University Press, 2006), 6.

24 Anthony R. Ceresko, *Introduction to Old Testament Wisdom: A Spirituality for Liberation* (Mumbai: St. Pauls, 2000), 33.

25 John J. Collins, *Jewish Wisdom in Hellenistic Age* (Louisville, KY: Westminster John Knox, 1997), 54.

righteousness and the fear of Yahweh are interpreted as fundamental values in the quest for wisdom. In the instructional discourse, the Book of Proverbs inspires individuals to seek wisdom, and to learn the dynamic of justice in social relations. The Deuteronomic influence concerning the integration of wisdom and law is further argued in the following discussion.

2.1. The Deuteronomic Influence on Wisdom Writings

Moshe Weinfeld initiated one of the valid arguments on the sapiential interpretation of Torah in wisdom discourse. In his writing, he identified wisdom influence upon the legal and hortatory speeches of Deuteronomy and Deuteronomic influence on sapiential wisdom. Weinfeld states that the Deuteronomist no longer conceive of 'wisdom' as cunning, pragmatic talent, and the possession of extraordinary knowledge, but interpreted wisdom as knowledge and understanding of proper behavior.[26] The interpretation of Torah in Proverbs is widening from the common understanding of Torah as laws and statutes of God to its association with wisdom and understanding. Further, the concept of 'long life,' 'riches and honor,' 'reward and punishment,' could have successfully come from the circle of scribal sages employing the literary resources found in Deuteronomy. Weinfeld recognized that the vocabulary such as 'to bind,' 'to keep,' 'to teach,' and the interpretation of justice is similar to that of Deuteronomy.[27] The didactic idioms, the pedagogical presentation of the Deuteronomic historiography on 'the fear of YHWH' or 'fear God,' and the concept of good life are typical of Deuteronomistic ideology.[28] In addition to this, the Deuteronomic influence in various texts of the Hebrew Bible is observed and wisdom and law are argued as having a common origin for a specific purpose. Both wisdom and law seem to have been borrowed from the understanding of Law and wisdom in AWA and they originated in the tribal society for bringing social harmony and order.

2.2. Wisdom and Law as Having Common Origin

The emergence of wisdom and law might have originated from a tribal society and gradually developed in the later stage to meet the need of the society. Traditional wisdom serves to transmit its inherited values to represent a form of moral basis functioned in a conventional society for an agreed pattern of behavior. Joseph Blenkinsopp understood law and wisdom as having had a common origin. He acknowledged that Proverbs has numerous parallels with the Egyptian instructions and there are similarities between case law and

26 Moshe Weinfeld, *Deuteronomy and the Deuteronomic School* (Oxford: Clarendon Press, 1972), 255-257.

27 Weinfeld, *Deuteronomy and the Deuteronomic School*, 255-257.

28 Weinfeld, *Deuteronomy and the Deuteronomic School*, 298-299.

proverbial sayings, and the apodictic sentences of law and the instruction.[29] In the process of adaptation and indigenization, Torah is assimilated to wisdom for the establishment and maintenance of order in the tribal society. According to R.N. Whybray, Blenkinsopp identified some similarities between case law and proverbial sayings, and between apodictic sentences of law and the instruction.[30] Whybray stated that Blenkinsopp understood law and wisdom as having had a common origin related to the concern for the establishment and maintenance of order in the tribal society.[31] Whybray further described wisdom as associated with the Word of God, the Spirit of God and the Law.[32] Wisdom can be identified with the Law, in which the scribes or the wise men might have possessed one's inherent knowledge as well as borrowed from one's neighbor and makes the Law as a principal subject of the study.[33] The Book of Proverbs interpreted the Mosaic Law in wisdom instruction and thus it is vital to examine its relationship and how such laws are incorporated in wisdom instruction in Proverbs.

2.3. The Relationship of Mosaic Law and Proverbs

David L. Brooks argues that both Law and Proverbs have similar topics that can be compared and contrasted.[34] Brooks maintains that the redactor and the compiler of the Book of Proverbs are aware of the Law and he presents an argument that the law or Torah is completed only after exile. He identified that Proverbs developed some aspects of the Mosaic Law such as adultery, weight, and measures, cursing one's parents, the poor, and 'the fear of YHWH.'[35] Brook's findings are similar to that of Weinfeld which support the relationship of Torah and the Book of Proverbs. Furthermore, the concept 'the fear of YHWH' deserves special attention since 'fearing God' is the focal concern of the Book of Deuteronomy (Deut. 6:2, 13, 24; 8:6; 10:12, 20; 13:4; 14:23; 17:19; 28:58; 31:12-13). The notion of 'hearing,' obeying,' and 'keeping' the instruction in one's heart are typical of Deuteronomy presentation of the Toraḥ.The similar usage of the phrase 'fear God,' binding and keeping God's commands is presented in a rhetorical speech in Proverbs (Deut. 6:6-9, 13; 10:12; 11:18-20; Prov. 1:7; 6:20-22; 7:2-3; 9:10). The injunctions about the

29 Joseph Blenkinsopp, *Wisdom and Law in the Old Testament: The Ordering of Life in Israel and Early Judaism* (Oxford: University Press, 1995), 51.

30 Blenkinsopp, *Wisdom and Law in the Old Testament*, 51.

31 R. N. Whybray, *The Book of Proverbs: A Survey of Modern Study*, vol. 1, ed. Robert Morgan (Leiden: E.J. Brill, 1995), 29.

32 R. N. Whybray, *Wisdom in Proverbs* (London: SCM Press, 1965), 11.

33 Whybray, *Wisdom in Proverbs*, 21.

34 David L. Brooks, "The Complementary Relationship Between Proverbs and Moses' Law," *CTR,* 5/1(2007): 3-32.

35 Brooks, "The Complementary Relationship Between Proverbs and Moses' law," 24-31.

removal of boundaries (Deut. 19:14; 27:17; Prov. 22:28; 23:10) is parallel to Prov. 22:28; 23:10; 11:1 and 20:10, 23. The Book of Proverbs and Deuteronomy exhorts kindness to the poor (Deut. 15:11; 24:14; Prov. 14:21, 31; 19:17; 31:9, 20). Deuteronomy and Proverbs teach that vengeance belongs to God (Deut. 32:35; Prov. 25:21-22). The instruction concerning the impartial judgment (Deut. 1:17; 16:19; Prov. 24:23; 28:21) is observed and the concept of justice stands prominent (Deut. 16:20; Prov. 10:2; 11:4, 19; 12:28; 16:31; 21:21).

2.4. The Relationship of Law and Wisdom

Wisdom saying does not appear only in the Book of Job, Proverbs, Ecclesiastes, and Ecclesiasticus but, it is also mentioned in the Psalms and other books such as prophets and historical narratives, (as for example, the figure of Joseph as a young sage). [36] David Daube states that the Fifth Commandment 'Honor thy father and thy mother' in Deuteronomy is derived from wisdom; particularly from ancient wisdom.[37] Deuteronomy describes its laws as wisdom stating "And you shall keep and obey the statutes" (Deut. 4:6). The statement proceeds to say that observing the statutes is wisdom (חכמה) and understanding (בִּין) in the sight of the nations and when they hear all these statutes, they will say, surely a wise (חכם) and understanding (בִּין) nation. In Deuteronomy, the phrase 'hearken to the statutes,' and 'the voice of God,' or even simply 'hearken' (Exod. 20:12; Deut. 5:16) conveys wisdom terminology. Another revealing term which is common is דרך (the way) in which one should go and the phrase 'to walk in the way' is associated with 'God's, ways,' 'to turn from or after, a direction' is attached with rewards and long life.

The concepts of wisdom in the Book of Proverbs are not accidental, but they are connected to a theological discourse concerning social relations in the Post-exilic period.[38] Bernd U. Schipper analyzed that, the influence of Deuteronomy on Proverbs 1-9 conveys that Wisdom and Torah is a late-exilic literature and this period influences the composition of the Book of Proverbs up to the final layer in Proverbs 30.[39] The argument the author

36 David Daube delivered two sets of Gifford Lectures at the University of Edinburgh. The work of volume 1 is titled as *The Deed and the Doer in the Bible* in September and October 1962, which appeared as a book from the Templeton Press in 2008; and volume 2 is titled as *Law and Wisdom in the Bible*, in which he delivered in April and May 1964. David Daube, *Law and Wisdom in the Bible: David Daube Gifford Lectures*, vol. 2, ed. and comp. Calum Carmichael (West Conshohocken, PA: Templeton Press, 2010), vii. 4.

37 Daube, *Law and Wisdom in the Bible*, 25-28.

38 Bernd U. Schipper, "When Wisdom Is Not Enough! The Discourse on Wisdom and Torah and the Composition of the Book of Proverbs," in *Wisdom and Torah: The Reception of 'Torah' in the Wisdom Literature of the Second Temple Period*, JSJSup., vol. 163, eds. Bernd U. Schipper and D. Andrew Teeter (Leiden, Boston: Brill, 2013), 55.

39 Schipper, "When Wisdom Is Not Enough!," 57.

presented here is that wisdom instructions share similar terms as Torah (Prov. 3:1; 6:20) and commandment (Prov. 7:2, 3 in 3:3; 6:20, 21; 7:1).[40] In the composition of the Book of Proverbs, the concept of wisdom is reduced from a theological concept to everyday knowledge. In connection to this, one can observe that in Judaism, Ben Sira interpreted Torah in wisdom discourse and such interpretation embraces the covenantal commandments (Sir. 3:1-6) and social law of Deuteronomy (Sir. 4:1-6; Cf. Deut. 15:7-11).[41] The author might have depended on Proverbs to produce his book of "wise instruction and apt proverbs" (Sir. 50:27) and thus argue that Proverbs represents at least part of a literary definition of 'wisdom' in the mind of the Post-exilic author.[42] Ben Sira understanding of wisdom is firmly rooted in Torah as presented in Proverbs.[43] Ben Sira further affirms and widens the concept of Torah which has been incorporated by the sages and scribes in the Book of Proverbs.

3. The Centrality of Torah in the Post-exilic Period

Torah is the central integrating factor around which all other features of religious activities are organized in the formulation of the Hebrew scripture.[44] David M. Carr assumed that the exilic and the Post-exilic periods appear to be the central times of the rise of a Torah document both for its existence as well as the authorization of it as a legal status. Wisdom and Law in ancient Israelite might have emerged from tribal rural setting and developed over the period of time in different stages of redaction and compilation and finally took its shape of adaptation and culmination in the Persian Period.[45] It is, therefore, important to study the authorization of Torah and how Torah is integrated as wisdom and wisdom associated with Torah values.

3.1. The Authorization of Torah in the Persian Empire

Leo. G. Perdue describes that during the Persian Period, the scribes collect and compose their writings and archiving of important literature and Torah is

40 All three instructions intend to lead to a successful life in Proverbs is expressed by the root היה which is used in 3:2 in relation to the length of days and years of life, and ודך היים as disciplinary reproof and a way to life in 6:23. Further, שמר מצותיוהיה, 'to keep my commands and live' in 7:2. Schipper, "When Wisdom Is Not Enough!," 59-60.

41 Richards A. Horsley, *Scribes Visionaries and the Politics of Second Temple Judea* (Louisville/ London: Westminster John Knox Press, 2007), 120.

42 Gerald T. Sheppard, *Wisdom as a Hermeneutical Construct: A Study in the Sapientializing of the Old Testament*, BZAW 151(Berlin/ New York: Walter de Gruyter, 1980), 15-16.

43 Collins, *Jewish Wisdom in Hellenistic Age*, 54.

44 John Bright, *A History of Israel* (London: SCM Ltd., 1960), 418.

45 Carr, "The Rise of Torah," 40.

fundamental in the world-view of the sages during this period. [46] In Proverbs, one discovers that the sages addressed the simple to seek wisdom guided by the teachings of the Torah in their activities and social roles. As such, the literary forms and themes of Proverbs differ from the Pre-exilic texts particularly texts that have undergone sapiential redaction. According to Perdue the teaching of the sages is to be located in the different period of historical events, and social circumstances and their teaching reflect diverse encounters regarding moral systems, views of God, comprehensions of human nature, and religious understanding.[47] The writings have shaped the Jewish identity and provided insights for the reconstitution of the perceptions of oneself and the later generations. Moreover, the literary tradition of the sages comprises of material culture yields relevant epigraphic, symbolic, artistic and architectural evidence for the reconstruction of the socio-historical location of sapiential literature.[48] In addition to this, Gary Knoppers argues on the association of the legal laws of the local communities with that of the central administration of the Persian regime.[49] He asserts that the Achaemenid Empire portrays the most interesting, difficult, and important subjects in the study of the authorization of Torah. He observed that the local law and regulations are authorized through imperial consent as long as those local regulations did not contradict imperial regulations and interests. Perhaps a much stronger claim is recognized than a general description of the Persian crown on initiating and permitting a local law book. It is difficult to understand how Jewish law codes became imperial law and how Yahweh's law became the king's law in the Persian Period. Knoppers stated that the Persian authority seems to have put pressure on collecting and framing of the indigenous law book in which the Jewish community was one of them. The charge to the task was carried out by Ezra. He is known as "a scribe in the law of the God of heaven" (Ezra 7:12, 21), commissioned by the king and his seven counselors "to conduct an inquiry concerning Judah and Jerusalem regarding the law of one's God in their possession" (Ezra 7:14). There is a possibility that Nehemiah reinstated the ancient decrees and the service duties of the priests and Levites as a subsequent of the Persian authorization. But, Nehemiah rarely cited Persian imperial sanction as the basis for any of the policies that he has implemented. Knoppers argues the Persian Empire as highly centralized and tightly defended Persian policy. The Persian government allowed local leaders to be active players in shaping policies

---

46 Leo G. Perdue, *The Sword and the Stylus: An Introduction to Wisdom in the Age of Empires* (Grand Rapids, MI: Willian Eerdmans Publishing Company, 2008), 195.

47 Perdue, *The Sword and the Stylus*, 3.

48 Perdue, *The Sword and the Stylus*, 3.

49 Gary Knoppers, "An Achaemenid Imperial Authorization of Torah in Yehud?" in *Persia and Torah: The Theory of Imperial Authorization of the Pentateuch*, SBLSymS 17, trans. and ed. James Watts; (Atlanta: Society of Biblical Literature, 2001), 115-134.

within their communities and publish their indigenous traditions as Persian law.[50] It is fascinating to promote indigenous legal instruction but for what purpose such laws were promoted is a question. Liberation of one community does not rely on preserving and promoting one's tradition or legal instruction, but how those traditions and legal sanction enhance liberation to the oppressed sections is a question. Thus, the Persian authorization of preserving indigenous law has led the sages and scribes to develop a hermeneutical approach that addressed Torah in wisdom instruction.

3.2. The Hermeneutical Construct of Torah-Wisdom in Post-exilic Period

The notion of wisdom had encountered a process of transformation in Israel from the understanding of wisdom as a practical skill to a form of philosophical reflection which culminated in a concept of hypostatization.[51] The hermeneutical construct of wisdom influenced is observed in legal, prophetic materials, and the historical book. Sheppard argues that one can often measure quite tangibly how the author conforms to the parts or the whole of a non-wisdom biblical text into a redaction-like representation of it in a new context concerning wisdom.[52] Sheppard describes the association of Torah in wisdom as a hermeneutical device of the Post-exilic author. The authenticity of Torah and its interpretation in wisdom as ideological and practical is further argued in Sheppard's writing.[53] The argument states that in the name of unity the order of the canonical material in the early stage shows that unity displayed lies more in the hermeneutical principles used than in the material itself.[54] Sheppard argues that Torah as a term functions as a hermeneutical idiom or construct which designated the subject matter of both the first part and the whole of Scripture. The use of Torah as an interpretative rubric becomes a lens through which one can search the entire Scripture concerning its hermeneutical constructs. Thus, Torah in the Post-exilic Judaism is not only integral to the formation of the Hebrew Bible but found their mandate in the resources of the earlier tradition. As a result, the term 'wisdom' underwent modification and the merging of law and wisdom in Post-exilic period conveys the struggle for justice among sub-groups. The struggle for justice is further examined in the context of the socio-economic and political crisis of the Persian Period.

50 Knoppers, "An Achaemenid Imperial Authorization of Torah in Yehud?" 115-134.

51 Sheppard, *Wisdom as a Hermeneutical Construct*, 6.

52 Sheppard, *Wisdom as a Hermeneutical Construct*, 14.

53 Gerald.T. Sheppard, "Canonization Hearing the Voice of the Same God through Historically Dissimilar Traditions," *Interpretation* 36/1(1982): 21-31.

54 Sheppard, "Canonization Hearing the Voice of the Same God through Historically Dissimilar Traditions," 21.

4. The Socio-Economic and Political Crisis in the Post-exilic Period

The political crisis of the Post-exilic period might have upsurges the socio-economic injustice of the Jewish community. In this context, wisdom saying exhibits a greater significance in the Post-exilic period than in the Pre-exilic period as the Jewish immigrants sought to redefine their lives under the Persian regime.[55] The instruction regarding the struggle between the powerful rich and the powerless poor can be identified as a socio-economic concern encountered by the Jewish community in the Post-exilic Period. The theological significance of Torah in wisdom instruction to the disadvantaged sections (the עָנִי, אֶבְיוֹן, דָּל, אַלְמָנָה, מַחְסוֹר, רָשׁ and the יָתוֹם) is described in symbolic and conceptual imagery. In Proverbs Torah values is associated in the context of wealth and poverty of the righteous and the wicked. A symbolic interpretation of Torah can be identified in the vocabulary of honor and dishonor, 'way,' 'life,' 'running,' and 'walking.' Such terminologies depict individual's life-span and activities on earth as a journey that one walks through it. In addition to this, Torah-wisdom presents the saying and instruction as a confrontation to the power-rich and the attitudes towards the powerless poor.

4.1. The Powerful- Rich and the Powerless-Poor

The socio-liberative reading of wisdom discourse indicates a fresh perspective to the understanding of law and wisdom. Regarding the term 'poor,' Proverbs portray two categories that drives the poor to poverty. First, because of Laziness (Prov. 6:10-11; 10:4, 5, 26; 13:4; 14:23; 15:19; 19:24; 20:4-5; 21:25; 22:13; 24:30-34; 26:13,14,15,16) and drunkenness (Prov. 23:20-21, 31-). Second, the poor as a result of injustice in a form of bribery (11:24; 13:23, 25; 13:25; 22:16, 22; 23:21; 28:15; 30:14;) exercise by the rich and the powerful oppressor. The poor because of injustice is the concern of the study particularly in the context of wealth and poverty of the righteous and the wicked. The portrayal concerning the rich and the poor witness the moral and ethical issues of the condition of the rich towards the poor (10:15-17; 13:22-23; 14:31-32; 15:25-27; 19:1-4; 21:13-14; and 22:7-9, 16). It is asserts that during this period Israel seemed to have suffered from the effects of heavy taxation (Nehemiah 5:1ff) which resulted in debt slavery.[56] Further, the influential Jewish leaders who were in the service of the Persian were an arm of the foreign oppressor.[57] Even though the Jews

---

55 Milton P. Horne, *Proverbs-Ecclesiastes: Smyth & Helwys Bible Commentary* (USA: Symth and Helwys Publishing Inc., 2003), 22.

56 Charles E. Carter, "The Province of Yehud in the Post- Exilic Period: Soundings in Site Distribution and Demography," in *Second Temple Studies: 2 Temple and Community in the Persian Period*, JSOTSup., 175, eds. Tamara C. Eskenazi and Kent H. Richards (Sheffield: JSOT Press, 1994), 139.

57 Geo Widengren, "The Persian Period," in *Israelite and Judean History*, eds. H. Hayes and J. Maxwell Miller (London: SCM Press, 1977), 533.

during this period found its new way of living by adapting its existence within the Persian Empire, they were not free from the socio-economic oppression.[58] Prophet Nehemiah witnessed the peasantry encountered in debt from heavy taxation and exploitation by the wealthy resulting from the corresponding disintegration of family structure and village community (Neh. 5).[59] In such a crisis, the Book of Proverbs addresses wisdom in 'the fear of YHWH' as ethical values in which justice, righteousness and the fear of the Lord is construed (Prov. 1:3, 7; 2:8-9; 9:9, 10; 10:11, 20, 21, 30; 11:9; 16:8; 21:3, 15; 22:8, 29:7). These principles are social and ethical concerns of Proverbs. The study on the significance of Torah in the Book of Proverbs is an effort to envisage wisdom, not as mere intellectual knowledge, but as practical advice in which the younger generation are called to observe and implement.

4.2. Torah-Wisdom Address Injustice of the Post-exilic Period

The socio-economic oppression is strategically employed under the Persian Empire to expand and enlarge the economic and political stability. Such policy intensifies the problem of injustice to the disadvantaged sections. Perhaps one of the reasons that inspire the sages to interpret the principle of Torah in wisdom discourse was to confront the problem of injustice in the Post-exilic period. Regarding the notion of justice, Proverbs bear similarities with the wisdom and percepts of AWA. Protection of the widow, the orphan and the poor is a common policy in Ancient West Asian wisdom discourse.[60] Hence, justice is interpreted as associated with the character of the wise and the Saying inspires the hearers about the execution of justice to the oppressed. The teaching urges the rich to share their resources with the poor and discourage any discrimination towards the poor and the afflicted of the society (Prov. 11:24-25; 14:21, 31; 19:7, 17; 22:9; 28:27). Such instruction of order is shaped in the Commandments to build a moral community. The representation of Torah in Proverbs as mentioned above reflects the Mosaic and Deuteronomic law. It is assumed that the formulation of the moral good in the directives of the commandments is an attempt to define the character of the law not only as orienting towards the common-good but also as a norm of reason.[61] Hence, the inclination of the concept of wisdom as secular in its approach finds its religious expression in the moral essence of Torah. In addition to this, the concept of order and freedom is further depicted in human social relations. Such relational

58 Widengren, "The Persian Period," 538.

59 Horsley, *Scribes Visionaries and the Politics of Second Temple Judea*, 22.

60 F. Charles Fensham, "Widow, Orphan, and the Poor in Ancient Near Eastern Legal and Wisdom Literature," in *Studies in Ancient Israelite Wisdom*, selected with a prolegomenon by James L. Crenshaw (New York: KTAV Publishing House, Ins., 1876), 161.

61 Miller, *The Way of the Lord*, 137.

order is not primarily oriented toward a broad hierarchy of human relationship, though some hierarchy is assumed alongside relationship.[62] Oppression and dominance are terms associated with individual's social relations in which humankind as social beings relate and interact daily in the community.

Justice and righteousness as described in Proverbs is presented as the primary concern of wisdom discourse. The fundamentals of justice in Proverbs emerged to promote social justice, protect the interests of the community, and the restriction of power to balance the rights of different possibly competing groups in society.[63] Wisdom in Proverbs does not include only the perception of the logical consequences but, also challenges the socio-economic inequality.[64] Wisdom in Proverbs is construed as knowledge of the created order that conveys its origin from God.[65] The sages of Israel in their attempt to discover harmony and social order, they suggested that one has to follow the Torah-values as an ethical code of conduct.[66] The pursuit of wisdom in the imagination of the sages in Proverbs is to embrace 'justice,' 'righteousness,' 'truth,' and 'order.' The purpose of the search for 'order' is communicated in terms not simply to satisfy the curiosity of seeking knowledge for one's benefit but, its purpose is primarily pragmatic.[67] Thus, Torah is associated with 'justice,' 'righteousness,' 'way,' 'life,' 'wise,' and 'foolish' in conceptual and symbolic discourse. The instruction on the protection of the disadvantaged is addressed as a confrontation to the wicked deeds of the powerful sub-group and the accumulation of wealth through false means to promote justice to the weak and powerless. The instruction regarding prohibitions of robbing the poor is assumed to have been addressed to the powerful rich who rob the land of the widows and orphans in the context of debts (22:22-23, 28; 23:10-11; 28:3-6, 27-28; 29:2, 7, 13-14; 30:13-14). The issues concerning the wicked as a contrast to the righteous are further presented from the perspective of the oppressive ruler who oppresses the poor.

The Relevance

The collection of the Saying in the Book of Proverbs is presented as a didactic teaching particularly to the youth of the Jewish community in the Post-exilic

62 Miller, *The Way of the Lord*, 63.

63 Christopher J. H. Wright, *Old Testament Ethics for the People of God* (Secunderabad: OM Books, 2004), 322.

64 Philip Johannes Nel, *The Structure and Ethos of the Wisdom Admonitions in Proverbs* (Berlin/ New York: Walter de Gruyter, 1982), 86.

65 Nel, *The Structure and Ethos of the Wisdom Admonitions in Proverbs*, 86.

66 Roland E. Murphy, *The Tree of Life: An Exploration of Biblical Wisdom Literature* (Grand Rapids, MI: William B. Eerdmans Publishing Company, 1996), 115.

67 Anthony R. Ceresko, *The Old Testament: A Liberation Perspective* (Mumbai: St. Pauls, 2009), 371.

community. As mentioned, the Persian Empire promotes the collection and the preservation of indigenous law and wisdom saying. Such occasion have led the Jewish scribes and sages to explore and develop diverse dimensions on the concept of wisdom. The dimension can be observed in the merging of wisdom and Torah as instructional discourse. The instruction is addressed to the 'child' and perhaps the younger generation on the value of wisdom. The significance of instruction to the younger generations is vital as they are the potential future leader of the society and without proper guidance and teaching they may be led astray or ends up in destructive lifestyle. The vision of a just society; equality, and individual's responsibility to one's community may not be realized if the child is unaware of the value of gaining wisdom. Thus, the home education plays as central towards nurturing individual's behaviors, attitudes, and actions. In addition to this, human social relations are not isolated, but it influenced the broader aspect of the social group and social organization. The interpretation of wisdom is essential to mediate contemporary society in general and indigenous Khasi society in particular. It is assumed indigenous community employs one's traditional wisdom to convey spiritual values to promote order and healthy social relations in the community. Regarding this, indigenous Khasi wisdom instruction initially functioned as parental instruction in the home. The instruction consists of ethical values that have had an active role in building justice in the society.[68] The sages of Israel employ Torah values in wisdom discourse to the Post-exilic Jewish community. Likewise, the hermeneutical approach of interpreting indigenous values is vital in addressing issues facing contemporary Khasi Society.

Concerning indigenous wisdom saying of the Khasis, the *Teaching of the Elders* (*Ka Jingsneng Tymmen*)[69] is an important text as it relate with value-orientation and character development of the child towards a healthy social relation. The instruction or admonition guides and encourages the community about social behaviour and code of conduct with an aim to bring justice and harmony in the society. Besides, the *Teaching of the Elders*, the indigenous poems and maxims address the issues of wealth and poverty and the importance of justice. In the pre-literary stage, the teaching is communicated orally from parents to children. The 'around the hearth' (*Sawdong ka lyngwiar dpei*), is an actual configuration of the oral-based foundations of family education in the

68 Esther Syiem, *Oral Discourse in Khasi Folk Narrative* (Guwahati: EBH Publisher, 2011), 2.

69 The instruction *Ka Jingsneng Tymmen: Shaphang Ka Akor Khasi ha ka Rukom Rwai Phawar* was first published in *U Khasi Mynta* in February 1897. The collection was later added and published in two sections in a book form in 1902 (Part I) and in 1903 (Part II) by R.S. Berry. *Ka Jingsneng Tymmen* means 'The Teachings of the Elders' or 'The Counsel of the Elders,' Bijoya Sawian, *Ka Jingsneng Tymmen (The Teaching of the Elders)*, (Shillong: Ri Khasi Press, 2005), ii.

Khasi society. The parental teaching is documented after the development of the Khasi script. The *Teaching of the Elders* and some of the proverbs of the indigenous Khasis are collections that have emerged during the colonial rule in India. The collection of the Saying seems to be uncritical to the existing colonial power and oppression, and their retrospective thought on the ideal repositories of wisdom and knowledge were unquestioned.[70] However, these instructions serve as an important text to contemporary Khasi society when western influence has seeped to the extent that indigenous culture and traditions are under threat of being lost.[71] The social values are moral principles function as instructional discourse towards nurturing individual's moral and social activities of the Khasis community.[72] The goal of instruction guides and protects indigenous community's cultural beliefs and lifestyle, and the Saying portrays the rich oral tradition of their myths and legends.[73]

Wisdom instructions in Proverbs are praxis-oriented and aim to challenge the community on the obsession of power and wealth earned by dishonest means. The interpretation of Torah values inspires individuals concerning the execution of justice. The interpretation of gaining wisdom in Proverbs is assumed to have presented as a unique Jewish discourse. Concerning this, the study of wisdom regarding 'the fear of YHWH' is interpreted in the indigenous Khasi understanding of *Tip-Briew-Tip-Blei* (knowing humankind and knowing God). The phrase *Tip-Blei* 'knowing God' interprets one's understanding of God that subsequently connects one's responsibility towards humankind. Wisdom is the faculty to know what God expects of humankind on earth. The ability to know God is consequent upon a shared sense of community that weaves society together.[74] The term *Tip-Briew* 'Knowing humankind' is associated with a community's healthy relationship and harmonious living with each other.[75] It implies character, attitudes, actions and the ability to hold on to moral and ethical values of the community. The concept of *Tip-Briew-Tip-Blei* is essential to indigenous Khasi community as it is life-affirming particularly in relation to social behaviour and in building a just and healthy community. This principle guides, nurtures and protects individuals from involvement in the unhealthy behaviour. The concept of justice and righteousness is understood in the term *Ka Hok* (justice, righteousness, truth) to the indigenous Khasi. Further,

70 Syiem, *The Oral Discourse in Khasi Folk Narrative*, 46.

71 Payel Dutta Chowdhury, "Depiction of the Khasi 'Teachings of Elders': A Study of Radhon Singh Berry Kharwanlang's "Ka Jingsneng Tymmen,"" *Pune Research: An International Journal in English* 2/1(2016): 1-2.

72 Nongkynrih, *Around the Hearth: Khasi Legends*, viii.

73 Chowdhury "Depiction of the Khasi 'Teachings of Elders': A Study of Radhon Singh Berry Kharwanlang's "Ka Jingsneng Tymmen,"" 5.

74 Syiem, *Oral Discourse in Khasi Folk Narrative*, 2.

75 jaitdkhar, *Ka Niam-Ki-Khasi: Ka Niam Tip-Blei-Tip-Brieu*, 6.

the phrase *Kamai ia ka Hok* (righteous earning or to earn righteousness) is believed to be the decreed given by God. *Ka Hok* stands as the ultimate, eternal source of divine law.[76] In truth and justice, (*Ka Hok*) lies the brilliance of light, courage, and strength, seeking wisdom and discovery of knowledge, also giving succour in periods of darkness, uncertainty, and afflictions, guiding a person to the right direction.[77] God revealed himself to humankind through his justice and righteousness (*Ka Hok*).[78] The phrase *Kamai ia ka Hok* depicts the individual's integrity and the sense of being truthful and just. However, these concepts are being faded in contemporary Khasi society, as indigenous values are disintegrated. Such changes are experienced in the disparity between the rich and the poor, the powerful and the powerless. Contemporary Khasi community is tackling with social violence and multi-faceted socio-economic exploitation in which the advantaged sections exploit the poorer social sub-group. Further, the character and behavior of the wise is linked with honour which is interpreted in the phrase *Tip Burom-Tip Akor* (to know the honour of the etiquettes of life). In addition to this, the association of wisdom with character is known as *Ka Buit-Ka Akor* (skill and demeanor). The term *Tip Burom-Tip Akor* 'to know the honor of the etiquettes of life' is a concept associated with a social relationship that cautions individual's attitudes and behaviors. The social norms of *Tip-Briew-Tip-Blei*, *Ka Hok* and *Tip Burom-Tip Akor* are values that shape, mould, unite and bind human relationship and society together. However, these values seem to have becoming extinct from the Khasi community.[79] Contemporary Khasi society is tackling corruption, exploitation and the disadvantaged group of people is victim to such actions. The concept *Ka Hok* (righteousness and justice) is perverted in contemporary Khasi society. Injustices and inequality are prevalent in the socio-political, religious and economic that promotes conflict between the rich and the poor, the powerful and the powerless of the society.

Conclusion

The significance of Torah is argued from the assumption that the theological construct in merging Torah and wisdom is associated with the Deuteronomic interpretation of wisdom in Proverbs. Further, the relationship of 'Torah' and 'wisdom' can be found within various literary strata of the Book of Deuteronomy. The form and content of proverbial instructions are portrayed as

---

76 Sumar S. Sawian, *Golden Vine of Ri Hynniewtrep: The Khasi Heritage* (Guwahati: Vivekananda Kendra Institute and Culture, 2011), 8-9.

77 Sawian, *Golden Vine of Ri Hynniewtrep*, 9.

78 Sawian, *Golden Vine of Ri Hynniewtrep: The Khasi Heritage* 8-9.

79 Mawrie Barnes S.D.B, "Khasi Society and the Impact of Modernity; Challenges to Integrity and Identity", *Tribes of North-East India Issues and Challenges*, eds., B.K. Medhi, R.P. Athparia & K. Jose SVD, New Delhi: Omsons Publications, 2009, 176.

having conformed to the ethical values and social norms of the Deuteronomic Torah in which the Mosaic Torah is presumably conveyed. The dimension of wisdom in a human social relationship is acknowledged, and the diverse communicating devices are depicted as an attempt to engage Torah within the realm of wisdom instruction. Hence, the Book of Proverbs deepens the concept of wisdom that leads to praxis-oriented social relations in which the Book of Proverbs asserts as 'the way of wisdom.' The socio-economic and political complexity of the Post-exilic Israel is further manifested in the Post-independent Khasi society of North-east India. The quest for justice is focal point of the Book of Proverbs and the concept of *Ka Hok* is prominent to indigenous Khasi wisdom instruction. Wisdom instructions are praxis-oriented and challenge the community from the obsession of power and wealth earning by dishonest means. The teaching inspires the individual's responsibility to uphold and execute justice. The interpretation of gaining wisdom in Proverbs presents a unique Jewish discourse of Torah values. Indigenous wisdom of the Khasis addressed the importance of individual's social relation and the teaching focus on values that can bring forth justice in the community. Thus, the notions of justice, righteousness, and the fear of the Lord can be vibrant if they are interpreted from one's indigenous understanding. Wisdom instruction of the indigenous Khasi society has the possibility to negate contemporary issues of discrimination between the rich and the poor, the advantaged and the disadvantaged. Wisdom instructional discourse in the Book of Proverbs can be meaningful if it is described from indigenous wisdom instruction. Further, the concept of wisdom in the Book of Proverbs can impact to a greater extent to contemporary Khasi society as both texts emphasise on socialization, behaviours and conduct that can bring forth healthy social relation.

14

The Rich in Matthew
A Socio-Economic Reading (Abstract)

Keciziuying Siang

The writer of the first Gospel, Matthew, appears to have a positive attitude towards the rich. It is observable that stories bearing positive images of the rich which are found in his sources are reproduced. For instance, the story of a centurion, probably a rich and a socially outstanding person, taken from Q (Mt 8:5-13// Lk 7:1-10), and the story of a tax collector who became one of the twelve disciples of Jesus, taken from Mark (2:13-17// Mt 9:9-13; Lk 5:27-32), are retold. But most of the parables and stories that bear negative images of the rich found in the other two Synoptic Gospels, for example, the parable of the dishonest manager (Lk 16:1-13), the parable of the rich fool (Lk 12:13-22), the parable of the rich man and Lazarus (Lk 16:19-31), the story of the widow's offering where the rich are apparently condemned (Mark 12:41-44// Luke 21:1-4), are absent in Matthew. Besides, Matthew's first beatitude which is slightly different from that of Luke seems to signal an accommodative approach to the rich as in this particular pericope Matthew has no "woe" against the rich, whereas Luke has four "blesseds" and four corresponding "woes" against the rich (Lk 6:20-26).

However, the assumption that Matthew has a positive attitude towards the rich poses a difficulty due to the presence of two seemingly negative passages concerning the rich. The first passage is the "God-mammon" logion (6:24// Lk 16:13), and the second passage is the story of the rich young man (Mt 19:16-30// Mk 10:17-21; Lk18-18-30) who apparently refused to follow Jesus due to his riches. The two passages pose a difficulty to the supposition that Matthew has a positive view of the rich.

Therefore, taking Matthean explicit and implicit texts concerning the rich at face value, two different sets of questions may be asked: Firstly, why has Matthew retained stories about rich persons that bear a positive picture of the rich? Why are most of the negative stories of the rich and the disparaging remarks made on them absent in his account: is it that he had no knowledge of them, or is it to serve his purpose and achieve his goal by avoiding them? Is Matthew's approach to the rich conditioned by his background and the context of his community? Secondly, if Matthew has concern for the rich, then why are seemingly negative passages still retained? Is Matthew contradicting himself in his understanding of the rich? These are some of the questions that the research looks into, especially by taking seriously the socio-economic context of the author and his community.

In investigating Matthew's understanding of the rich, four passages are taken into account: Matthew the tax collector (Mt 9:9-13//Mk 2:13-17; Lk 5:27-32); The rich young man (Mt 19:16-30 // Mk 10:17-31; Lk 18:18-30); the first beatitude (Mt 5:3// Lk 6:20); the saying on serving two masters (Mt 6:24// Lk 16:13). The main reason behind the selection of these four passages is that they can be grouped into two sets. The first set (the first two passages) belonging to the triple tradition is about two supposedly rich persons who responded differently to the call to follow Jesus; the second set (the last two passages) belonging to the double tradition is perhaps sayings of Jesus that implicitly concern the rich. In each set one can see two apparently contradictory – positive and negative – views of the rich.

In examining Matthew's view of the rich, two main methods are employed: The first is social/sociological criticism. Ekkehard W. Stegemann and Wolfgang Stegemann's model of social description of the first century Mediterranean world is employed in analyzing the socio-economic status of Matthew's community. Behind Stegemann and Stegemann's social description model lies the assumption that "opportunities and social positions of people depend not only on their personal characteristics and abilities but also on the 'distribution system' of their society," and that distribution can be determined by three 'basic elements': *power*, *privilege*, and *prestige*. Stegemann and Stegemann employed these three variables in determining a person's social stratum in the first century Mediterranean societies, which resulted in dividing the ancient societies into two strata: 'upper-stratum groups' and 'lower-stratum groups' or 'elite' and 'nonelite.' In other words, in trying to assess the social inequality of the ancient Mediterranean societies, they followed a *dichotomous model* where the existence of the third (middle) stratum is denied. However, to do justice to the social differentiation within the elite and the masses of the people, the terms upper stratum groups and lower stratum groups are employed, which are synonymous with the terms elite and nonelite and upper stratum and lower stratum. That means even within the two strata there are various layers and groups of people that made up the strata.

Based on Stegemann and Stegemann's model of social stratification, the available data found in the Gospel itself are analyzed in determining the socio-economic status of Matthew's community. This model of social stratification fits well the study as the theory considers a person's economic condition to be one of the prime factors in determining one's social position.

The second method employed here is partly adapted from the groundbreaking work of M. Gnanavaram, *Treasure in Heaven and Treasure on Earth: Attitude towards Poverty and Wealth in the New Testament Communities and the Early Church,* in which the author applies redaction criticism extensively besides the traditio-historical method. Normally, redaction criticism is interested in the theological emphases of the evangelists. However, in Gnanavaram's work, redaction criticism is judiciously employed to determine the socio-economic interests of the evangelists. Thus he claims that redactional activities of the evangelists are not always theological, they also bear their socio-economic interests. In this present study, following Gnanavaram's use of redaction criticism, a given text is examined from the socio-economic perspective. However, it is important to note that Gnanavaram does it from the margins' viewpoint, whereas the present research gives importance to the rich.

In employing redaction criticism the following methodological concerns are noted: 1) In examining a particular saying of Jesus, or parable, or any other pericope, the changes in the sources are noted. Is Matthew's version different from Luke's account if their source is Q, or has Matthew altered the Markan source if he is using Mark? The alterations, changes, omissions, additions, placement of material, etc. are then interpreted with a view to ascertain whether Matthew has socio-economic interests in doing so. 2) Has Matthew conserved his source materials? If so, what is the significance of conserving such materials? 3) The *seams* in the Gospels are the introductions, conclusions and transitions which connect with other pericopes, and they often provide significant clues to the intended purpose of the writer. Most of the time it contains much of the author's own vocabulary and point to an evangelist's particular reasons for including a particular pericope. Thus due attention is given to these *seams*.

The research, employing social criticism and redaction criticism in the investigation on Matthew's attitudes towards the rich, arrives at some key findings which include the following:

1) Matthew's Redactional Changes Suggest his Accommodative View of the Rich

After considering extensively four passages which reflect Matthew's attitude concerning the rich, it is evident that i) Matthew has purposefully chosen the story of a supposedly rich tax collector despite the negative image of tax collectors of antiquity (Mt 9:9-13). It is the first evangelist who not only names the tax collector as Matthew in the call narrative but also categorically states that this Matthew the tax collector is one of the twelve disciples of Jesus (Mt 10:1-4), whereas this categorization is absent in Mark and also in Luke (cf. Mk 3:13-19a; Lk 6:12-16). ii) In reproducing the Markan story of the rich man (Mk 10:17-21//Mt 19:16-30), several Matthean redactions could be observed: in Mark, so also in Luke, the young man is outrightly put to shame by pointing out that he still lacked one thing; whereas in the Gospel of Matthew, the rich young man confesses himself his own lack, thus avoiding embarrassment. In Luke the rich man is further put in an uncomfortable situation by telling him directly "[h]ow hard it is for those who have wealth to enter the kingdom of God!" (Lk 18:24b); while in Matthew, so also in Mark, this particular comment is uttered only in the hearing of the disciples, after the rich man had left the scene grieving (Mt 19:22-23; Mk 10:22-23). Only Matthew provides the condition – "If you wish to be perfect" – of selling all his possessions and giving the money to the poor; if not he appears to be acceptable as long as he does the Law. On the contrary, in Mark as well as in Luke, disciples are called to a life of impoverishment. Matthew's use of the word 'grieving' (*lupou,menoj*), which impelled biblical scholars to arrive at a conclusion that Jesus' challenge was evidently rejected by the rich young man, may also bear a positive outcome as in Matthew grief appears compatible with a resolve ultimately to obey. In Mark, so also in Luke, the disciples are portrayed as still possessing wealth like the rich man, whereas Matthean disciples are seen following Jesus after having left everything. Perhaps they are seen as 'the first' in discipleship. Thus the logion, "many who are first will be last, and the last will be first" (19:30), leaves a positive anticipation that those who are now last, including the rich young man, possibly could be first in the eschatological kingdom. iii) Matthew's *oi`ptwcoi tw/| pneu,mati* (Mt 5:3) seems to be closer to the Old Testament concept of *ynI['/wn"['* which has multifaceted meaning rather than to the classical Greek concept of *ptwco,j*. This understanding fits well the socio-historical and economic context of Matthew's community as they appear to be more urbanized and wealthier as compared to that of Markan and Lukan community members. Matthew might have employed his redactional phrase "in spirit" in order to include both the rich and the poor members – the *maka,rioi* – of his community. This assumption possibly gives the best reason why the woe sayings against the rich (cf. Luke 6:24-26) were not found in the first Gospel. iv) The God-mammon logion (Mt 6:24) stresses on absolute and unqualified discipleship, and at the same time it reflects Matthew's view of wealth in discipleship. It appears that the first evangelist is not against having property or wealth, but only when it takes the place of God – wealth becoming Mammon. What is more remarkable in this logion is the placement of the material. Matthew and Luke's arrangement of the material are entirely different from each other. Matthew has placed it along with other material dealing with wealth and possession (Mt 6), whereas Luke has placed it in the context of the parable of the dishonest (rich) manager, where the manager was condemned for his indulgence in the dishonest wealth (Lk 16:9, 11). Moreover, it is important to note that other Lukan apparent negative accounts of the rich, which appear within the central section of the Gospel (Lk 9:51-18:14), are absent in Matthew, for example, the story of the rich man and Lazarus (16:19-31), the parable of the rich fool (12:13-22). Thus all of Matthew's redactional changes, addition and omission of material, and his placement of material suggest his positive approach towards the rich, probably because of the economic condition of his community.

2) Matthew's Redactional Changes Bear his Socio-economic Interests

The first evangelist's audience was mainly of Jewish origin and a few from a Gentile background, who probably lived in one of the cities of Syria, where a large Jewish population was then residing. Matthew's community perhaps began to take shape within the last three decades of the first century CE, during which the Jews also began to reorder themselves especially after the first Jewish war (70 CE). Matthew's community, in the process of defining themselves as a Christ-confessing community, faced bitter persecutions from the then contemporary Judaism. Besides, though Matthew's community appears to be more urbanized and wealthier compared to that of Mark or Luke's community members, economic disparity within the members of the community prevailed, which perhaps became one of the potential threats to the tranquility and unity of the community. Matthew's community struggled not only with purely religio-theological issues but also with concrete socio-economic problems. Matthew, bearing in mind all these religio-theological issues and socio-economic realities and experiences of his community, perhaps reshaped the Gospel material for the service of his community. Thus, in the study it has been observed that redactional changes are not only for theological intentions but bear socio-economic implications.

3) The Old Testament and Other Jewish Writings Perhaps Influenced Matthew in his View of the Rich

In the Old Testament, God is frequently attributed to be the source of riches and also the one who blesses his faithful with many riches. Particularly in the Pentateuch the rich are generally seen as those being blessed by God for their faithfulness to him. However, in the poetical and wisdom books, there appear two types of rich persons – the corrupt rich and the upright rich. On the one hand the wicked rich are seen as oppressors and exploiters of the upright poor; they are also condemned for their undue reliance upon their wealth; these wicked rich are the antitheses of the poor. On the other hand the upright rich are regarded as those who receive God's favour for their obedience to his will. In short, poetical and wisdom books praised the upright rich, whereas they condemned the wicked rich. In the prophetical books the idea of the righteous rich does not appear. Particularly, the eighth century prophets saw the Israelites' society comprising of broadly two classes of people – the rich and the poor. The rich are condemned for their evil practices in their dealings with the poor, for relying on their riches, and for their self-indulgences; whereas the poor are considered as the helpless righteous who are being exploited and oppressed, and who experienced untold miseries at the hands of the corrupt rich. However, it is to be noted that wealth in itself is not condemned, but the accumulation of it through corrupt and evil practices. Intertestamental writings, particularly Sirach and the Dead Sea Scrolls maintain the belief that riches are from the Lord and He rewards the righteous and the faithful with wealth. Especially Ben Sira, the author of Sirach, stresses that wealth is a sure sign of God's blessing, which should be used for the service of God, for others, and for oneself. Similar to the authors of the poetical and wisdom books, Ben Sira also notes two types of rich persons – the wicked rich and the upright rich. He commends the rich who are blameless, honest, and pure in their dealings; however, he criticizes the corrupt rich who acquired their wealth by exploiting the poor and weak. Similarly, in 1 Enoch the distinction made between the rich and poor is sharp. The rich are considered sinners who practice all sorts of evil and wickedness and boast in and rely on their wealth, while the poor are considered as humble who do not set their minds on earthly riches but upon the Lord; the poor are considered righteous and upright who would receive blessings in heaven. Unlike the book of Sirach and 1 Enoch, the Dead Sea Scrolls do not present us explicitly the idea of righteous rich, or corrupt rich. This may be because the Qumran community considered themselves as the community of the poor – 'the poor in spirit.' They regarded themselves as God's elect and thus the righteous ones; whereas others, including the rich, are considered to be impious and wicked, destined to be destroyed. However, the Qumran community also looks forward to a time of great reversal of power and riches, when the ultimate prosperity of the community will be realized. Therefore, it is apparent that Matthew's view of the rich is to some extent influenced by his Jewish scriptures.

4) Maintaining Healthy Tension Between Discipleship and Wealth

In the study it is seen that most of the material of Matthew's first discourse deal with discipleship and wealth. Particularly Matthew 6, as observed in chapter 3, reflects the issue of wealth in discipleship. As mentioned earlier Matthew nowhere regards wealth as evil per se; possessing possessions, as reflected in the story of the rich young man (19:16-30), appears to be acceptable if one could keep the Torah. It is apparent from the narrative of the call of Matthew the tax collector (9:9-13) that the first evangelist does not necessarily negate possession of wealth; he does not altogether view wealth as an obstacle to discipleship. However, Matthew strongly condemns wealth taking the place of God. The God-mammon logion (6:24) demands absolute and unwavering discipleship; the Matthean Jesus seeks for an uncompromising commitment to God's will and purpose, which is also the hallmark of the Jews as the people of God in the Old Testament and in the Dead Sea Scrolls.

Moreover, it is observed that Matthew repeatedly reminded his readers about giving. As most of Matthew's members were from the lower strata of society, there is an emphasis on doing acts of mercy in the Gospel. Especially Matthew 6 deals more with wealth and giving: Matthew opens chapter 6 (vv 1-4, Matthean own material) with an instruction on giving, which is perhaps an extended idea of his fifth beatitude (5:7); giving alms to the poor is thus generally understood as storing up treasures in heaven (6:16), and the saying on the sound eye of 6:22-23 could be also understood in terms of generosity. Certainly, in the story of the rich young man, Matthew with his own redactional phrases emphasizes on 'good deeds' (19:16) and love for one's neighbors (19:19b). Thus the command to sell and give to the poor (19:21) is perhaps the social and practical aspect of discipleship. Matthew's continual mention of helping the poor is perhaps to address the issue of his community. Though comparatively the Matthean community in general appeared to be wealthier than the Markan and the Lukan communities, most of the Matthean community members were poor. And so, probably, Matthew's goal was to alleviate poverty by encouraging the relatively richer members of his community to help the poorer members.

5) Wealth has a Place in Heaven

For Matthew, it seems, wealth, social aspects of discipleship, and future reward are interrelated. He sees wealth as something to be precious and good if gotten justly and valued it appropriately; riches are to be seen as divine blessings, to be used not for selfish ends but for the benefit of those in need, and in which he saw an eschatological reward. For instance, in Matthew 6:1-4, as much as it emphasizes the right way of doing acts of mercy, it also stresses on reward (cf. 5:7); likewise giving to the needy is equivalent to storing up treasures in heaven in 19:21 (cf. 6:19-21). Matthew's admonition of giving (perhaps to the wealthy who possessed wealth and who were thus in a privileged position to extend help) to the poor thus has futuristic eschatological implications – reward in heaven. Matthew's teachings on wealth, giving, and reward are well connected; they bear socio-ethical and religious connotations. In other words, the just rich are seen as not just those who have received divine favor (in terms of wealth) here on earth but also those who will receive divine favor (in terms of reward) in heaven, if they used their wealth in helping the poor and needy. Moreover, before concluding his Gospel with the Epilogue (26:3-28:20), Matthew ends his fifth book and the last discourse with the saying on "the judgment of the nations" (25:31-46), where he sets forth good works to the poor, weak, and oppressed as the only criterion for the final judgment. It is therefore observable in Matthew that wealth has religious and eschatological significance.

The findings of the present study certainly shed light on the issues of wealth and the wealthy, Christian discipleship and wealth, and on how to be rich in the midst of the majority poor like in our country India. Some of the findings, which are also in line, to some extent, with the indigenous social and moral values, bear practical implications for indigenous Christians in particular and Christians in India in general.

Contributors

Rev. Dr. V. J. John serves as Professor in the department of New Testament at Bishop's College, Kolkata and the North India Institute of Post-Graduate Theological Studies (NIIPGTS). He was the Dean of doctoral studies (2012-19) of NIIPGTS and was elected President of Society for Biblical Studies in India (SBSI) for the biennium (2016-2018).

Rev. Dr. Vanlalnghaka Ralte is Professor of New Testament and Principal of Aizawl Theological College. He has been engaged in various committees of Senate of Serampore College (University) and has had an enormous contribution in Mizo Bible Translation.

Rev. Dr. K. Jesurathnam is an ordained minister of Telugu Baptist Church. He is currently Friedemann Golka Professor of the Old Testament and the Chairperson of the Biblical Department at the United Theological College, Bangalore. He is the author of a number of books and articles in the field of the Old Testament.

Dr. Jose Varickasseril obtained licentiate in Sacred Scripture from the Pontifical Biblical Institute, Rome & at the École Biblique and Hebrew University (Jerusalem). He has his doctorate in Biblical Theology (from the Pontifical Urban University, Rome) and doctorate in Spirituality (from the Salesian Pontifical University, Rome). Currently he is teaching at Sacred Scripture and Theology and serves as co-pastor in a congregation.

Dr. Tekayaba earned his MTh from United Theological College and D.Th (Old Testament) from Senate of Serampore College (University). He formerly taught at Leonard Theological College, Jabalpur. Currently he is an Academic Dean of Correspondence Course and faculty at Discipleship Bible College, Dimapur, Nagaland.

Rev. Dr. B. Lalnunzira is an Associate Professor at the Aizawl Theological College, Aizawl. He teaches Old Testament and Biblical languages. Currently he is Head of the Department of the Old Testament at Aizawl Theological College, and Secretary of the SBSI.

Dr. Zakali Shohe is Associate Professor of New Testament and the Academic Dean at Trinity Theological College in Dimapur, Nagaland. She is the co-editor of *Theology In-Context* (TTC, 2010) and has authored a monograph *Acceptance Motif in Paul: Revisiting Romans 15:7-13* (Frankfurt: Peter Lang, 2017).

Father Laurence Culas is a priest of Archdiocese of Trivandrum (Latin), Kerala. He secured Doctorate in Biblical Theology (Catholic Institute of Toulouse, France). He teaches Scripture at Bodhi Institute of Theology, Tillery, Kerala. Presently he is the President of Catholic Priests Conference of India (CPCI), Secretary of Catholic Biblical Association of India (CBAI), President of the SBSI, and Coordinator of Pastoral Commissions in the Archdiocese of Trivandrum.

Sr. Virginia Rajakumari Sandiyagu is a member in the Congregation of Sisters of St. Anne, Bangalore. She holds a doctorate in Biblical Theology from Katholieke Universiteit Leuven, Belgium. She has authored a book named *Women as Eyewitnesses to the Christian Kerygma: The Galilean Women in the Redaction of Luke, an Exegetical Study of Luke 8:1-3*, and few articles in National and International Theological Journals.

Gregory Thomas Basker is currently Associate Professor of New Testament and Christian Origins in The United Theological College, Bangalore, India. He holds a Dr. Theol. from the University of Heidelberg, Germany, in the field of Biblical Hermeneutics.

Prema Vakayil belongs to the Congregation of Carmelite Sisters of St. Teresa (CSST). She holds a Doctorate from St. Peter's Pontifical Institute, Bengaluru and a Post Doctorate from Tantur Ecumenical Institute, Jerusalem. She teaches New Testament at St. Peter's Pontifical Institute, Bengaluru.

Dr. Joseph Lalfakmawia is from Mizoram and he currently serves under the Mizoram Presbyterian Church as Probationary Pastor. He recently earned his doctorate (New Testament) from NIIPGTS and Senate of Serampore College (University).

Dr. Enolyne Lyngdoh earned her MA degree from secular college and D.Th (Old Testament) from Senate of Serampore College (University). Currently she is Assistant Professor at John Roberts Theological Seminary, Shillong.

Dr. Keciziuying Siang is from Nagaland. He earned his doctorate (New Testament) from Senate of Serampore College (University). Currently he is an Academic Dean at the Academy of Integrated Christian Studies, Aizawl.